FULFILLING THE CIRCLE:
A STUDY OF JOHN DONNE'S THOUGHT

This book assumes that we can understand Donne's works much better if we take them as a whole. The book also assumes that the principles of consciousness, of epistemology and psychology, are the backbone of his thought. In light of these assumptions, Terry Sherwood concentrates on principles of reason, bodies, and suffering that unify Donne's works. These principles reflect how Donne assimilated the complex spiritual and intellectual currents of his time. More important, these principles inform the centre of important works written throughout Donne's long and varied literary career.

TERRY G. SHERWOOD is a member of the Department of English at the University of Victoria.

TERRY G. SHERWOOD

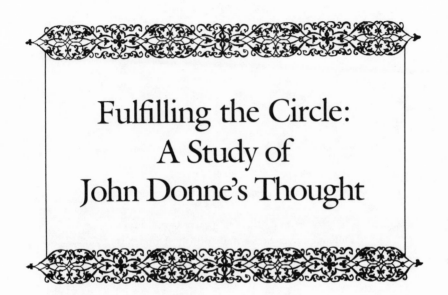

Fulfilling the Circle:
A Study of
John Donne's Thought

UNIVERSITY OF TORONTO PRESS
Toronto Buffalo London

© University of Toronto Press 1984
Toronto Buffalo London
Printed in Canada

ISBN 0-8020-5621-0

Canadian Cataloguing in Publication Data

Sherwood, Terry G. (Terry Grey), 1936–
Fulfilling the circle : a study of John Donne's thought

Includes bibliographical references and index.
ISBN 0-8020-5621-0

1. Donne, John, 1572–1631 — Criticism and
interpretation. 2. Donne, John, 1572–1631 — Religion and
Ethics. 3. Christianity in Literature. I. Title.

PR2248.S53   821'.3   C83-098420-8

This book has been printed on acid-free paper.

FRONTISPIECE: Effigy of Dr John Donne, St Paul's Cathedral

COVER: Portrait of John Donne reproduced
by permission of the Dean of St Paul's

TO NANCY

Acknowledgments

While working on Donne, I have enjoyed the generosity of other scholars. At Berkeley Donald Friedman and Hugh Richmond encouraged my early interest. Later at Victoria, Thomas Cleary, David Jeffrey (now of the University of Ottawa), and Robert Schuler all read and helped improve individual chapters. Edward Berry bravely read the whole manuscript, as did Patrick Grant, who for years has kindly allowed me to pester him with questions about Medieval and Renaissance thought. Arthur Barker of the University of Western Ontario gave timely encouragement at an important stage in the book's development.

Chapter Two includes portions of two articles published earlier: 'Reason in Donne's Sermons,' *A Journal of English Literary History*, 38 (1972), 353–74; 'Reason, Faith, and Just Augustinian Lamentation in Donne's Elegy on Prince Henry,' *Studies in English Literature*, 13 (1973), 53–67. Chapter Seven is a version of 'Conversion Psychology in John Donne's Good Friday Poem,' *Harvard Theological Review*, 72 (1979), 101–22.

The writing of this book was supported by a Canada Council Leave Fellowship. Its preparation for publication was greatly aided by Judy Williams, who copy-edited the manuscript at the Press, and by Susan Cripps, who assisted in proofreading and preparing the index at Victoria. The publication of this book is made possible by a grant from the Canadian Federation for the Humanities, using funds provided by the Social Sciences and Humanities Research Council of Canada, and a grant to the University of Toronto Press from the Andrew W. Mellon Foundation.

My biggest debts are to Graham, Megan, and especially Nancy, for their sustaining gifts of heart and mind.

Contents

INTRODUCTION

1

Fulfilling the Circle

One primary reason for modern interest in Donne's lyrics is the taut, intellectual self-consciousness in these poems. But fondness for the lyrics at the expense of Donne's other works has tended to distort our view of Donne. Our estimate of the epistemological and psychological principles informing his portrait of human consciousness has also suffered. A more balanced understanding of how Donne viewed the soul and its motions requires the larger context of all the works and, in particular, those of his maturity. A long view of his writings reveals consistent principles that reach fruition in the mature religious prose.

To say that later works offer a necessary perspective on earlier works is not to prejudice understanding of earlier works, nor is it to allow the older man to dictate to the younger. Instead, it is to say that the mature works construct one essential context in which to approach troublesome elements in the earlier works. This is true of the epistemological and psychological notions that are the subject of this study.[1] We find consistent basic principles in Donne's preoccupation with the ways in which the rational soul knows and uses its various knowledge, both natural and supernatural. And we find a similar consistency in his self-conscious observations of the rational soul and its relationships to the body. Thus, to follow the lines of Donne's development either way, backwards or forwards, increases our understanding greatly. The variety of genera and literary intentions in Donne's works does present special problems; but solutions can best be achieved by remaining within Donne's works and by taking advantage, in particular, of the explicit and comprehensive exposition in the sermons. Applications to even the more private and secular love poetry can be revealing.

Such a long view of Donne's works validates the 'metaphysical' tag in assessing his principles of consciousness. His 'metaphysical' principles are not mere subjective points of reference for him, as some have argued.[2] Although the motions of consciousness are the dramatic centre of most of Donne's works, his conceptions of epistemology and psychology, so crucial in this drama, are necessarily related to these objective metaphysical realities. Accordingly, this introduction to Donne's epistemology and psychology necessarily sets out essential metaphysical principles as expressed in the religious prose. These quite orthodox formulations are the mature and complete expressions of ideas and intellectual tendencies also present in Donne's earlier thought.

To begin with, an orthodox notion of Creation formulates the polar opposition between creation and annihilation at the heart of his thought. For him this orthodox notion sets terms for the relationships between heaven and earth, eternity and time, and the divine and human natures. An example from the *Devotions upon Emergent Occasions* demonstrates how the individual, in body and soul, must embody the principles of Creation. While invoking this metaphysical backdrop, Donne expresses his characteristic rational consciousness of the body and of his own suffering. Reason wrings the figurative and typological significance from the events of Donne's illness. The rational soul finds in misery the deserved punishment for both shared Original Sin, this 'miserable condition of Man' ('1. Meditation,' p. 7), and also for Donne's personal sin. This corrective illness will bring him into conformity with Christ, but within the context of Creation.

In the fourteenth devotion the physicians' consideration of the 'criticall dayes' in his illness leads Donne to turn to a consideration of time. His frame is the Genesis archetype, the week of Creation. This is a basic frame for Donne's mature notions of salvation history, time, typology, Covenant, Election, sin, suffering, and participation between God and man. This also is the basic frame for examining his notions of epistemology and psychology. Donne's 'criticall dayes' remind him that God has given these points in time; the urgency of this illness inspires a proper use of time, in terms of the original Creational pattern. Only this pattern can prepare man for eternity; and Donne must understand not only his immediate experience, but also his entire life in terms of this pattern. He must view the illness as the first day; the 'light, and testimony' of his conscience as the second; preparation for the Lord's Supper, the third; his death as the fourth; his resurrection, the fifth; Last Judgment sixth; and, finally, everlasting Sabbath ('14. Expostulation,' pp. 72–6). Belief in this salvational pattern enables him to place his own immediate temporal experience – when considered, known, felt – in the pattern that fulfils Creation, and hence time. Thus, consideration, knowledge, and feeling participate in this most inclusive metaphysical frame. Donne's treatment of this frame and its parts reveals its far-reaching significance in his thought and, more immediately, its significance in his notions of epistemology and psychology.

I SOME CONSTITUENTS OF CREATION

Donne was preoccupied with Creation. His first detailed exposition, in the *Essays in Divinity*, contributed to his preparation for Holy Orders, it is thought, and was probably written as early as 1607, perhaps as late as 1615;[3] his fullest treatment is in three 1629 sermons on Genesis. Yet his continuing interest is revealed in such diverse works as 'The Storme,' 'The Calme,' 'A Valediction: of Weeping,' 'A Nocturnall upon S. Lucies Day,' *The Anniversaries*, and many other sermons. In the sermons, in which Donne applies the events of Creation as types for the recreation of the sinful soul, he develops most fully his lifelong interest in Creation to configure the soul's condition. As we will see, the relationship between the Word and the Spirit in Creation is Donne's basic paradigm for God's role in recreating the sinful soul. And Creation is the basic for his theology of participation that hinges on the likenesses established between the Creator and his creatures. The human role, in enhancing the human likeness defaced by sin, necessarily involves principles of recreational epistemology and psychology.

There are familiar orthodox markings in Donne's conceptions of Creation and recreation. The Genesis story of Creation expresses God's loving will overflowing to create being, by informing a material world through a temporal sequence. That six-day temporal sequence established the relationships between form and matter, God and man, and eternity and time. With the Holy Spirit hovering over the waters, God spoke and all was created sequentially in time. The Holy Ghost applied forms inherent in the *Logos*, the Word and Wisdom of God, the mind of the Father. The act of Creation established time as the proper dimension for the relationship between God and man, and between form and matter. One result is that man necessarily must follow God's way spiritually and physically through sequential time. The nature of earthly existence assumes such movement.

When repairing the created world, God followed his own precedent established at Creation. The Fall had unhinged creation, reversing created being toward nothing and disjointing time. God again traced the Creational pattern, first through prophetic promises inspired by the Spirit, but most fully when the Spirit overshadowed Mary as he had Chaos.[4] The Word is thus incarnated according to the same pattern. By no means opposed to Creation, the Incarnation enacts the same principles to fulfil them. Like the Incarnation

Christ's life, death, and resurrection are temporal events which are the pattern for salvation when spiritually interpreted (humility, obedience, suffering, crucifixion of sin, rebirth). The Incarnation furthers a recreation that applies the old principles and rejuvenates time. The Incarnation is the central event within a metahistorical format embracing the principles of Creation: prophetic promise, its fulfilment in the incarnate Word, and the Spirit's later application of Christ to members of his Body, the Church. These events pattern a six-thousand-year metahistory concluded by the Last Judgment and followed by eternal Sabbath, the New Jerusalem of redeemed believers incorporated in Christ. History follows the six-day Creational pattern.[5]

However, Creation and metahistory interest Donne primarily as contexts for understanding human experience. Redemption through the Word creates anew; and the running parallels between Old and New Creation are a central wellspring of analogical and metaphorical energy in Donne's works. In a 1619 Lincoln's Inn sermon, Donne, in exhorting young listeners in the language of Ecclesiastes 12:1 to 'Remember now thy creator in the dayes of thy youth,' builds a full set of analogues between Creation and regeneration. These range from the 'first day ... thy knowledg of Christ' to 'a desire of a spiritual Sabbath in the seaventh' (*Sermons*, II, 243). Donne's exhortation follows its Creational sequence to its climactic fulfilment. A purposeful recreation must inform sequentially, hence fulfil actual time, here the days of youth. This fulfilment occurs in the human consciousness, thus expressing both the metaphysical and psychological sides of Donne's notion of Creation.

At this point we need to trace the backbone of this notion, that is, the working relationship between the Spirit and the eternal Word. The implications for Donne's mature thought about human consciousness are profound. We find a traditional Christocentric theology that also accommodates the Spirit's expanded role in contemporary Protestantism.[6] Orthodox and consistent with Scripture,[7] Donne appropriates power to the Father, wisdom to the Son, and goodness to the Holy Spirit (*Sermons*, V, 88). His elucidation of the Son and the Spirit likewise follows traditional lines: 'the Sonne is the word and wisdome of God, and the holy Ghost is the goodnesse, and the purpose of God; that is, the administration, the dispensation of his purposes' (*Sermons*, IX, 58).[8] In proceeding both from the eternally generated Son and from the Father, the Spirit applies the Word and Wisdom of God. At Creation, brooding upon Chaos, the Spirit imposes form when God speaks, thus applying the Word: '*The Spirit of God ... breathed upon the waters*, and so induced, or deduced particular formes' (*Sermons*, IV, 251). The informing act hangs upon God's spoken Word. Donne inherits the assumption in Christian Platonism that created forms are derived from Ideas in God's mind attributed to the Word. The Ideas are associated with the Son, the perfect Likeness generated in the Father's self-knowledge or, in the linguistic formulation, his self-expression, his Word.[9] That perfect Likeness is the model for all created likenesses to God, whatever their levels of being, hence cinching closely together the Word and the Ideas, in which all created forms participate through likeness. Donne says:

When as *Dicere Dei est intelligere ejus practicum*: when God would produce his Idaea, his pre-conception into action, that action, that production was his *Dixit*, his saying ... In the act of Creation, the Will of GOD was the Word of God; his Will that it should be, was his saying, Let it be. (*Sermons*, IV, 102)[10]

Donne's point, that all created forms are preconceived according to divine Ideas[11] and that Creation was the work of the full Trinity, supports the crucial nexus in his thought between the Spirit and the Word. He frequently reminds his listeners that the Spirit and the Word were both necessary for Creation.[12]

This connection between the Spirit and the Word leads us back to human consciousness since recreation necessarily follows the design of that connection. The Spirit and the Word have respectively different implications for Donne's thought. The Spirit is the agent of recreation: 'The Spirit of God wrought upon the waters in the Creation, because he meant to doe so after, in the regeneration of man' (*Sermons*, IX, 104). Through the Spirit's actions God is present in man; and eternity, present in time. The Spirit moves, fecundates, and informs the human consciousness, the Church, and human history, either maintaining or interrupting principles of nature. Just as he proceeds eternally from the Word and the Father, and just as he informs Chaos according to eternal impressions in the mind of God, the Spirit also proceeds into human hearts and applies 'the Mercies of the Father, and the Merits of the Son, and *moves upon the face of the waters*, and actuates, and fecundates our soules, and generates that knowledge, and that comfort, which we have in the knowledge of God' (*Sermons*, IX, 93). Moving believers through the Scriptural Word or the minister's spoken word, the Spirit actuates understanding, knowledge, and love of truth incarnate in Christ and his teachings. The Spirit's intimate motions in human faculties, like the imprinting of matter according to Eternal Ideas in God's Word, guide a fulfilling Creational principle. To do the Spirit's bidding is to know this principle in one's own fulfilment in time.

Likewise, to follow the Spirit is to experience the principle by which creatures participate through likeness in the Creator. By sustaining the created world and regenerating believers, the Spirit enhances the participation of all creation in God. The prayer concluding Part One of *Essays in Divinity* assumes that participation is one article of Creation:

And as, though thy self hadst no beginning thou gavest a beginning to all things in which thou wouldst be served and glorified; so, though this soul of mine, by which I partake thee, begin not now, yet let this minute, O God, this happy minute of thy visitation, be the beginning of her conversion, and shaking away confusion, darknesse, and barrennesse; and let her now produce Creatures, thoughts, words, and deeds agreeable to thee. (p. 37)

Man's tripartite soul participates by natural likeness in its triune Creator God, but fulfilled participation requires God's help to remove sin's deformity. The traditional vocabulary of imprinting,[13] which expresses Donne's conception of participation, unites all creatures through likeness to the Creator, either as the lesser trace or the greater likeness: 'And thus *Per filiationem vestigii*, By that impression of God, which is in the very beeing of every creature, God, that is, the whole Trinity, is the Father of every creature' (*Sermons*, III, 266). Likeness varies as the degree of being; image exceeds trace; and the tripartite spiritual soul has *filiationem Imaginis*, not just *filiationem vestigii* (*Sermons*, IX, 83). Repeatedly Donne examines the significance of that imprinted Image: 'we have, in our one soul, a *threefold impression* of that image ... A *trinity from the Trinity* ... the *Vnderstanding*, the *Will*, and the *Memory* (*Sermons*, II, 72–3). Donne splices the notion of filiation, enriched by Scripture, to the long-lived notion of graded likeness, *vestigiae* and *Imagi Dei*.[14] The father of the rain (Job 38:28) and of lights (James 1:17), God delegates power to man (Psalm 8:6), also filiated to Him, to rule all his creature-children (*Sermons*, VII, 417–18). They are *vestigia*; man is *imago*. However, only in Heaven, when knowing as known, does the human Image fulfil its likeness to God; there, '*we shall be made partakers of the Divine nature* (2 Pet. 1:4); Immortall as the Father, righteous as the Son, and full of all comfort as the Holy Ghost' (*Sermons*, VIII, 236). The imprinted human Image can reach progressively toward that fulfilled heavenly participation through the Spirit's regenerative motions that restore the damaged likeness.

The Spirit reforms the soul according to the Word as the Model for all form. If we shift our focus from the Spirit to the Word, we approach Donne's theology of Creation and recreation from another promontory. Again, we find Donne's coalescence of metaphysical and psychological realities. Seen in terms of the Word, man's fulfilling participation in God is a growing conformity with the Incarnate Word in both soul and body. Conformity, by restoring the human composite, restores the ultimate object of Creation.

Man's body is 'Gods Master-piece' (*Sermons*, VII, 259), an 'Illustration of all Nature; Gods recapitulation of all that he had said before, in his *Fiat Lux*, and *Fiat firmamentum*, and in all the rest, said or done, in all the six dayes' (*Sermons*, VII, 272); and his soul, climactically breathed in by God, is imprinted with his likeness. The Fall casts a shroud over the body; it hobbles the soul's self-governance and slackens its mastery over the body. A saving pattern that rehabilitates body and soul through purposive actions restores Creation: to this end the Word, Image for all form, 'will weare ... flesh.'[15] Again, the Spirit applies the Word in time, overshadowing Mary while the Image of all forms enters her womb (*Sermons*, X, 129).

Flesh serving spirit, humility, obedience, mortification of sin, suffering, and resurrection – the Incarnate Word illustrates a new Creation, a recreation. With the body turned purposefully to spiritual ends, its bonds with the soul are drawn together anew by following the pattern of saving behaviour. In turn, the tripartite soul finds the Creator in the Incarnate Word; this perfect Image manifests the whole Trinity in Christ's power, wisdom, and goodness. Human reason, will, and memory assimilate these virtuous conditions by following their incarnation in Christ's actions. As a result, man's likeness to God is refurbished. The Word participates in human nature so that man may participate in God's:

When God hath made himselfe one body with me, by his assuming this *nature*, and made me *one spirit* [1 Cor. 6:17] with himselfe, and that by so high a way, as making me *partaker of the divine nature* [2 Pet. 1:4], so that now, *in Christ Jesus*, he and I are one ... (*Sermons*, X, 117)

Christ's suffering in the flesh points the way to restoration. By taking up the Cross of affliction, penitential suffering, and responsive Calling, man discovers his inherent likeness:

... That when God affords thee, this manifestation of his Crosse, in the participation of those crosses and calamities that he suffered here, when thou hast this signe of the Son of Man upon thee, conclude to thy selfe that the Son of Man Christ Jesus is comming towards thee; and as thou hast the signe, thou shalt have the substance, as thou hast his Crosse, thou shalt have his Glory. (*Sermons*, VIII, 319)

Conformity to Christ's suffering which participates in his saving merits is disciplined by the visible Body of Christ, the Church.

To recapitulate briefly, Donne's mature thought coheres through relationships of imprinted likeness between the Creator and participating creatures. When the Fall cripples participation, the original human imprint, created by the Father through his Word and Spirit, must undergo repair according to the same pattern. Under the overshadowing Spirit, Mary's womb fills with the incarnate Word; similarly, the Spirit applies Christ's merits to believers through a recreative development that repeats the six days of Creation. Man is the final achievement of both Creation and recreation; but recreation demands man's efforts as well as God's. A member of Christ's Body, man must heed the Spirit's motions, to conform to the suffering Christ, in both body and soul; this mutual participation between man and God incarnates the principles of the Word as a vivid presence within man's behaviour. Suffering with Christ not only reforms the disturbed valencies binding body and soul, but also dramatizes within the individual's experience the metaphysical forces that create and sustain all existence.

II RECREATION THROUGH TIME

We have observed how a broad metaphysic based on principles of Creation is Donne's context for viewing human consciousness. A corollary with far-reaching significance for the composite soul and body is that sequential time is the medium for both Creation and recreation. The vivid temporal awareness in the lyric poetry is expressed in later works in time's progressive fulfilment within human consciousness. We find that the metahistorical powers of re-creation, that is, of divine Covenant and the history of salvation, are mediated to the individual through the Holy Spirit. The fulfilment of history and time is achieved in the individual's conscious and willing participation in God through the Spirit's recreative motions. It follows that the fruition of time, its fullness, becomes a function of human epistemology and psychology.

Two elements in Donne's Covenant theology[16] are important in his conception of time and its relationship to Creation. First, the principles of Covenant explain further the ties between Creation and recreation through time. That is, the need for the Eternal Covenant between the Father and the Word and the later covenant between God and man in time assumes the causation of Creation damaged by the Fall. Significantly, the eternal Decrees of Reconciliation and of Election and Reprobation promise God's recreative power through Christ the Word.[17] Second, God's Covenantal promises guarantee man's recreated participation in God through time. Covenants with man, beginning with Adam and Abraham, then others later, and finally each Christian believer, ensure the Christian's participatory likeness with God established in Creation, but weakened at the Fall. Just as 'every creature hath *filiationem vestigii*' and 'every man hath *filiationem imaginis*,' so also 'every

Christian hath *filiationem Pacti*' when 'taken into the Covenant' which God makes with the Elect (*Sermons*, VIII, 286). The *filiatio Pacti* guarantees participation established at Creation; for the Covenant, whenever repeated in human history, restates a promised relationship with the Word, ever present in prophecy, however unfulfilled before the Incarnation. In short, the notion of Covenant promises a new Creation.

Predictably, the Word is one common denominator between Donne's notions of Creation and Covenant. Whereas the Word is the source of form in Creation, the promise of recreation in the Covenant also applies the Word. First covenanted by the Decree of Reconciliation, the Word is the Messiah promised to Adam, then promised again later in a specific Covenant 'to one people, to the Jewes, to the seed of *Abraham*' (*Sermons*, V, 70). In his commitment to circumcision as a sign of the promise, Abraham confirmed God's Covenant, that is, 'the *Messias*, who being to come, by a carnall continuance of *Abrahams* race, the signe and seale was conveniently placed in that part' (*Sermons*, VI, 193). Abraham's Covenant with God foreshadows the fulfilled Covenant between Christ and the faithful Christian. Thus, Donne can claim 'my portion there' with Abraham's seed (*Sermons*, V, 70). Like Abraham's, his temporal life can be recreated according to principles covenanted through the Word.

The other predictable common denominator in Donne's notions of Covenant and Creation is the Holy Spirit, who is both the divine informing agent in Creation and also the seal of the Covenant in the believer's temporal life: 'Now all promises of God, are sealed in the *holy Ghost*; To whom soever any promise of God belongs, he hath the holy Ghost' (*Sermons*, V, 109). The Spirit of Promise seals both externally and internally – externally in Baptism, the ceremonial acceptance into Christ's Body. The Spirit offers Christ to the believer in a 'new Creation,' again 'moving upon the face of the waters in the Sacrament of Baptisme' (*Sermons*, IX, 93). And the Holy Spirit speaks externally in the Scripture, the Holy Word, which embodies God's promise (*Sermons*, V, 229). The Spirit also applies the promises of Christ's Covenant externally through the Church's other Sacraments, its ordinances, and the minister's spoken word. More important for this study, the Spirit applies these promises internally by assuring the believer that he participates in Christ's Covenant. This internal witness to man's spirit is also the Spirit's seal,[18] which respects the needs of consciousness.

And, since that seal occurs in time, it is central in the fulfilment of time, which, as we will see repeatedly, is Donne's context for understanding consciousness. Just as man's likeness to God is renewed through the Spirit's internal and external motions, time is fulfilled simultaneously by the Spirit moving within the believer. Although the human soul will be recreated fully only in Eternity, this renewed likeness nonetheless develops in time as a new creation. The several vocabularies expressing Donne's conception of meta-history characterize this internal change: metamorphosis of the Old Covenant into the New, fulfilment of type in antitype, and achievement of prophecy in history. Barbara Lewalski finds Protestant assumptions in Donne's typol-ogy. The individual Christian recapitulates in himself both Old and New Testament experience: 'God works in us precisely as he works in history.'[19] Christ fulfilled prophecy in the fullness of time; likewise, the believer, pur-suing Christ's pattern, may fulfil time in his own life. Sin's persistence, even in the erected believer, restrains full participation in God and retards fulfil-ment, which is necessarily developmental and never perfect in time. Yet time and history continue to seek their recreative goals in the human fullness expressed in the Incarnation and offered later to those who respond to the Spirit's motions to follow the pattern of the Incarnate Word.

The Spirit's descent at Pentecost configures that enduring offer of fullness. The paradigmatic relationship between the Spirit and the Word is again enacted, recalling the overshadowing of Mary at the Annunciation (*Sermons*, IX, 241). Pentecost not only confirms Christ and his teachings, but also be-comes the pattern for the pouring of Grace in every Christian consciousness, that is, the Advent of Christ[20] repeated through the Spirit's administration. The Spirit infuses, fills with the fullness of the Word by speaking in Scripture, in the Church's Ordinances and Sacraments, in the minister's sermons, and, more intimately, in devotional practices. In a re-enactment of Pentecost, the Spirit 'shall fill you all (according to your measure, and his purpose) and give you utterance, in your lives and conversations' (*Sermons*, IX, 241). The Spirit, promised to believers by Christ, teaches what Christ taught in order to satisfy man's desire to know:

He shall teach you [John 14:26], He, who can not onely infuse true, and full knowledge in every capacity that he findes, but dilate that capacity where he findes it, yea create it, where he findes none, *The Holy Ghost ... (Sermons*, VIII, 254)

Progressively, the Spirit fulfils the believer with the fullness[21] that is Christ, the incarnate Word.

Donne's central paradox of developing 'fulfilment' and achieved 'fullness' in time needs to be understood in terms of the connection between meta-history and the individual consciousness. As noted, the week of Creation establishes the design for developing time; and the Fall requires a realignment of that design through the Word, who enters time to fulfil it. As fullness itself, the incarnate Word manifests the values for the proper realignment of time, first in Promise, in prophetic announcement filled with the Spirit's wisdom. But then this promise itself reaches fulfilment in Mary's womb overshadowed by the Holy Ghost. Time is fulfilled thereby: literally filled full, through the entrance into history of the Word, who is the fullness of the Godhead.²² However, fullness does not contradict time's own continuing, developing sequentiality, which follows Christ's pattern. Although Christ's own fullness was contained in each moment, his life paradoxically developed in a pattern of birth, suffering, death, and resurrection. That pattern itself will be completed in the spiritual lives of erected, conforming believers. The Spirit will fill these members of Christ's Body, the Church, according to Christ's pattern.

The 'circle of time' (*Sermons*, II, 313) dissolves this apparent contradiction between, on one hand, time's achieved condition in Christ and, on the other hand, continuing fulfilment, between simultaneous resolution and developing movement in time. The principle of participating likeness between God and man, in the pattern of Christ's life developing circularly in time, is the central notion. Like Christ's life, Christian history is an irreversible circle of sequential events from beginning to end, ever informed by God who 'fills every place' (*Sermons*, II, 217), as the circle's omnipresent centre. The circle, one of the 'most convenient Hieroglyphicks of God' (*Sermons*, VI, 173), expresses further implications of participating likeness between God and man. Christ, his life, the Church, man's soul, man's life, and the history of salvation – all are 'circles.' Thus, like man's soul, time is God's creature made in his likeness, for God himself is an unending circle containing both a beginning and an end in himself (*Sermons*, IV, 96). Also, man's life, whether recreated or fallen, develops in a circle. Recreated life begins with a body and ends at Resurrection with a glorified body (*Sermons*, VIII, 97). The fallen life is also 'made with a Compasse,' passing 'from point to point,' from dust to dust (*Sermons*, II, 200). Recreated time follows the pattern of the Incarnate Word, the Alpha and Omega (*Sermons*, III, 187–8), the 'fullness' of the circular God who takes human form and enters time to set it back properly on its circular track. That is, the circular God shows how to renew the temporal human cirle (*Sermons*, IV, 68). Similarly, Christ's Body the Church is a 'chariot' moving 'in that communicable motion, circularly; it began in the East, it came to us, and is passing now, shining out now, in the farthest West' (*Sermons*, VI, 173). To find God's 'fullness,' the centre of time's circle, more clearly manifested in some places and times, and not others, does not suggest a retreat from the circumference of time's circle; rather, it suggests the discovery of possibilities inherent at any point in time. Fullness can be achieved in any believer, but not absolutely, only in the condition of fulfilling, on the circumference of time.[23] In that sense, the 'day' of fulfilment, of the fullness of time, is omnipresent in the fulfilling pattern of Christ's birth, life, and death (*Sermons*, VI, 333). The centre can be found on the circumference; Christ's 'fullness' informs time in its pieces and in the whole, everywhere present and available, but never completed in the earthly lives of Adam's heirs.

Likewise, Christ's Body never completes its earthly fulfilment, owing to limitations in its members. Although the Body does participate partially in the fullness of its Head, it will enjoy unqualified fullness only when history completes its hexameral development and time's circle is filled completely. Conformity with Christ's suffering earns that reward. And the individual member deserves more as he participates increasingly in that fullness and consciously understands the psychology of his participation. Like the Head, each member must suffer for others, like Paul, to fulfil Christ's suffering in his own flesh for the Body's sake (Colossians 1:24). That he thereby fulfils, fills up the circle of time, for both himself and the Body, expresses two halves of the same truth. In that fulfilment Donne's theology of Creation and his theology of recreation become one.

To return to the important point: it was Donne's special gift to portray life on the circumference of time's circle by finding metaphysical forces vividly effected in the soul and body. This gift was consistent with a theology that viewed man as the goal of Creation and his tripartite Image of God, the fulfilled faculties of the rational soul, as creation's best likeness to God and hence the best means to reach him. Donne's temporal immediacy assumes that human life is understandable only in terms of movement on the circumference of the circle. A rational being with a physical body, man lives in pain as his temporal condition; and the metaphysical forces that create, sustain, recreate, and draw him to fulfilment become humanly understandable only as they inform man's temporal understanding and knowledge. That heightened temporal awareness – ratiocinative feeling, conscious of the material body and its experience – continues to attract modern readers. Donne's attention to suffering, however traditionally Christian, appeals to us less. But Donne's temporal consciousness assumes that what a person knows and feels is a function of his pain. Donne's mature theology of participation, likeness between man and God, emphasizes that knowing, loving, and comprehending God require suffering in soul and body, in conformity to the Cross. Recreation through conformity can be measured only in the most immediate psychological and physical terms.

III SOME RUDIMENTS OF DONNE'S EPISTEMOLOGY
AND PSYCHOLOGY

Donne's mature thought completes a development that was based in Donne's own nature. As suggested, Donne's end gives one necessary position for viewing his works as a whole, for assessing his direction along the circumference of his circle. Donne's 'nice speculations of philosophy' in the love poetry and the satires, which unsettled Dryden,[24] reveal a need for precise terms to express his participation in metaphysical forces. The sense of being poised in vivid but connected moments in time, between the forces of creation and annihilation, remains constant, as does his clear sense that forces controlling existence must be measured through likeness to immediate human experience. The need to understand these forces remained constant, although it became more educated and theological. Similarly, there is a constancy in the epistemological and psychological principles expressing that continuing impulse. These central principles are the primary subject of this study; and in Part One we will see how Donne's respective notions of reason, body, and suffering should be assessed by training one eye on the full exposition in the sermons.

This approach is necessary in evaluating reason's primary role in Donne's epistemology and psychology. Many Donne critics have found scepticism where it did not exist, and others have seriously underplayed reason's importance in relation to memory and will. But Donne's conviction of reason's dominant powers lies at the heart of his thought. Reason erects the strategies of argument; it is the operative faculty in Donne's wit; it is 'our connexion / Of causes'[25] that comprehends the relationships between God and creation; and it is the 'doore of faith' (*Sermons*, IX, 360), achieving the wisdom that establishes the foundations for the will's several steps. Reason's dominant role does not suppress the will's full experience or lessen Donne's impatience with the Stoic's muffled emotions. In Donne's works the will's experience is rich and varied: passionate longing in both secular and divine love, honest grief, faith's assurance, and the fullness of joy. Nor does an emphasis on reason withstand a many-voiced assertion in recent scholarship that Donne encouraged the power of memory along an Augustinian course;[26] but it does reset a balance badly disturbed by overly strenuous claims that memory dominates Donne's mature epistemology and psychology. Donne was not a rationalist. But he considered the tripartite soul a genuinely rational soul, however aware of its own limits and activities. Reason's self-scrutiny is not scepticism; rather, it illustrates the same justice that scrutinizes the soul's other faculties as well. Reason's self-trickery, fraud, and misguidance merely emphasize that, not propped up by elevating emotional conviction as in the poems of resolved love, or by divine assurance as in the sermons, reason can yield to earthly distortions. Yet it remains the primary agent for achieving knowledge and for assessing the soul's full experience.

The body's relationship to its infused soul likewise remains stable in his works. Donne's celebration of the body rejects the Platonist's queasy distaste. Although both reason and will 'see' God in Glory, Donne also asserts with Job that '*in my flesh I will see God*' (*Sermons*, III, 112). The resurrected and glorified body fulfils the earthly body's goodness. Rational consciousness includes a charged sense of residence in a body indelibly part of the human composite, though distinct and also separable in death. This relationship between the rational soul and the material body connects such markedly diverse, but fundamentally sympathetic, works as 'The Extasie' and the *Devotions upon Emergent Occasions*. In the love lyric the lovers return to their bodies, which 'Did us, to us, at first convay' (54), in order that 'Weake men on love reveal'd may looke' (70). Their bodies, 'ours, though they'are not wee' (51), are essentially distinct, but necessary for the souls and their relationships to others. This dualistic placement of body and soul in essentially different, but related, dimensions, adhering by an essential 'allay' (56), supports the division between the meditation and the expostulation in the *Devotions*. The body's illness occurs in nature, but the spiritual interpretation of illness distinguishes the body from the soul, which reads the body's experience emblematically and typologically. Distinct, though not separate, the body's experience is the necessary occasion for the soul's. Here, again, others will read the body's experience.

The body's goodness and its service to the soul support Donne's basic epistemology, conveniently distilled in a 1629 sermon. Although faith 'be of infinite exaltation above understanding,' which is 'above our senses,' yet 'we come to understand' by the senses and to 'beleeve' by the understanding (*Sermons*, IX, 357). Here is Donne's clear sense that knowledge begins with immediate, palpable bodily experience. Ecstatic lovers who first entwine their hands on 'A Pregnant banke' (2) are essentially compatible with the sick Donne in the *Devotions*. There, the Spirit communes, not directly to the soul, but indirectly through the body's experience, which reason must interpret.

Donne's consciousness of the body heightens the importance of the traditional microcosm-macrocosm notion in his thought. As half of the human composite and the fulfilment of material creation, the body is the central datum in the physical world. All material existence points to the body through the correspondences relating the microcosmic body to the macrocosmic physical and social worlds. The resulting article in Donne's epistemology, that knowing these correspondences is necessary to understand the soul's experience, simply expresses an elemental consciousness of the body in Donne's psychology. Similarly, this consciousness underlies Donne's understanding of human society, necessarily a collection of human bodies, whether now in time or later in Glory. Donne gravitates naturally to the traditional paradigm that communities are Bodies like human bodies; Christ is the church's Head and the king the kingdom's Heart. Souls require bodies, which require associations with other bodies. Donne's deepest instinct is always to fulfil these requirements. Accordingly, the rational soul must know the implications of its own unbroken bodily consciousness and of the body's immediate experience. Although the paradigmatic correspondences, of body to physical world and to community, are stable and universally applicable, their application must adjust to local circumstances. Reason must examine the body's experience in these terms. Through the body, God guides man's relationships to the world, other men, and God himself; emblematic interpretation of the body's experience follows accordingly.

Thus, the rational soul, keenly aware of its interdependence with the body, must know the leigitmate claims of both body and soul in terms of the controlling metaphysical principles. This awareness, which braces Donne's epistemology and his understanding of human psychology, is itself shaped by human suffering, the essential condition of earthly life. To assess the composite of body and soul is to explore its condition of suffering. Many of Donne's most familiar works – 'A Valediction: of Weeping,' 'A Nocturnall upon S. Lucies Day,' 'The First Anniversarie,' *Holy Sonnets, Devotions upon Emergent Occasions, Deaths Duell* – are expressions of suffering: sorrow, mourning, misery, lament, affliction, and pain. The assembled powers of consciousness must evaluate the significance of pain in body and soul. Man is an afflicted being both punished and saved by suffering. Here is a deep, traditional Christian root. Pain and death, God's contradictory punishment and purification from sin, convert sinful love for the creature into love for God, either directly or indirectly through virtuous love for the creature. Yet not all grief purifies. For the aggrieved lover of 'A Nocturnall,' death continues love's pain; and his grief at parting ('absences / Withdrew our soules, and made us carcasses,' 26–7) predicted his anguish when his lady died. Such grief parallels the remembered love-suffering for Donne's 'profane mistresses' ('Holy Sonnet, XIII,' 10). Although excessive suffering for a lost creature suggests a sinful affection, Donne consistently endorses the natural, affectionate expression of grief that opposes Stoical denial. Nonetheless, even that grief shares the general misery inherited from Adam.

Donne's solution to misery is conformity to the suffering Christ. One consequence in the sermons is his adaptation of Paul's conviction that he could '*fill up that which is behind of the afflictions of Christ in my flesh, for his Bodies sake*' (*Sermons*, III, 332). Obedience to God's will, by welcoming suffering as his punishment and evidence of his favour, metamorphoses suffering into joy. But joy can only fulfil, not transcend, earthly suffering. Death is the only escape from this earthly condition, even for the regenerate. By definition, human consciousness must attune itself, in knowing and feeling, to this condition.

In demonstrating the importance of Donne's notions of reason, body, and suffering in his epistemology and psychology, Part One concentrates on the individual notions themselves. Part Two shifts the perspective to the varied ways in which these notions shape important works written by Donne in different literary forms and at different times: 'A Valediction: of Weeping,' *Holy Sonnets*, 'Goodfriday, 1613. Riding Westward,' and *Devotions upon Emergent Occasions*. Parts One and Two both assume that we can 'dilate,' as Donne might put it, our understanding of his works by locating the part in the fulfilment of the whole.

Consciousness is the dramatic centre of the works discussed in Part Two. Donne himself speaks in all but 'A Valediction: of Weeping,' and even there Donne's personal experience may occupy the foreground.[27] The important point is that events of consciousness are Donne's primary source of literary energy; and these works clearly enact those principles examined severally in Part One. Nevertheless, there can be no absolute separation between the importance of epistemological and psychological principles for Donne and his personal consciousness that infuses his works. That these principles are manifested in writings clearly enlivened by Donne's own experience simply adds convincing evidence of their importance in his thought. And the fact that these writings define the experience of consciousness according to shaping metaphysical forces makes them characteristic of Donne's thought in general. The assumptions underlying these works prepare us, finally, for *Deaths Duell*, the conclusion to Donne's life and to this study of his thought. *Deaths Duell*, though written and delivered at a later time in Donne's life, is simply the final part added to a consistent whole.

PART ONE

2

Reason

When Donne, speaking in unison with St Paul, says 'I know nothing, if I
know not Christ crucified' (*Sermons*, v, 276), he expresses his desire for conformity in epistemological terms. By no means a rationalist's notional consent,
this experiential knowledge expresses the erected motions of the full soul and
body, following a saving pattern. Penitential self-knowledge, encouraged by
the Spirit's recreative motions, no less than a fulfilled love of God and a
sufferer's active Calling in Christ's Body, describes that 'knowledge.' Yet in
a sharpened reason lies the cutting edge of this knowledge and in the more
constricted notional knowledge lies its foundation. The will and the memory
contribute their own forms of knowledge, the will through love and faith,
the memory through living recall; but both forms depend upon rational
knowledge and continue under reason's advisement. The power of recognition, of discernment, is essentially reason's, whether in the mature religious
consciousness attuned to the Spirit or in the earlier self-consciousness of the
love poetry. Reason erects the structures of recognition and applies knowledge, whatever its sources, to serve that recognition.

Assessment of reason in Donne's works must include both his discussion
of the faculty itself and the forms it uses. If we had to account only for
Donne's explicit discussions in the sermons, rightly labelled a 'veritable de-
fense of reason,'[1] the matter would be less vexed. But the secular love poetry
leaves such explicitness until later, in spite of a ratiocinative mode characteristically dependent on logical forms which Donne's Renaissance audience
knew well as the 'rule of reason.'[2] However, the complications arising from
Donne's witty chop logic, together with the naturalism, libertinism, or cynicism of some Donne personae, have been increased by the continuing
popularity of Donne's secular love poetry at the expense of later works.
Though the commentary on Donne's logic, argumentation, and dialectic is

extensive,[3] disagreement about why Donne deploys formal strategies of reason as poetic statement remains lively.

The great variety of critical responses[4] both admits that reason's posturing is essential in the love poetry and also reflects the contradictions that result from Donne's shifting personae. These several faces lend support to the view that Donne is a poseur[5] responding variously to a refracting external reality. We can allow that this tendency is present without having to concede that it defines his essential nature, since some faces emerge more forcefully than others. The criteria for judging which are most important should come from inside, not from outside Donne's works. Accordingly, determining his attitude toward reason is better served by noting that Donne flatly rejects rational scepticism publicly in his Prince Henry elegy. Henry's death seems to destroy both a coherent reality and the manner of apprehending it. Yet reason, after momentarily rejecting its own capacities, finds in them the power to meet the demands of temporal events.

This pointed rejection of rational scepticism displays the foundation on which Donne's defence of reason in the sermons is built. This rejection cannot be underestimated in assessing the central role that reason plays in Donne's thought. Reason establishes the principles necessary for accepting revealed truth, evaluates the implications of that truth, and prepares for further belief. But reason's importance is not limited to establishing religious truth. Its role as the tripartite soul's primary faculty is consistent with its centrality in the life of faith. Although Donne clearly demonstrates the importance of the will and memory, it is reason, in both its discursive and intuitive dimensions, which guides moral and spiritual experience. Donne's characteristic ratiocination throughout his works is consistent with his conviction that the goal of human existence is the *visio dei*, reason's unimpeded comprehension of God in heaven.

Reason's eminence in Donne's thought necessarily rejects modern claims of his scepticism and also cautions against establishing the wrong contexts for examining reason in the love poetry. Again, the Prince Henry elegy gives a necessary clue. The poem unequivocally assumes that reasoning is the necessary adaptation to time. As we will see, the love poetry shows the same assumption, as well as the corollary that we need not view reason's missteps as evidence that Donne sceptically rejected it. Donne's later works explicate this assumption in some detail; and the sermons build on it a fully articulated conception of reason as the predominant faculty in saving knowledge of Christ. Such knowledge saves man, in time, for eternity.

I REASONING IN TIME: THE LOVE POETRY

Much recent commentary sensitive to the importance of time in Donne's poetry has made necessary connections between Donne's dramatic immediacy and the explicit pressure from temporal events. On one hand, Donne's speakers are brightly aware of the moment; on the other hand, they are threatened by the treacheries of temporal change. The very nature of the poetry is to stand in the vividly realized present to answer that threat. Robert Ellrodt sees a poetry of 'presence' that finds the eternal within separated, discrete moments in time.[6] Ann Ferry likewise finds Donne keeping within time, but warring against it to win what he needs to preserve value against change.[7] Taken together, Ellrodt's sense of an eternized present and Ferry's sense of toughened sequential growth approximate the impulse in Donne expressed later in the fulfilment of time, the dilated moment that remembers its place in a developing sequence. In the love poetry Donne's several personae, whatever their likenesses or unlikenesses, perceive and experience in temporal sequentiality. In these poems logical and temporal development may be the same, at least mutually regarding, and Donne's poetry works from the assumption that syllogistic or dialectical development is movement in time. In fact, Donne appears to perceive time by means of rational formulations. Thus, discursive reasoning is itself a figure for time.

To say that he wants to transcend[8] or dissolve time is to misunderstand Donne, for whom reasoning itself follows a temporal sequence. In 'The Anniversarie' the 'everlasting day' (10) that 'no to tomorrow hath, nor yesterday' (8) contradictorily needs the reminder, on this first anniversary, that there was a yesterday just as it anticipates a goal, tabulation of threescore years. The clumsiness of the quantitative measure ironically confesses the inexperience of these very human lovers, who view heaven as simply further development along this temporal continuum:

> But soules where nothing dwells but love
> (All other thoughts being inmates) then shall prove
> This, or a love increased there above,
> When bodies to their graves, soules from their graves remove. (17–20)

The doubleness of 'prove' identifies experiencing with demonstrating rationally, and thus confesses that the speaker is seeking evidence to control his fears of change. His temporal consciousness cannot think beyond change.

The poem clarifies two kinds of sequence. The first is connected to the body in a daily world of physical change. The second is connected to the soul and is paradoxically chorded: 'Running it never runs from us away' (9).

The difference cannot forget the likeness, the rhythm of sequential motions: the 'Running' of spiritual time suggests some of the sequential movements of the physical world. This similarity, which is inextricable from the dissimilarity, that it never runs away, is found in the compatible union of body and soul. Love which inhabits both the physical and spiritual realms cannot escape the demands of sequential consciousness in either realm.[9]

Experience as 'proof' and, as Donne says later, a minute in time as a 'syllogisme' (*Sermons*, x, iii) suggestively express how Donne perceived experience and thereby elucidate for us his often imperceptible modulations between logical and dramatic expression. It follows that not all of Donne's logical constructions need submit to the stringent logician's eye, which orders logic into a cool service of abstract truth and not into the active struggle to discern and to clarify the events of temporal experience. The dramatic movement abides by many of the same principles of temporal motion as the intellectual movement does; neither promises completion or stasis, but instead each instigates further development. Donne assumes movement before, during, and beyond the poem. Both dramatic and rational movement are, by their very natures, reflexive with outer and inner stimuli that deflect and extend the movement without stopping it. In the witty confection 'Womans Constancy,' the virtuoso speaker juggles his taste for detached sexual pleasure with his face-saving male desire to maintain the upper hand. His conditional conclusion, in assuming the lady to be a worthy intellectual match, seeks to nullify her strategy by predicting it:

> Vaine lunatique, against these scapes I could
> Dispute, and conquer, if I would,
> Which I abstaine to doe,
> For by to morrow, I may thinke so too. (14–17)

His conclusion expects a counterargument seeking her advantage; and this anticipated dialectical movement furnishes these lovers' time continuum. They, not dispute itself, bear responsibility for any moral uneasiness caused by the poem.

Reasoning conceived as movement in time tells much about the assumptions of Donne's paradoxical argumentation. The mode of formal paradox is. a mainstay of Donne's early art, both in the arguments of the *Juvenilia* and in the shape of the drama in many love poems. Deliberate fallaciousness seeks fulfilment, not only in the bedevilment of its own chop logic, but also in the concurring dialectic with the reader's counterargument.[10] The final truth played in the intellectual game is not necessarily a mocking parody of reasoning, but reasoning's defence against itself as well as its own pleasure. Such a defence recognizes that reasoning is a continuing activity in time that corrects the misuse of reason.

In 'Communitie' the speaker's argument identifies the foundations for the Christian counterargument against his blunt naturalism. His goddess Nature, not God, created (10) women 'things indifferent' (3), neither good nor ill. Donne's irony notes that God's human creatures were likewise not pronounced good, but for the different reason that goodness is the will's achievement. The speaker thus clumsily strips away the soul by denying its potential for goodness. Women are edibles for common use, to be devoured like 'fruits' or 'meat' or the 'kernell' (19–24). The licence of selfishness not only defies the charity of spiritual love, but also any emotional engagement at all ('wee may neither love, nor hate,' 11). Charity's sacrifice of self is inverted by the sacrifice of others instead. The speaker's careful argument clearly defines its principles of value ('Good wee must love,' 1), the reasons why women fail ('But since shee did them so create,' 10), and the way they might have fulfilled the principles of value ('If they were good ... ', etc., 13). The form for the counterargument is ready-made.

In 'Loves Infiniteness' the temporal dialectic of argument and counterargument unfolds not between poem and reader but within the speaker's mind. The structure of logical conditionals is dismantled singly, then reconstructed to express his changing understanding of his love. Increased understanding itself progressively fulfils love, and the poem's several conditional structures formally invite refinement of that understanding. This logical formulation begins immediately: 'If yet I have not all thy love, / Deare, I shall never have it all' (1–2). The speaker's desire for 'all' must expand beyond a quantitative understanding intoned by sexual need, to the quantitatively unconfined spiritual love. In love, the objectified 'have' (1) must yield to the subjectified 'Be' (33). The monetary language of business (e.g., 'purchase,' 'bargaine') yields to the less rigid, but likewise categorical, 'gift of love' (9) and finally to the mutual vivification of natural growth. Even the rooted love, that owns the 'ground' (21) of growth, acknowledges a constriction through ownership that is released through the growth of mutual engraftment.

The poem's title, not Donne's own,[11] strikes slightly off key unless wisely ironic, since the speaker's desire for 'all' is satisfied by reference to botanical growth. This botanical notion, which lacks infinity's unconfined reach, is fitted to his instinct for objective quantification, hence to his essential nature. Moreover, botanical growth predicts further development consistent with the temporal consciousness of the speaker. The ratiocinative line does not outlive itself, but allows for further progress that answers the demands of changing experience. That the poem's logical resolution may be literally momentary agrees with the poem's temporal development.

The flawlessly plotted logic of 'A Valediction: forbidding Mourning' acts not toward a nervously achieved resolution of love, like 'Loves Infiniteness,' but out from it, not evolving toward a temporal end, but logically prescribing a mode of temporal action informed by mutual belief. Counterargument is neither invited nor expected; the argument to convince, clarifying to confirm shared assumptions, grapples with mutual fears while standing securely on mutual emotional and spiritual conviction. A pattern of logical comparisons would build that conviction into dignified action. These comparisons all embrace motion. The poem first builds comparisons that separate these spiritual lovers from earthly lovers: as quietly as virtuous men die so must the lovers part; trepidations of the spheres differ from 'Moving of th'earth' (9). Later, there are comparisons explicating their spiritual love: their love endures 'expansion, / Like gold to ayery thinnesse beate' (23–4); they are 'two so, / As stiffe twin compasses are two' (25–6), she at the centre like one leg, 'leanes and hearkens' (31), he on the periphery to 'obliquely runne' (34).

In the ambiguity of the introductory 'As' (1) lies the keynote for merging logical and temporal movement ('As virtuous men passe mildly'away'). The ambiguity temporarily allows either a logical comparison or an adverbial clause of time. The delimiting 'So' (5) then sets the logical frame, only to stretch it while developing the elaborate comparison between the actions of love's clergy with those of dying saints:

> So let us melt, and make no noise,
>   No teare-floods, nor sigh-tempests move,
>   'Twere prophanation of our joyes
>   To tell the layetie our love.
>
> (5–8)

This poem reaffirms that, for Donne, logic is understandable only as a function of a rational consciousness shaped by expectations of temporal sequence; in the elaborated comparisons between spiritual union and the motions of expanding gold and circling compasses this fact is most forcefully present. The poem accepts motion as the creature's way; the comparisons everywhere sort out the motions that concern the human composite of body and spirit, most explicitly in the 'Moving' (9) earth versus the trembling spheres, the separation that will physically 'remove' the lovers' bodies, the compass's 'fixt foot' that will 'move' after its wandering mate (27–8). This discursive depiction of spiritual motion makes no claims to exhaust a love 'Inter-assured of the mind' (19), so 'refin'd / That our selves know not what it is' (17–18). Yet human reason has the gift to apprehend partially what it cannot comprehend totally, seizing a share of truth with the terms of its own temporal consciousness. Discursive reason cannot do otherwise; such apprehension is its life, its responsibility, and its mode of salvation.

'A Valediction' shares Donne's habitual insistence, evident throughout his works, on setting analogical comparisons that conceive a participated reality through a logic of likeness. An older tendency in Donne scholarship, to doubt Donne's belief in real ontological connections between analogical thought and outer reality, is threatened by a more conservative estimate of Donne's intentions.[12] Nor need a rigorous logic of analogy contradict an equally energetic 'logic' of paradox. On one hand, Donne believed that reason could discern real emblematic parallels between the Cross and outstretched swimmers, and shipmasts and yardarms ('The Crosse,' 17–24). On the other hand, reason is not excluded from apprehending divine paradoxicality: 'The Father having begot a Sonne most blest, / And still begetting, (for he ne'r begonne)' ('Holy Sonnet, xv,' 5–6). Analogical comparisons stress similarity, but assume dissimilarity; paradox uses similarity as a lure to emphasize dissimilarity. A world view like Donne's that discovers *vestigii Dei* in creatures conceives likeness between physical and spiritual, temporal and eternal, creature and Creator; but it denies absolute identity, hence also announces differences. Analogy and paradox can measure the same reality, but from different perspectives. Dissimilarity scans the great distance between man and God, who has 'begott' a Sonne and yet paradoxically still begets. Similarity shortens that distance by depicting God in terms of man:

Propagation is the truest Image and nearest representation of eternity. For eternity it self, that is, the Deity it self seems to have been ever delighted with it: for the producing of the three Persons in the Trinity, which is a continuing and undeterminable work, is a propagation of the Deity. (*Essays in Divinity*, p. 69)

Reason's need for both analogy and paradox readily admits that paradox confirms reason's own limitations. Yet it is reason that apprehends that to have 'begott' whom one is still 'begetting' or that lovers can 'dye and rise the same' ('The Canonization,' 10) is incomprehensible.

Analogy and paradox can be handmaidens of the same truth, differently complexioned, but with discernible likeness of feature. In 'Loves Growth' the co-ordination between analogy and paradox suggests further how Donne adapts logical form to fill the complex needs of temporal consciousness. Donne modulates from analogy into paradox, first setting points of likeness between love's growth and natural growth, then clearly stressing the concurrent unlikenesses. The speaker's actual love contradicts Platonic authority that would substitute a literary experience ('no Mistresse but their Muse,' 12) detached from real human events. Thus, love that 'sometimes would contemplate, sometimes do' (14) will not separate soul from body, nor disallow temporal change. Closely worked analogies with natural phenomena and natural seasons assert real correspondences between the microcosmic composite of body and soul and the macrocosm. Sexual love changes 'as the grasse' (4), its spring increase, livened by the 'Sunne his working vigour' (10), turns his young man's fancy in correspondence to the heightened spring sexuality of natural creatures. Now physically 'elemented' (13), not 'pure, and abstract' (11), he can do. Donne exacts the harmonious correspondences between men and trees, between aroused but tender sexual love and the beauties of the trees' sexual events, between 'love deeds' and 'blossomes on a bough' (19). This sexual love carries upward, inspiring spiritual increase consistent with the body's union with the soul.

That union inspires the co-ordination between analogical and paradoxical expression in the poem. The analogical movement in the second stanza, from firmament to tree to water to heavenly spheres, describes a concourse acting in both directions between terrestrial and celestial, as between body and soul:

> And yet not greater, but more eminent,
>> Love by the spring is growne;
>> As, in the firmament,
> Starres by the Sunne are not inlarg'd, but showne.
> Gentle love deeds, as blossomes on a bough,
> From loves awaken'd root do bud out now.
> If, as in water stir'd more circles bee
>> Produc'd by one, love such additions take,
>> Those like to many spheares, but one heaven make,
> For, they are all concentrique unto thee;   (15–24)

The poem steps back down to earth in the tree image, to recall the earthly domain of human love. The concentric water circles carry back to the celestial spheres, but the preparatory descent first pushes against this upward movement. This counterforce explains Donne's progression into paradox. What the celestial analogy adds in spiritual elevation to the concentricism and union of the water circles it loses by eliminating the fruitfulness of biological growth. Thus, the poem returns partly to the analogy of the natural year, but rebuilds it as paradox according to a human mould:

And though each spring doe adde to love new heate,
As princes doe in times of action get
New taxes, and remit them not in peace,
No winter shall abate the springs encrease.   (25–8)

To argue that Donne rejects the analogy between love's increase and natural
time[13] misses why he constructs his progression as he does. He takes pains
here to plant man in the natural world, beginning love's growth in sexuality
revived by the spring sun. The paradox that each spring adds new heat
immune to winter's abatement celebrates the wonder of a physical and spiritual human composite. Donne's analogies deeply inscribe the likeness that
discovers man as part of nature, ignoring momentarily the unlikeness owing
to man's spiritual nature. The concluding paradox leaves man, properly for
a being of body and soul, both in and out of nature, in and out of natural
time. It is reason that finds him there; and both analogy and paradox serve
his quest.

Paradox's inner dialectic between likeness and unlikeness, only implicit in
analogy, here captures the dualism of body and soul. Donne's poetry plays
up and down this progression between analogy and paradox to denote concurring dimensions of actuality. The tendency to regard Donne's paradox as
confessing his rational scepticism forgets reason's clear eye in paradox's complex vision. In 'Loves Growth' the sharply cut analogies confirm believed
correspondences between man and the created world with a clarity and sharpness of distinction that is characteristic of Donne's 'metaphysical' mode. Paradoxical experience of love's increase includes that clear-eyed analysis, just as
the experience of faith offered by Donne's sermons includes reason's con-
comitance. Experience collapses unlikeness onto likeness, leaving the sorting
out to reason as part of the soul's necessary apprehension of changing experience.

The complex intimacies between analogy and paradox further suggest
reason's perception of change. Like 'The Anniversarie,' 'Loves Growth' enters
two interrelated dimensions, respectively through body and soul. The search
for natural analogies for love experience acknowledges the cycle of sexual
change, while the paradox pulls the spirit away from the full seasonal cycle
and modifies the principle of natural motion without excluding it. The ex-
acting likenesses between man and nature paradoxically submit to juxtaposed
unlikeness that brings man within the additional dimension of growth. There
spiritual accumulation, becoming more 'eminent,' is the law of motion. Yet
the paradox holds man as body and soul in both dimensions. The categories
of reasoning, of logic and paradox, are to be seen as the attempts of an

essentially temporal consciousness to express the modes of its changing experience without violating its habits of perception.

As noted, Donne affirms this necessary connection between reason and the requirements of time as an article of basic conviction in the Prince Henry elegy. As also noted, the absence of explicit discussion of discursive reason in the love poetry has eroded our grounds for agreement about patterns of reasoning there. For a poet less logical, less argumentative, less dialectical, the consequences would not be so disruptive for criticism. In Donne's case, our estimate of his poetic sensibility, of meaning in the love poetry, and of its relationship to later works are all at stake. Hence, the Prince Henry elegy has a particular significance by setting a fixed point for evaluating reason. The continuing movement of reasoning itself as the beginning of value for man in time is a critical assumption there as in the love poetry. Reasoning's truth or falsity is a measure of Donne's respective personae and their special temporal pressures, not of reason itself. Its essential validity is not at stake.

II SCEPTICISM REJECTED: THE PRINCE HENRY ELEGY

Yet the Prince Henry elegy offers a much broader index to Donne's notion of reason than a flat rejection of ultimate scepticism. Donne not only finds in reasoning the floor of consciousness, but the rudimentary tie to other humans. Conceived as part of a dialectic between himself and an informed inner readership, the poem itself is a sophisticated expression of that tie to other humans through reason. The most arresting fact about the poem, however, is that Donne finds confirmation for his treatment of reason in Augustine. Given Augustine's profound influence on Donne's thought, this fact should not be surprising, if it were not for the received notion in Donne scholarship that Donne's anti-intellectualism and scepticism follow from his Augustinian spirituality.[14] Significantly, Donne looks to *The City of God* for confirmation of reason, finding there a broad context in which the problem of scepticism is inseparable from other problems of mortality such as grief, love, and social ties. For both Donne and Augustine, human consciousness must make constant adjustments to the ruptures of time, in ways that maintain essential ties with others. Donne's poem suggests to both his coterie and his public audiences how this rupture can be understood.

Elsewhere, I have discussed in detail how the poem's coterie audience influenced its content. As noted, the poems of Edward Herbert and Henry Goodyere have a particularly close relationship.[15] By affirming that memory will preserve the prince's value, Herbert gives an explicitly Platonic solution to the problem caused by Henry's death. Herbert's Platonic epistemology is answered by the epistemological form of Donne's poem, with its discussion of the shock to his two 'Centres,' reason and faith.[16] Donne's solution to the shared event is a refutation of scepticism that demonstrates an Augustinian, and not a Platonic, solution. The close links between Donne's and Goodyere's poems reveal that his friendship with Goodyere encouraged the fullness of Donne's Augustinian content.

The centre of Donne's Augustinianism in his elegy lies in the rejection of scepticism. This rejection must be the beginning of any assessment of Donne's attitude to reason. The Prince Henry elegy centres on a fundamental irony: the paradoxical conflict between two constants, mortal uncertainty and continuing value. To accommodate this paradox is to deny ultimate doubt and scepticism. Ironically, the speaker's powers of reason and faith are never really threatened, only his earlier presumption of absolute knowledge and belief. For Donne, the possibilities of reason and faith are constant, however clouded by shock of human weakness; and man advised of his limitations can resolve his mortal uncertainty. Hence, the irony of the poem's conditional ending does not undercut the speaker as does the earlier irony. That is, his request to know the 'historie' (96) of Henry's lady, as a means of establishing Henry's continuing influence on others, does not assume that she will be found. Yet he believes in the *possibility* of one like Henry's beloved, even if her actual existence is uncertain. We find that Donne's irony is central in the poem's crucial rejection of rational scepticism. Ruth Wallerstein perceived in broad outline Donne's Augustinian solution to scepticism, that the mind finds the 'grounds' of both reason and faith in its own 'operations.'[17] What she did not perceive is that his ironic treatment of his speaker is an essential expression of that epistemological issue, and that *The City of God*, as we will see, was Donne's specific Augustinian source.

Human presumption, which is the main target of Donne's irony, lies behind the speaker's exaggerated assertion that Henry's death has killed both reason and faith. The speaker has viewed Henry as a consummated illustration of the unity of reason and faith, since Henry's presence was rational confirmation of human possibility. That is, Henry's very presence immobilized European monarchs who recognized his virtue and feared his future actions. Thus, he prevented 'rumors of warrs' (42) and justified belief that his necessarily peaceful reign would have emblematized 'eternall' peace (36). Accordingly, his death made such belief 'heresie' (43) and killed faith itself. Likewise, reason 'our connexion / Of causes' (65–6)[18] is destroyed, since reasoning from cause to effect is interrupted: whereas Henry's life had proved that certain events caused certain understandable results in Fate's temporal 'chaine' (71), Henry's death opened a hiatus in that chain since he had been the 'only subject Reason wrought upon' (70). The speaker's willingness to see Henry as definitive proof of the mortal powers of reason and faith is presumption. His understanding of reason and faith has hardened into an attempt to ignore mortal realities that these faculties must constantly accommodate. The irony is that his reason and faith continue in spite of his exaggerated grief and shock.

Donne found in *The City of God* a type for such presumption. In belittling the Pagan's audacious attempt to manipulate fate, Augustine asserts that 'fate' is of God if taken to mean 'the whole connection and train of causes [omnium conexionem seriemque causarum] which makes everything become what it does become.'[19] By extending 'conexionem ... causarum' to include logical relationships, while at the same time preserving the Augustinian meaning in the 'links' of fate's 'chaine,' Donne includes in *conectere* both fate and the means of understanding it. Like Augustine's Pagans, Donne's speaker has presumed to control fate: he has assumed that he could understand it completely, since the living Henry seemed to be rational proof of ultimate human potential (19–20). The speaker's exaggerated shock, expressed in the assertion that thwarted rational expectations destroy reason, is the exploded presumption of absolute understanding. Like Augustine, Donne is confronting God's often inscrutable purpose with man's desire for absolute understanding.

The speaker's overconfidence preceding Henry's death and his despair afterwards both deny the proper limits of mortality, which are re-established in the poem's climactic turning point. Though death has harshly reminded him of his limitations, his human powers do remain:

> But, now, for us, with busie proofs to come
> That we'have no Reason, would prove wee had some:
> So would just lamentations. Therefore wee
> May safelier say, that wee are dead, then hee.　　　(77–80)

Rediscovered reason and the proper expression of grief are the necessary beginnings for the outward movement to love, in the search for Henry's beloved as a bridge to God. Thus, understanding Donne's 'proofs' of reason and 'just lamentations' lies at the heart of the poem's meaning. And it is here that the influence of *The City of God* becomes most significant as we see by first examining Donne's treatment of reason and then of 'just' lament.

For Donne the climactic reconstruction of meaning begins in reasoning itself as a testament to reason and knowledge. The very existence of rational 'proofs' precludes absolute scepticism. For both Augustine and Donne rational consciousness itself establishes reason. In *The City of God* Augustine defines the tripartite basis of consciousness: existence, knowledge of existence, and love of it. 'For we both are, and know that we are, and delight in our being, and our knowledge of it' (*City*, XI, xxvi).[20] The first act of consciousness is thus indubitable rational knowledge of existence that refutes the Academics' extreme scepticism that all knowledge is deceptive: for, even to be deceived presupposes that one exists and has rational knowledge of his existence (*City*, XI, xxvi). Donne's argument clearly echoes Augustine's:[21] rational 'proofs' that reason is dead presuppose the use, and hence the existence, of reason.

Donne's juxtaposition of 'reason' with 'just lamentations' clearly ties rational consciousness to a proper expression of human grief. Having rehabilitated his rational consciousness, Donne's speaker has the attendant capacity to recognize 'just' limits. Augustine's discussion of self-recognition in the tripartite consciousness and of its inner sense of the 'just' inspires Donne's statement. Augustine says: 'For we have another and far superior sense, belonging to the inner man, by which we perceive what things are just, what unjust – just by means of an intelligible idea, unjust by the want of it ... By it I am assured both that I am, and that I know this; and these two I love, and in the same manner I am assured that I love them' (*City*, XI, xxvii). This 'inner sense' is a determinant of the 'just' (quo iusta et iniusta sentimus) and affirms truth for the rational mind. Accordingly, Donne's rehabilitated speaker can now assess a 'just' expression of grief.

Significantly, in Donne's poem it is another human's death which momentarily blinds the speaker to his own humanity. And it is the link through love, by seeking the prince's beloved, which will finally reaffirm the possibility of meaning. The very movement outward from re-established reason to other humans for confirmation of the individual consciousness is Augustinian. Augustine argues that man, after he discovers his own tripartite consciousness, looks to other men for confirmation of that consciousness: 'and yet, as we cannot of ourselves know how long they [i.e., the three parts] are to continue, and whether they shall never cease to be, and what issue their good or bad use will lead to, we seek for others who can acquaint us of these things, if we have not already found them' (*City*, XI, xxviii). Likewise, man is bound to other men by love. Just as each man loves God's image in his own tripartite consciousness, he loves other men's love of the Good in themselves and others. However, death knifes through such social ties, denying the means of confirming one's own consciousness, and removing the objects of love.

For Augustine a 'just lament' admits the need to express the resulting human pain, while recognizing the inevitability of such ruptures in a fallen existence; likewise, it recognizes that the possibilities of loving man and believing in God still remain. Augustine says that Cicero's fatherly lamentation for his dead child in *Consolation* is not the 'just' believer's cry salved by hope and belief in heavenly peace (*City*, XIX, iv). But Donne's speaker does achieve such a realization in 'just lamentations.' Thus, the climax defines the speaker's mortality in Augustinian terms. No longer presumptuous or despairing, he can accept his rational powers and his grief as irrevocable birthrights of fallen man.

The final therapy for the reconstructed reason is the link with another human. As noted, the poem's movement outward to Henry's lady traces an Augustinian pattern of confirmation. Augustine's treatment of the uncertainties of necessary social ties also moulds this discussion of Henry's lady. She would have duplicated his rare virtue, and their 'oathes, which only you two never broke' (94), would have denied the perfidies of friendship discussed by Augustine as constant dangers in friendship. The delimiting 'only' emphasizes the rarity of such relationships which, as Augustine says, are ever threatened by vicissitudes by which 'even the best of men are broken down or corrupted, or are in danger of both results' (*City*, XIX, viii). Henry's love assures the possibility of such relationships even if his death was itself a disruption; the speaker has only to hear more of the 'historie' of that love. Here the Augustinian emphasis on the uncertainty serves Donne's irony, for the elegy's affirmative conclusion is hedged in by the intentional mystery of the lady's identity. He *does not know* that she exists, only that *if* she did and *if* he knew the 'historie' of her love and could meet her, he could 'pardon fate my life' (91) and accept his own continuing existence. The more we demand her historical identity, the more we blur the symbolism of his search and miss Donne's point that such uncertainties describe mortality.

This uncertainty sums up the epistemological issue raised by the poem. The conclusion ironically poises the balance between man's desire for clarity and certainty, and the temporal forces disturbing it. At the same time that Donne is demonstrating the profounder ironies in this balance, he is offering an Augustinian synthesis that shows the problems of scepticism to be inseparable from other problems in human existence. Donne's basic Augustinian assumption requires that belief in God, which can accept the vicissitudes of temporal life, depend upon the priority of reason and its continuity. Donne's irony assumes that the temporal moment always forces 'Industrious' man (72) to struggle for 'busie proofs' that are difficult, possible, necessary, however darkened by uncertainty. As emphasized earlier, this is the root assumption in Donne's conception of reason. That Donne chose a major occasion to affirm the importance of reason, for a select coterie as well as a wider public audience, and that he worked out this affirmation using an Augustinian vocabulary set clear terms for assessing the status of reason in his thought.

III THE AUGUSTINIAN FOUNDATION

In the broader field for exposition in the sermons, Donne's treatment of reason works consistently on this Augustinian ground. The unsettling counterthrust has come from modern critics, not from Donne himself. They have argued that the theological basis of Donne's religious intensity lies in an Augustinian tradition of spirituality and in anti-Thomistic Renaissance scepticism and fideism, both of which are supported by Reformation attacks upon reason. However, such argument has too often diverted necessary attention from the exact status of reason in Donne's sermons. The importance of reason is considerably greater and its role in his faith more intimate than has been granted. The critics' emphasis upon Augustinian spirituality has not accommodated the rational elements in the sermons, which are congenial to both Augustine and Aquinas, and which inform content and literary form. Likewise, Donne's differences from Calvin, whose influence pervaded English Protestantism, have not been defined clearly enough. The sermons show that Donne assimilates Calvinistic elements into a basically Augustinian conception of reason while strongly endorsing the powers of reason and its necessary contribution to man's temporal life.

To affirm that Donne strongly endorses reason is to face a long line of dissent arguing for Donne's scepticism and fideism.[22] Although such arguments rightly stress Donne's constant demarcation of reason's limits, they turn a blind eye to Donne's epistemology, which makes reason integral in spiritual life. Previous discussion has turned on the relationship between reason and faith, while neglecting Donne's resolute emphasis upon reason's priority in time. Donne's 1629 encapsulation of his basic epistemological assumption bears repeating: 'by our senses we come to understand, so by our understanding we come to beleeve' (*Sermons*, IX, 357). This statement conforms to Aquinas's notion that all knowledge begins in sensory knowledge,[23] from which reason abstracts the universal characteristics and governing universal principles, a Natural Law 'imbedded in nature'[24] and comprehensible to all men. As Donne puts it, the 'light' of reason enables man to 'discerne the principles of Reason' (*Sermons*, VII, 310) in the natural world. Rational knowledge of principles structuring the natural world is a necessary precursor to faith, since man can determine certain truths about God on the basis of these principles:

The *reason* therefore of Man, must first be satisfied; by the way of such satisfaction must be *this*, to make him see, That this World, a frame of so much harmony, so much concinnitie and conveniencie, and such a correspondence, and subordination in the parts thereof, must necessarily have had a workeman, for nothing can make it self ... (*Sermons*, III, 358)

Reason also shows that this workman, whose Providence watches over the world, necessarily deserves our worship and that he has set forth the terms of worship in written Scripture, the source of 'all Articles of our Beliefe' (*Sermons*, III, 358). Such rational knowledge is prior, in time, to faith. '*Knowledge* cannot save us, but we cannot be saved without Knowledge; Faith is not on this side Knowledge, but beyond it; we must necessarily come to *Knowledge* first, though we must not stay at it, when we are come thither' (*Sermons*, III, 359).

The rational acceptance of Scripture is crucial in Donne's epistemology, further illustrating reason's priority to faith. Of course, simple acceptance of the Bible as God's Scripture is not itself sufficient for belief, but simply takes one to the threshold of faith. Thereafter, each article of faith and each act of belief is founded upon rational knowledge; and in each individual case, rational understanding precedes faith. For example, although the Resurrection defies rational understanding, belief in it rests upon rational conviction. Man reasons: since God is all-powerful, he is capable of raising Christ from the dead; since God is good, he will do what is best for man (*Sermons*, III, 96). Likewise, other parts of the Bible prove that the Resurrection must be believed (*Sermons*, III, 99). Thus, once accepted, the Bible itself provides evidence for proving or substantiating certain religious truths. Christ's miracles prove his divinity, and hence give reason for believing in him as God (*Sermons*, III, 296). Here, as elsewhere, belief presupposes reason, since rational acceptance of the Bible must occur before the miraculous events can be believed. And belief in miracle – and here is a point to be stressed – becomes the rational premise for subsequent belief; alternating acts of reason and belief lead to the ultimate belief in Christ's deity. By necessity reason is part of the *modus operandi* of faith, even though paradoxically denied complete comprehension of its own premises as it moves higher in the realm of faith. Not only is reason not excluded from the realm of belief, it is necessary to belief, exercising a continual priority. Donne's insistence upon this rational justification of belief, as a means of suggesting reason's importance, shows that he found it an important pattern for the way in which the mind first refers experience to rational scrutiny. This does not make Donne a rationalist, or deny the depth of his spirituality or religious emotionalism. But it does oblige us to see his desire to understand as a constantly moulding factor in his religious experience.

The status of reason before and after belief is anatomized further in Donne's distinction between the 'common Reason' and the *'new facultie of Reason'* of the 'regenerate Christian' (*Sermons*, III, 359). And the Augustinian form of this distinction undercuts assertions that Donne belonged to the 'anti-intellectual tradition of Augustine.'[25] Donne argues that natural knowledge is attained by the 'common Reason,' a neutral force, serving good or ill ends. 'All the wayes, both of Wisdome, and Craft lie open to this light, this light of naturall reason' (*Sermons*, III, 360). The same faculty, with the same basic powers, operates in either case, but the ends differ; that is, the same 'common Reason' that participates in the invention of printing or artillery develops the 'humane Arguments' (*Sermons*, III, 359) that bring man to accept Scripture. In the regenerate Christian, however, true understanding that leads to wisdom requires an act of the will whereby, with humility and prayer, reason works to understand and love the truth found in Scripture. The *'new facultie of Reason'* is thus reason aided by faith, and seeking wisdom. Frank Manley correctly relates Donne's distinction, between the 'common Reason' and the 'new facultie,' between knowledge and wisdom, to the Augustinian distinction between *Scientia*, 'knowledge of this world only,' and *Sapientia*, 'knowledge of this world and the next.'[26] To examine, in greater detail, the Augustinian basis to Donne's thought in this regard is revealing.

Augustine divides the faculty of reason into two functions, *ratio* (or *ratio inferior*), leading to knowledge of temporal things, and *intellectus* (or *ratio superior*), leading to wisdom or knowledge of the divine.[27] *Ratio* is the discursive reason, which moves from one kind of earthly knowledge to another; *intellectus*, however, refers to intuitive understanding of higher truth. In its higher reaches *intellectus* is necessarily aided by faith, which bends the corrupted will, freeing reason to understand the truths of Christian faith. A point to bear in mind, especially in light of Donne parallels, is Augustine's assertion that knowledge must precede wisdom; *ratio* must precede the faith that leads *intellectus* to wisdom.[28] Augustine's famous dictum, *credo ut intelligam*, applies only to religious knowledge, which is dependent upon prior earthly knowledge, hence upon *ratio*; Augustine's emphasis upon the primacy of faith should not blind us to reason's part. As Gilson points out, the Augustinian conception of reason's relationship to faith consists of three steps: reason's preparation, the act of faith, then understanding the 'content of faith.'[29] Thus, the life of faith depends upon reason in both functions, *ratio* and *intellectus*, since, as Donne says, the 'Essence' of man is 'Reason, and understanding' (*Sermons*, I, 225). Further details of this dependence indicate the strong similarities between Donne's and Augustine's thought. For example, *ratio* and earthly knowledge constantly serve *intellectus* and wisdom. The discursive movement of *ratio* leads to understanding of higher truths, as in the constant needs of doctrine and Biblical interpretation, which utilize earthly knowledge within the life of faith. In comparison, it is useful to recall Donne's stairstepped alternation between reason and faith, as in the proof of Christ's divinity noted earlier. For Augustine, there is a 'discourse'[30] proper to wisdom (as well as to knowledge), and this is the discourse of theology, which depends upon reason in both functions. Only in moments of mystical contemplation is the mind free from its discursive movement altogether. As Augustine says, the faith necessary for wisdom is 'begotten, nourished, defended, strengthened' by the appropriate human knowledge.[31]

Failure to see detailed similarities between Augustine's and Donne's respective notions of reason has skewed modern understanding of Donne's use of Augustine. Donne's critics, unlike Donne himself, have too often accepted the distorted Reformation emphasis upon the non-rational in Augustine. Part of Donne's abiding interest in Augustine is rooted in Donne's attempt to create a role for reason consistent with both his own intellectual nature and his sense of human limitations; like Donne, Augustine had set the same task for himself. For Donne, the priority and continuity of reason, natural to a mind which constantly sought rational understanding, determined the contours of belief.

Donne's notion of man's intellectual needs and powers accounts for many elements necessary for assessing the sermons as literature. If reasoning is an important activity and if, as has been argued, Donne centres sermon style in psychic experience,[32] then we must necessarily assess reason's part in that experience. The recurrent vocabulary of logic and argumentation, and argumentation *per se*, must be explained. Donne's sermons are woven together from both rational and non-rational; to undervalue either is to unravel the literary fabric. As noted, reason's epistemological role is an especially crucial issue, expressing Donne's continual thrust to rational understanding. But reasoning for Donne pervaded the whole of Christian existence, ranging from moral choice to prayer. The consequences for the sermons as literature, in content, vocabulary, style, and structure, are profound.

An obvious indication of Donne's stress on rational effort is the language of formal logic, particularly the syllogism, occurring in widely varying contexts. The forms of Aristotelian-Thomistic logic and argumentation (i.e., syllogistic reasoning) are formal expressions of mental processes and are inextricable from Donne's conception of rational thought. For example, of God-given calamities he says that man must not judge calamity by the 'predicament of Quantity' (*Sermons*, VIII, 319). Another example is the '*Syllogismus practicus*' (*Sermons*, IV, 122) in moral choice, probable reasoning with conclusions syllogistically deduced from previous knowledge. Donne's analysis of reproof further suggests the importance of syllogism as a mental process. Reproof is a 'proofe, a proofe by way of argument' (*Sermons*, VI, 317) whereby, arguing syllogistically from certain moral standards, one tries to convince a wrongdoer of his error. Consequently, when, after delineating the syllogistic nature of reproof, he exhorts his auditory to self-reproof (*Sermons*, VI, 329) by convincing their consciences, he is invoking the internal syllogizing integral to moral rectitude. Behind Donne's interest in logic and argumentation is the notion that reasoning is the natural activity of a rational soul, whether rectified or fallen; that the 'common Reason' always operates, however debased its ends. Wayward argument in behalf of self, not God, is an adjunct to human perversity. Perverse reasoning is sin against man's essence, '*peccata cum ratione* and *cum disputatione*' in argument against God and the Church: 'we will reason, we will debate, we will dispute it out with God, and we will conclude against all his Arguments.' The sinful man enlists argumentative devices and knowledge of philosophy, perversely seeking a '*Quia*' and an '*Ergo*' against God, thereby abusing the rational process necessary for godly existence (*Sermons*, I, 225). In a word, the Christian is defined by right reasoning, the sinner by perverse reasoning. A similar principle describes the personae of the love poetry.

The frequent language of reason (i.e., formal logic) is explicit evidence of reason's importance for Donne; but the unexpectedness of reasoning in certain circumstances even more tellingly announces just how integral reasoning, logical thought, and argumentation are in his Christian consciousness. Prayer is a good case in point. Donne singles out the 'for' in a prayer of Jacob, introducing Jacob's reason for asserting his unworthiness. The prayer proceeded not from mere habit or custom, but from 'debatement, and consideration and reason' (*Sermons*, I, 277). 'He praises not God, he prays not to God, he worships him not, whatsoever he does, if he have not considered it, debated it, concluded it, to be rightly done, necessarily done' (*Sermons*, I, 278). Prayer assumes prior rational consideration. That Donne illustrates the rational content of prayer with Scripture relates to a likewise unexpected interest in the logic of Scripture. A verse from Paul's letter to Colossians is part of a Pauline argument, with the 'for' a particle of connection as well as argumentation (*Sermons*, IV, 283). The first clause – '*For, it pleased the Father, that in him should all fulnesse dwell*' – is an 'Inference' drawn from preceding verses. The logical form warns that man is not to accept religious matters 'meerely without all reason, and probable inducements' (*Sermons*, IV, 283). This interest in the logical substratum of Scripture is fully consistent with Donne's emphasis upon the constancy of human reasoning.

Donne's notion of rational activity is also recorded in more subtle ways.

Donne argues that a Christian's actions best indicate his assent to the Bible, becoming 'arguments for it to others, to convince them that doe not, and confirme them that doe beleeve in it' (*Sermons*, I, 299). The word 'argument,' although a figure for the effect of moral example on others, suggests that the cognitive response approximates the discursive process of reasoning, with others' actions as premises for one's own actions. Donne's characterization of memory is likewise revealing:

The Memory is as the conclusion of a Syllogisme, which being inferred upon true propositions, cannot be denied: He that remembers Gods former blessings, concludes infallibly upon his future. (*Sermons*, VIII, 262)

As in the previous example, Donne, by discussing a non-rational process in rational terms, translates one mental process into another approximating it. Terms from argumentation or inference, used as reference points for other mental activities, affirm perhaps even more convincingly than explicit discussions of rational forms that the syllogism for Donne embodied an indelible pattern in human consciousness of temporal sequence.

Joan Webber contends that Donne's sermons reveal his growing awareness that non-rational dimensions of meaning are the more important, and that his style became more associative and less logical as a consequence. However, the discursive, inferential elements of his thought must be fully assessed. Webber rightly emphasizes Donne's 'meditative' style which, she argues, is the attempt to make prose an accurate form for thought itself. She argues that in *Biathanatos* Donne discovered that syllogistic organization is an artificial form superimposed upon thought.[33] Rather, the mind moves associatively, seizing thoughts or fragments of thought in a much less predetermined manner than is characteristic of the more linear, syllogistic development. Meditative style in Donne is the offspring of an increasing dependence upon memory,[34] which functions like the modern unconscious, spontaneously recalling instinctive truths and aspects of one's experience. Accordingly, Donne is much less likely to reason from proposition to proposition. Admittedly, any account of Donne's mature prose must assess its segmentation, its denial of Ciceronian order. But to invoke the Augustinian memory, asserting Donne's desire to abandon syllogistic order, and not stress Donne's acceptance of the syllogism as natural discursive thought, is to misread Donne's notion of rational activity. Donne's loosening of syllogistic structure does indicate an increasingly sophisticated notion of mental activity. For example, Donne's characteristic exfoliation of qualifying clauses and phrases often seems to loosen argument, submerging it in intervening sentence elements. By stretching syllogistic thought to embrace ideas emerging, sometimes associatively, in a particular thought sequence, Donne makes prose embody less structured cognitive materials. However, the remaining bones of syllogistic argumentation usually form a skeleton for his thought, even in non-argumentative passages. The syllogism is rarely dismembered completely.[35]

This syllogistic substratum is an essential element in Donne's so-called meditative style. His repeated description of sermons as 'meditations'[36] makes his notion of meditation here very significant. As in the following examination of the sinner's misuse of reason, he discusses meditation as part of reason:

But when we come to sin, upon reason, and upon discourse, upon Meditation, and upon plot, This is *Humanum*, to become the Man of Sin, to surrender that, which is the Form, and Essence of man, Reason, and understanding, to the service of sin. (*Sermons*, I, 225)

Elsewhere, David prepares for confession: he recalls his sins to his memory, then 'considers' how to rid himself of them, then resolves to confess. This 'consideration' or 'meditation' is a rational effort necessary for devotion: 'And such a premeditation, such a preconsideration, doe all our approaches, and accesses to God, and all our acts in his service require' (*Sermons*, IX, 303). For Donne, the words 'consideration' and 'meditation' are virtually interchangeable and fall within the sphere of reason. Donne never explicitly differentiates between meditation and consideration, on one hand, and argumentative proof, on the other. However, his discussions *per se* of proof and argumentation, as in his discussion of miracle as proof for Christ's divinity (*Sermons*, III, 295), are tightly argued and rigorously syllogistic. In contrast, his sermon style is generally much looser, but informed by its syllogistic substratum. His conception of whole sermons as 'meditations,' and sermon parts as 'considerations,' forces us to say that meditation for Donne included syllogistic thought. As noted, he does make it explicit that syllogistic thinking is indigenous to reason and that meditation is a rational process.

That Donne's meditative style also accommodates the less structured behaviour of memory is fully consistent with Donne's Trinitarian psychology, which co-ordinates the memory, reason, and will. Augustinian psychology appeals to the less stubborn memory in order to bend the Fall-weakened reason and will, to direct them to their proper ends in understanding and loving God. But, this is not an either-or choice, to the memory or to the reason and will. Recollecting man's debility and God's blessings moves the will through fear and love for God; the will, in turn, guides the ever active reason in search of knowledge of God. Human life involves continuous co-operation between man's three faculties. Donne's conception of his sermons as 'meditations,' and of meditation as a function of reason, cautions against over-emphasizing the role of memory in this co-operation. The elements of argumentation and rational exploration of doctrine, which are essential in both Donne's and Augustine's faith, follow necessarily from the rectification of will and reason. Reason always operates, but finding its proper end depends upon an activated memory and healthy will. That memory acts like the conclusion of a syllogism for Donne suggests that reason and memory inform, restrict, and characterize each other in their close interaction. Some of Donne's sermons may appeal primarily to the memory, just as others appeal primarily to the reason or will; but any approach to the sermons should alert us to the continuity of reasoning, which constantly interacts with materials gathered from the memory, and which is basic to exhortation.

Donne's analogical metaphor is another important element of reason in the sermons. One tendency in modern criticism is to regard Donne's figurative language as a retreat from reason, as another example of his appeal to emotion;[37] but such arguments rest uneasily with Donne's contrary assertion that the Holy Ghost is a 'Metaphoricall, and Figurative expresser of himselfe, to the reason, and understanding' (*Sermons*, IX, 328). Donne's notion of metaphor refers to the Augustinian division, noted earlier, of reason into *ratio*, the discursive reason, dealing with earthly things, with knowledge; and *intellectus*, the intuitive understanding, leading with the aid of faith to wisdom. Dennis Quinn points in the right direction by arguing that 'Biblical rhetoric springs from the double nature of Christ,' and that the preacher imitates the 'divine process visible in Scriptures' of applying Christ's merits to men.[38] For Augustine, the Incarnate Word is the pattern for the Biblical Word, on which the preacher models his rhetoric, including his poetic figure. And we do well to recall that Augustine argues that the double-natured Christ is known through both *ratio* and *intellectus*: the temporal, physical side of Christ, the events performed in time, belong to *ratio*; and his divine nature, to *intellectus* aided by faith. It is in Christ that knowledge and wisdom reach the perfect balance:

Through Him we reach on to Himself: we stretch through knowledge to wisdom; yet we do not withdraw from one and the same Christ, 'in whom are hidden all the treasures of wisdom and of knowledge.'[39]

Understanding Biblical figure, which manifests spiritual truth in physical form, follows the same pattern. The Augustinian 'similitude' functions analogically; a physical referent leads to a spiritual truth, *ratio* leads to *intellectus*. For example, the 'wise serpent' is the regenerate 'new man,' who is like the serpent which, 'having forced its way through narrow openings, sheds its skin and renews its vigor.' *Ratio* yields knowledge of the snake, 'knowledge of things' that leads to understanding the spiritual analogue, the 'new' man.[40] As Donne says, Scriptural figure works on 'reason, and understanding,' that is, reason in both dimensions. And here we have the basis of Donne's compulsion, manifest everywhere in the sermons, to explain the analogues in his metaphors.

A good example can be found in a sermon on Penitential Psalm 3:28. To emphasize the Church's significance, Donne delays equating the Church with the Biblical 'way,' tantalizing the auditory into need for complete elucidation; then, in a beautiful, poetic passage, he makes the equation:

They did see that Pillar in which God was, and that presence, that Pillar shewed the way. To us, the Church is that Pillar; in that, God shewes us our way. For strength it is a Pillar, and a Pillar for firmnesse and fixation: But yet the Church is neither an equall Pillar, alwaies fire, but sometimes cloud too ... Our way, that God teaches us, is the Church; That is a Pillar; Fixed, for Fundamentall things, but yet a moveable Pillar, for things indifferent, and arbitrary.

Donne's eloquence subserves rational meaning; the Church, as the 'way,' takes on the Pillar's characteristics, all of which are clearly, rationally articulated. Later, Donne reiterates the analogue between 'way' and Church; the 'Evill man' is a constant threat, even though the Christian 'go in the right way, the true Church' (*Sermons*, IX, 362–3). The auditor's rational faculty is never at rest.

To recapitulate, any critical description of the sermons must account for integral rational elements which characterize Donne's thought. For Donne, the priority of reason is a salient clue to the essential rational nature of human consciousness. His interest in logic, particularly the syllogism, in a variety of human experiences, including prayer, reproof, moral choice; his interest in the logical dimension to Scripture; his notion of 'meditation' and metaphor as rational – all attest to the pervasiveness of rational consciousness and its demands. That Donne saw misdirected reason as corrosive to belief is not inconsistent with the needs of this consciousness, nor is the increasing emotional glow in his religious life. He saw reasoning as a constant, for the sinful and the rectified; for belief itself needs help from an active reason while it directs reason to its proper end in understanding divine truth and living a rectified life. The important distinction, not yet sufficiently embraced by

Donne scholarship, is that Donne's reason does not contradict other elements of his Augustinianism, but is, on the contrary, informed by an Augustinian rubric: man as a rational creature must reason before and after belief. Donne's 'common Reason' is the Augustinian *ratio*, necessary for the knowledge that obeys and aids wisdom, the domain of *intellectus*.

IV THE REFORM INFLUENCE

As elsewhere in Donne's thought, Augustine's thoroughgoing influence emerges in special ways. The Augustinian rational components, boldly present in the foreground, are the foundation for Reform influences. Unlike many of his Protestant contemporaries, Donne affirmed the tripartite Augustinian soul against the more contemporary Reform notion that subordinated the memory to the reason and will. A closer look, however, reveals a more complex realignment that admits contemporary pressures as well. In fact, the memory in Donne has nothing like its scope in Augustine;[41] and its considerable importance in Donne does not prevent its disappearance when Donne slips into a natural contemporary idiom addressing only the understanding and the will. Yet Donne was not sympathetic to Reform denigration of the reason. Rather, he entrusted to reason a virile co-operation with Grace, while embracing the Reform emphasis upon the Spirit's role. The indwelling Spirit was one of the most salient epistemological and psychological factors in Donne's maturity. Similarly, a popular Reform vocabulary for describing mental processes – discernment, confirmation, assurance, impression, and sealing – is tailored to Donne's own needs and sets him very much in his contemporary Protestant context.

The persuasive influence of Calvin, whom Donne admired greatly (*Sermons*, III, 101), supported English Protestant conceptions of the human soul and the Holy Ghost's tutelage. Calvin divided the soul into the understanding (intellectus), which had the 'office' to 'distinguish (discernere) between objects,' and the will, to act on these distinctions.[42] Through free choice, reason would direct the appetite and temper all organic motions.[43] The Fall blinded the rational intellect and bound the once free will, hopelessly perverting the once erected soul and its offices. No longer could reason know God's will manifested in creation, and no longer could the will freely choose to obey that Will without divine enablement. Benighted, ignorant, reason no longer discerns and knows God's nature and will; even the most ingenious are 'blinder than moles'[44] and have no rational capacity for divine ends, whatever their prideful political and technological skill.[45] Once sound and erect, now maimed and puny, the soul can be repaired only through divine initiative.

The centre of Calvin's epistemology and psychology is the Holy Spirit illuminating the darkened mind and renewing the perverted heart. The Spirit applies the Word, repairs the damage for which costs have been paid by the Incarnate Word. Christ's sacrifice cancels the debt to divine justice; the events of his life, teachings, and Passion host patterns for fulfilled being and acting; and his nourishing presence resides in Scripture, the Church's sacraments and ordinances, and the preaching of the Word. His Spirit is the divine agency of his application, and human faith the object of his restorative notions in the reason and will.

Calvin's weighted emphasis on faith aggressively denigrates natural reason's capacity to know God, but does not lay reason aside. Significantly, faith speaks a metamorphosed language of rational epistemology; and, more, faith is a 'firm and certain knowledge (cognitionem)' of God that is 'both revealed to our minds and sealed (obsignatur) upon our hearts through the Holy Spirit.'[46] Supernatural knowledge of faith is reason drawn beyond itself by the Holy Ghost. That the transformed reason is accompanied by the vocabulary of natural reason expresses the continuing participation of the natural mind in the supernatural experience. And Calvin's energetic attack upon the emasculation of natural reason does not disbar a propped-up reason from participating in religious experience, as the reworked vocabulary of reason indicates. The 'knowledge' (alternately: cognitio, scientia, notitia) or 'recognition' (agnitio) of faith transcends 'comprehension' (comprehensio, apprehensio) dependent on sense perception. Although the mind is 'persuaded of what it does not grasp, by the very certainty of its persuasion it understands more than if it perceived anything human by its own capacity.' Such knowledge involves 'assurance' (certitudine, securitate) and not comprehension. To have more certainty than mere rational discernment, nonetheless, acknowledges the necessity of that rational ability (discernere, perspicere, apprehendere) as does spiritual discernment through faith.[47] Calvin repeats St Paul in 1 Corinthians 2:14: 'The natural man cannot receive (percipere) the things of the Spirit of God, for they are folly to him, and he is not able to understand (intelligere) them because they are spiritually discerned (diiudicantur).'[48] Paradoxically, the rational language of faith declares natural reason's failure while pulling reason upwards by the bootstraps of its own terminology. Discernment, understanding, knowledge – all semantically astride the chasm between fallen nature and the erected world of faith – discover the rational faculty on both sides of the chasm while exploring the hostility of dissimilar worlds. The discernment, understanding, and knowledge of faith are identified by the certainty that transcends comprehension and owes to the heart, the will,[49] not the reason. Calvin faulted Scholastic faith as mere rational assent denuded of the heart's 'confidence and assurance' (fiducia et securitate)[50] that engaged the heart's affection in love of God. The understanding of faith, enjoying the assurance and confidence of the heart's embrace, stimulates both head and heart to transcend themselves, but only under the Holy Ghost's tutelage.

Faith erected by the Holy Ghost carries man upward across the chasm between the natural and the spiritual. Calvin's exposition of the Spirit's role ever respects the inner co-ordination between reason and will; faith requires that the Spirit illuminate the reason while confirming and establishing the will:

The Spirit accordingly serves as a seal [sigilli], to seal up [obsignandas] in our hearts those very promises the certainty [certitudinem] of which it has previously impressed [impressit] upon our minds; and takes the place of a guarantee to confirm [ad confirmandas] and establish [constituendas] them.[51]

The Spirit supernaturally lifts the soul beyond its own understanding[52] by impressing and illumining the reason and confirming the will, yielding respectively the enlightenment and assurance of faith that 'know' God with certainty. The Spirit himself is the seal that guarantees, that seals the certainty of the faith he creates. Calvin's terminology, which predicts the commonplace epistemological and psychological vocabulary of much English Protestantism, including John Donne's, acknowledges the Spirit's motions as the major constituent that draws the natural soul into the supernatural activity of faith's 'knowledge.'

Yet these consistencies are redesigned by Donne's differences from Calvin, by and large determined by Donne's much greater respect for human powers. This is one major reason why we must resist Barbara Lewalski's persuasion that Donne's essential drift is Calvinistic.[53] The Spirit finds much more powerful human efforts in Donne than Calvin. Not that Donne does not often seem to strike our ears in harsher Reform tones, spitting out incriminations at the damnable human 'toad' (Sermons, I, 293), proclaiming the elitism of Election (Sermons, II, 325), or abjectly requesting the battering of Grace; he frequently seems to invite being tarred with a radical Reform brush. Yet Donne's revisions mollify such harshness. His conception of Election delays Reprobation until required by the individual's own actions in the present (Sermons, II, 323), even grants the possibility (since no human being could know for sure anyway) that all are chosen, but must freely accept the call through faith (Sermons, V, 53–4; II, 323). Similarly, his notion of the Incarnation suggests that all humans can be saved through Christ (Sermons, VI, 159). His elitism of the Elect similarly refutes Calvin's harshness; however abject the human toad, some men 'were sav'd without the knowledge of Christ,' through rectified reason (*Sermons*, IV, 119). Thus, for Donne natural reason is the 'doore of faith,' but for Calvin it is worse than a mole in divine matters. Donne's Augustinian argument against scepticism, plus reason's priority in time, reject the spirit of Calvin's rational abjectness; yet Donne learns well his Reform lessons about God's active presence in human understanding and acknowledges faith as a manner of knowledge.

An Easter sermon gives reason its rightful place as the necessary foundation of faith, the way for God's 'seal of faith.' Although the articles of faith are not amenable to reason but depend on revealed Scripture, reason must establish Scripture. Reason and faith, though different, are congenial, not 'continuall,' but 'contiguous'; 'they flow not from one another, but they touch one another, they are not both of a peece, but they enwrap one another.' Then a Donne statement that knows Calvin's epistemology: 'Faith it self, by the Prophet Esay is called knowledge; *By his knowledge shall my righteous servant justifie many*, sayes God of Christ; that is, by that knowledge, that men shall have of him' (*Sermons*, IV, 351). Though endorsing the necessary independence of reason, thereby drawing back forcefully from a Calvin-like scepticism, Donne's statement appreciates the psychological validity of faith's 'knowledge,' which engages the rational faculty beyond itself, differentiating reason's 'knowledge' from faith's. Yet Donne's adaptation of Isaiah 53:11 assumes that actual psychological experience of Christian belief blurs the exact boundary between the co-ordinated activities of reason and faith in the believer whose soul is fully directed in God. Rational comprehension fits into the full experiential understanding of faith that subsumes and fulfils it.

For Donne, reason tends to maintain its own individuality, even within the life of faith, thereby escaping the extreme destitution of Calvin's natural reason. Reason's discernment, its power to distinguish or perceive truth, is not swallowed up totally into the spiritual discernment of Calvin, but preserves its natural identity within the religious life. For example, Christian Sacrament necessarily is offered to men of 'understanding.' To take the Lord's Supper and 'not *discerne it*, (not know what they do)' (*Sermons*, V, 148) is to court danger. Habitually for Donne, discernment occurs under rectified reason's auspices. Clearly, this is only a difference in emphasis between Donne and Calvin, since Donne wants no rigid boundary between reason's knowledge and faith's. Yet the interplay between reason and the Spirit finds the edge of difference between Donne and Calvin. To 'prove and discerne the spirit' man must have 'so much reason, and understanding, as to perceive the maine points of Religion.' A 'naturall explicite reason' is not necessary 'for every Article of faith'; but reasons are necessary to prove that the Articles 'need not reason to prove them' (*Sermons*, IX, 384). Reason meets, discerns the Spirit in Scripture, satisfying its own independently firm demands. And reason's searching discernment must seek to recognize and open to the Spirit's illumination. 'Maintain that light, discerne that light, and whatsoever thy darknesse seemed, it shall prove to be but an *overshadowing of the Holy Ghost*' (*Sermons*, IX, 124). Rational discernment preserves the deeply etched lines of its human identity, while seeking the Spirit's instruction. Donne's use of Reform vocabulary reveals this difference from Calvin.

Nonetheless, Donne followed the Reform pattern whereby the Holy Ghost visits the reason and will. God through the Holy Ghost draws man by the faculties, 'the limbs of the Soul'; he 'enlightned their understanding' and 'rectified their will' (*Sermons*, I, 313) to invite the soul to the love embrace of faith. Donne also investigates the psychology of faith using the commonplace Reform terminology of confirmation and assurance. Having instructed reason, the watchful Holy Ghost establishes and confirms through the believer's assurance of Heaven (*Sermons*, IX, 352–3). 'If he be my Witnesse, he proceeds thus in my behalfe, his Spirit beares witnesse with my spirit, for mine inward assurance, that I stand established in his favour' (*Sermons*, IX, 229). Confirmation or establishment stands to assurance as contributing cause to spiritual or psychological effect; and assurance stands to faith as major product. One passage that acknowledges its explicit debt to Calvin denotes assurance as the distinguishing characteristic of faith, through near equation with it: 'they declared their faith, their assurance, that Christ could, and would help him' (*Sermons*, X, 74). It is the Holy Spirit that leads man to this faith; it is he that seals the assurance of salvation (*Sermons*, II, 262). Nonetheless, Donne continues to remind us that distinctions can be made between knowledge and the assurance of faith. For example, he distinguishes the different means whereby 'knowledge' and 'assurance' of the resurrection respectively accrue (*Sermons*, VII, 95). Closed to reason, the mystery of the Resurrection yields only to belief begotten by the Holy Ghost. 'We beleeve it immediately, intirely, chearfully, undisputably because we see it expressly delivered by the Holy Ghost' (*Sermons*, VII, 101). Rational knowledge prepares for faith and defends it afterwards, as the lantern the fire. Assurance is of faith, but Donne characteristically keeps us reminded of its debt to reason.

Assurance is the confidence, the certitude of heart, that describes faithful adherence to God's truth; it is the musculature of the erected will, strengthened, encouraged, exercised by God. The 'constant assurance' of faith (*Sermons*, X, 74) strengthens the believer against temptation, affliction, perplexity, and fear of death. The Spirit 'imprints in us a holy certitude, a faire assurance that he will never forsake us' (*Sermons*, IX, 345); when he 'shall separate you againe' in death, he 'will establish you with an assurance' of Resurrection (*Sermons*, VIII, 109). The Spirit's imprint establishes active patterns of felt psychological experience necessary to faith. For Donne, the manner of imprint invokes co-ordination between will and reason, and the Spirit and reason. Regarding Job and the importance of God's witness, Donne links witness to assurance; the Spirit's witness to the human spirit bears causally on the will's 'inward assurance, that I stand established in his favour' (*Sermons*, IX, 229). Whatever the vehicle that conveys the Spirit's witness or testimony, as I will indicate later in regard to conscience, the reason judges the will's change as evidence that assures the will further. That the Spirit enlightens the reason and establishes the will respects the natural psychological and epistemological pattern which refers will to the counsel of reason.

Confirmation or establishment, the means for achieving assurance, follows similar assumptions. Belief that follows understanding and yields assurance requires 'an establishment, a confirmation, by an incessant watchfulnesse' by God's Spirit (*Sermons*, IX, 352). The Spirit guides man from understanding, to established belief, to assurance of faith. He toughens and substantiates the will through reason his lieutenant. God manifests 'signes' of his Will in 'irradiations, illustrations of the understanding' for man to discern (*Sermons*, VI, 177). Reason then builds the foundations that establish the will. Confirmation and assurance are daily needs, and Scripture is necessary to meet that need. And Donne always brings reason to Scripture: 'He declares his will by his *Word*, and he proves it, he confirmes it; he is *Logos*, and he proceeds *Logically*' (*Sermons*, V, 103). The Holy Ghost, in Scripture and in the events of human experience, leads man up the scale of belief, from reason, to confirmation, to assurance, maintaining reason as the base line.

Thus, Reform elements in Donne's thought do mark the character of his mature epistemology and psychology, but, as with his Augustinianism, in accordance with Donne's own theological and spiritual temperament. Donne recognized in Augustine a congenial attempt to define the respective contributions of natural faculties and Grace; and he accepted Augustine's demarcation of reason into *ratio* and *intellectus*, while following his lead against scepticism. Donne's respect for human reason and his need for active divine aid led him to enunciate the rational elements in Augustine's thought, while acknowledging the Reform characterization of the Spirit's motions. The Reform elements of discernment, faith's knowledge, confirmation and assurance, like the Augustinian elements, are conscripted for Donne's larger purpose, a notion of saving knowledge that fulfils the human soul by engaging its full capacities. This 'knowledge' depends on the axis in Donne's mature thought uniting reason and the Spirit.

V THE JUDGMENTS OF CONSCIENCE

We have moved from considering reason's activities in the love poetry and
from Donne's rejection of scepticism in the Prince Henry elegy to considering
the Augustinian and Reform elements in his thought. We have thereby shifted
the accent from reason as a response to temporal events to more theoretical
principles in Donne's mature thought. However, to consider further the
relationship between reason and the Spirit is to remind ourselves that even
Donne's more theoretical considerations assume the pressures of life in time.
The epistemological and psychological events of his religious works, however
variable his explications of reason's or the Spirit's respective motions, assume
this axial relationship occurring in man's temporal experience. Much in Donne's
thought ramifies this assumption. Reason acts in a broad field that contains
the notions of conscience, participation, impression and seal, and spiritual
fullness; all these interdependent notions are indigenous to his theology and
spirituality, and define further the 'knowledge' gained in time that saves man.
To search reason's relationship to the Spirit is to find the common denominator in these notions and also to find that the believer's fulfilment in time
requires an active reason aided by the Spirit.

As to conscience, two principles form the matrix of Donne's conception:
first, that it is 'illumined and rectified' by the Spirit and that it also admits
'*humane arguments*' and, second, that conscience is man's '*Iudge*' and Scripture
his '*law*' (*Sermons*, IV, 216). The first assumes that the primary function of
conscience is rational, and that the Spirit behaves toward conscience as toward
the entire rational soul; the second denotes the legal function of conscience.
Yet this conception of conscience maintains ratiocination in time as the experiential constant in conscientious behaviour.

That the Spirit illumines and rectifies conscience is congenial with the
Reform framework of the soul, of reason and will. Donne's broadest depiction
of conscience encircles both faculties and their respective contributions to
conscientious behaviour. '*Conscience* hath but these two *Elements, Knowledge,
and Practise*; for *Conscientia presumit Scientiam*' (*Sermons*, VI, 256). Conscience
debates, concludes, and does; voluntary action concludes ratiocination. Not
itself a faculty of the soul, but a power of the soul's other faculties, conscience
enacts them in the domain of conscientious behaviour. Consistent with his
keen attention to reason, Donne carefully draws the lines of ratiocination in
the face of conscience, denoting the intimacy between understanding and
conscience. The '*Syllogismus practicus*' on the basis of 'former knowledge' of
what 'ought to be done' is the life line of conscience (*Sermons*, IV, 122). The
major premise is a known principle of right action; the minor premise is

achieved through self-knowledge of one's own actions; the conclusion follows deductively from the judgment rendered. Such self-knowledge is reason's achievement: to 'know' his sins man follows conscience in 'this scrutiny, this survey, this sifting' (*Sermons*, IV, 150), reason in its aspect of conscience, turned inward on the contents of memory, discerning to know, no less a rational examination of data toward *scientia* than less intimate rational activities.

The ultimate major premises of conscience's syllogism are God's law, known jointly by God and man: literally, con-scientia. God manifests his wisdom and truth in laws amenable to human understanding as guides for human behaviour. Before the Fall, rectified understanding needed only the law written in our hearts, the unsullied perception of Nature, remaining even now sufficient for the rectified Socrates or Plato (*Sermons*, IX, 82); Mosaic Law acknowledges that sin's damage permits such rectitude in few and offers a code for repair; the Gospel, in turn, fulfilled Mosaic Law with the New Law of Christ. What the Christian conscience knows jointly with God is his Law in all three manifestations, Nature, Law, and Gospel, as premises for rectified thought and action. Thus, conscience as 'judge' discerns law in his own heart and in Scripture.

Donne's concept of conscience looks to Law in the narrowest sense, as normative and pedagogical premises for specific actions, and in the broadest sense that finds the eternal Word as agent of Judgment inhabiting the human soul and advising the judgment of conscience. This broader acceptation recognizes all divine law as a manifestation of God's will expressed in his Word, embodied first in Creation, then in Law and the Prophets, then in Christ. The Word informs Nature, Mosaic Law, and Grace, as God's wisdom, as the truth of his Law; to know Christ in full experiential knowledge is to incarnate his truth, and know him as the principle of all action. Donne's near identification, first, between Christ and rectified reason ('*Christus Ratio*'), then, between conscience and rectified reason leads directly into his concept of experiential truth: 'Whosoever lives according to rectified Reason, which is the Law of nature, he is a Christian' (*Sermons*, IV, 119). The Law of Nature embraces both the divine truths and the rational means of apprehending them; Christian Law patterned after the righteousness of the Incarnate Word and embodied in Scripture similarly demands knowledge and vivified reason. Rectified reason, discerning and abiding by divine law, further incarnates that Law that manifests the Word: that is, Christ is imaged in rectified reason of the Christian, similarly in his rectified conscience (*Sermons*, V, 65–6). It follows that the reasoning of rectified conscience according to God's Law is an enactment of divine law, a manifestation of the indwelling Word.

Donnian conscience – everywhere circumscribed by the language of courts, judges, trials, witnesses, accusers, evidence, advocates, sentences – is conceived further in the ties between law, justice, and judgment. But Donne's broad theological assumption requires brief elucidation here. Divine justice, moved by its very nature, executes judgment through the body of Law. The respective manifestations of God's will in the Laws of Nature, Moses, and the Gospel declare the principles of obedience and also the consequences of disobedience, all according to divine Justice. Law embodies righteousness (or innocence) and satisfaction for violations committed, thus containing both standard and retaliation against infringement (*Essays in Divinity*, p. 87). The divine Judge expresses his own righteousness in demanding satisfaction for its violation. In its connections with Christ, divine judgment stands at the heart of Donne's theology and spirituality, for, as Donne asserts, quoting John 5:22: '*The Father judgeth no man, but hath committed all judgement to the Sonne*' (*Sermons*, II, 311).

The face of Donne's Christocentricism takes shape further thereby, as does his conception of rectified conscience as meting out divine judgment. Christ exacts all three determining events of Divine Judgment: the Judgments of Election, Justification, and Glorification in the Last Judgment. Christ judges; the believer in turn conscientiously ascertains and applies his judgments. In the Judgment of Election Christ separated the 'vessels of honour and dishonour in Election and Reprobation' (*Sermons*, II, 323); the believer in turn finds within himself a saving conviction that Christ died for him. In the Judgment of Justification Christ separates servants from enemies in the Church; for his part the believer must ask whether or not he has yielded himself fully to the Church's ordained 'application' of the Word and Sacraments of Christ Jesus that would justify him. The anticipated Judgment of Glorification previews Christ at the Last Judgment, separating sheep from goats: 'If you would be tryed by the third Judgement, do you expect a Glorification, or no?' Such expectation makes the believer reject past sin, loathe future sins, and eagerly welcome Christ's coming at any time (*Sermons*, II, 324). Like Justice, Judgment is a coeternal element of the divine nature; it is delegated to Christ the Son, whose Judgment Day carries through both eternity and the 'whole circle of time' (*Sermons*, II, 313). Man resides on the circumference of time's circle, and only by searching his own temporal consciousness can he find evidence of Christ's judgments of Election, Justification, and Glorification. It is conscience that arbitrates the search and judges the findings.

Fear of ultimate Judgment is pedagogical:[54] its lesson begins with the necessity of self-judgment. 'He that believes that God will judge him, is Gods Commissioner, Gods Delegate, and, in his name, judges himself now' (*Sermons*, VIII, 343). Conscience presides as judge, ordering the full internal tribunal in which man tries himself: he is cited, witnesses are called, evidence given, judgment made, and sentence passed according to God-given Law known jointly by man and God. Conscience's 'judgment' and 'evidence' engraft its legal to its rational function. Judgment, Donne tells us, is 'the last act of our understanding, and a conclusive resolution' (*Essays in Divinity*, p. 90); and evidence contributes to rational proof. The *syllogismus practicus*, applying general principles of Law to individual conditions known through rational self-discernment, reaches rational conclusions or 'judgments.' Thus, it is conscience that seeks, sifts, and judges the internal evidence for Election, Justification, and Glorification; as vice-judge, it enacts self-judgment under God's auspices. With the principles of Justice internalized, rectified conscience knows likeness to God, assimilating man to Christ in his function as Judge, incorporating in man the Justice, the Righteousness of the Word. To underline a crucial point: for the human creature, discursive rational judgment and 'legal' judgment become one.

VI REASON AND PARTICIPATION

It is the Spirit that internalizes, applies Christ's judgment in the human conscience; and, as anticipated earlier, the judgments of conscience illustrate the axis in Donne's mature thought joining the reason and the Spirit. How this is true in regard to conscience, however, is best discovered as part of Donne's fundamental notion of participation in God through likeness. The Spirit's inhabitation assumes the Son in the human soul, and the Father as well. An important Biblical source for this pivotal expression of Donne's notion of participation is Romans 8:16: '*The Spirit it selfe beareth witnesse with our spirit, that we are the children of God.*' The critical ingredients are the Spirit's witness of man's Election; Christ's merit that meets the demands of his own judgment; and Sonship to God the Father through adoption. The Spirit testifies to the conscience that, through participation in Christ's meritorious sacrifice made evident in man's erected behaviour, the believer has regained sonship weakened by the Fall. That is, he becomes like Christ the Son; he participates in God. Having received witness of Adoption from the Spirit, the believer cries '*Abba, Father,*' acknowledging the Father's inhabitation, through the Son, in the soul. This obligatory 'witnesse' not only discloses further legal implications of conscience and enters the legal dimensions of participation, but also manifests the Spirit's necessary epistemological and psychological contribution to the 'knowledge' of Christ that informs the soul and guarantees salvation. Thus, the Spirit's 'witnesse' locates that axis uniting human reason to the Spirit, and to Christ as well. Some detailed explanation of these points is necessary.

The Spirit offers his 'witnesse' in the 'triall' or 'judiciall proceeding' of self-judgment commanded by Christ (*Sermons*, v, 59). This trial seeking proof of man's sonship to God binds mutually: man to offer evidence of righteousness and faithful assurance of his sonship, and God to accept favourable evidence as legal title to rights as God's heirs. At bottom is the covenantal promise to the righteous, and Christ's meritorious sacrifice, applied by the Spirit and enabling human effort to meet the Covenant's legal demands. Man's self-judgment meets claims of both satisfaction and righteousness, both accusing sin and affirming righteousness. Both God and man must witness on man's behalf. Man's own witness is rectified conscience, clear-sighted evidence or 'proof' of 'testimony' of right thought and action. The Spirit also 'bears witnesse'; he 'pleads, he produces that eternall Decree for my Election' manifested in holy life (*Sermons*, v, 67). Just as the Bible under the Spirit's authorship is 'Proofe, Evidence of the will of God to man' (*Sermons*, v, 66), so is the Spirit's witness to the soul: that is, faithful assurance of Election. Such evidence proves the favourable Judgment of Election affirming man's sonship and legally entitling him to share the legacy of sonship with Christ.

The Spirit's witness to the rational human spirit announces his habitation 'in' man (*Sermons*, VIII, 266). The indwelling Spirit teaches the saving knowledge of Christ that enables man to participate in his tripartite God and alone leads him to heaven. The Spirit's pedagogy, saving knowledge of Christ crucified, God's resultant inhabitation in man, and man's participation – are all configured Biblically in Donne's treatment of Pentecost, and all relate to the axis uniting the rational human soul to the Spirit. A Whitsunday sermon commemorates Christ's promise to send the Spirit: '*(John* 14:20) *At that day shall ye know, that I am in my Father, and you in me, and I in you.*' Pentecost builds the paradigm: the Spirit's testimony as evidence to the Apostles, and to all believers, of their inheritance through Christ. Such evidence is 'knowledge which we have of our interest in God, and his kingdome here' (*Sermons*, IX, 233). To know through the Spirit proves inheritance; knowledge as way, knowledge of Christ in the Father ('*That I am in my Father*'), man in Christ through the Incarnation ('*you are in me*'), and Christ in man through the Spirit ('*and I in you*'). The 'evidence' is itself the 'way,' through which the Father is in Christ, God in man, and man in God through the Spirit's witness.

The language of 'knowledge' here reflects the verve of fulfilled spiritual experience, refusing to compartmentalize reason's knowledge from faith's, instead merging to co-ordinate them. This 'knowledge' embraces mysteries: the Trinity, the Incarnation, Redemption. And only faith holds mystery. Yet

the events proclaiming these mysteries are historical fact 'known' to the believer, unlike prophetic events of the Old Testament, which are only shadows
of the future. The 'Legacy' of fact 'is not only in a possibility, and in a
probability, and in a verisimilitude, but in an assurance, and in an infallibility,
in a knowledge, we know it is thus, and thus' (*Sermons*, IX, 234). Donne's
argument need not uncover its own foundations here: that rational substan-
tiation of Scripture defends the Bible's superiority to other Scriptures; that
a reason explicitly undergirds each article of belief; that Scripture itself is
rational; that events recorded in that Scripture may rest on faith, but offer
rational evidence for further events. Reason and faith may alternately lay the
bricks of 'historical fact' as convincingly as naked rational knowledge. Donne's
progression – possibility, probability, verisimilitude, assurance, infallibility,
knowledge – reaches 'knowledge,' but admits 'assurance' as an alloy, a conviction with faith's assurance. The Spirit's authorship of Scripture works the
stops of both reason and faith in creating understanding of historical fact
inherent in mystery, strengthening the habit of conviction.

The knowledge promised by Christ is experiential, not thinly notional,
but it builds reasoning and notional conviction so integrally into the structure
of faithful experience as to indicate its guiding pervasiveness. The drama of
Pentecost configures the Spirit's contribution to that knowledge, for the
'illustration of the holy Ghost' is necessary for the 'right understanding' of
Scriptures (*Sermons*, IX, 245). For the Christian, Scripture is the foundation
rock of belief, placed by the Spirit, its strength confirmed by reason: that
there is a God; that he speaks in Scripture; that the Bible is that Scripture.
The historical events and principles contained in Scripture similarly assume
rational proof to confirm them and to erect from them the outworks of faith's
'knowledge.' The Spirit illuminates understanding of Scripture, present help
aiding past authorship, confirming the foundation and constructing the out-
works of Scripture into the very experience of the believer. Pentecost configures the illumination of that reasoning believer. The illumined believer
may 'know' principles of the mysterious Trinity, e.g., that Christ is 'in' the
Father. Such mysterious 'knowledge' of faith assumes earlier rational justification of Scriptural authority, which in turn offers confirmation of its own
principles. The Spirit moves the will while illuminating the reason; both
motions contribute to faith's knowledge. The distinguishing line between
reason and faith progressively blurs, as believed principles, explicated by
reason and illumined by the Spirit, become the rational footing for subsequent
rational argument. As habit plays the principles of faith back and forth between the left hand reason and the right hand faith, these principles are
assumed by the ever active reasoning mind.

Most important, Christian experience itself confirms principles of faith's knowledge. Principles are 'known' as they are experienced, in such a way that reasoning, believing, and experiencing mutually invest the events themselves. That Christ is 'in' God, and man 'in' Christ, means little without actual experiential knowledge of Christ within: 'The largenesse and bounty of Christ is, to give us of his best treasure, knowledge, and to give us most at last, To know Christ in me' (*Sermons*, IX, 248). This experiential 'knowledge' touches the outward and inward events of erected Christian life: 'obedience to his inspiration,' 'reverent' use of Word and Sacrament, the Spirit's visits in effectual Grace. Only reasoned, explicit faith[55] can expect and recognize these events, though naked reason discerns their occurrence; both reason and reasoned faith thus 'know' the experience of Christ within. Understanding Biblical principle comes first, but only experience completes the knowledge of Christ within. The double perspective between principle and experience recalls the experiential basis while satisfying reason's justifiable need for manageable intellectual standards. Donne illustrates the gradual shift, between experiential 'knowledge' of Christ and that same knowledge changed to a principle, in terms of conscience; it is a 'Syllogisme that comes to a conclusion; Then only hath a man true knowledge, when he can conclude in his own conscience, that his practise, and conversation hath expressed it' (*Sermons*, IX, 248–9). Conscience translates experiential 'knowledge' of Christ's inhabitation into the premise of syllogistic proof. Right behaviour in turn reverses the direction by returning rational proof, hence rational 'knowledge' of Christ 'in' man, both to the believer himself and to others.

Throughout this Whitsunday sermon, Donne's broadened term 'knowledge' persistently alloys reason to faith as the central Christian experience of 'knowing' Christ. This alloy expresses man's participation in God, unswervingly respecting the character of the reasoning mind while assuming supernatural fulfilment through the Spirit. This 'knowledge' of Christ, by which man participates in his Triune God, is the lesson of Pentecost: '*shall ye know that I am in my Father and you in me, and I in you.*' The Spirit, who informs Creation according to the eternal Word, informed the apostles' power to communicate Christ, just as he informs Christ in the believer: 'the Holy Ghost applies the promises, and merits of the Son to us, and so is the Word of God to us too, and enables us to come to God' (*Sermons*, IX, 241). Through the Spirit's witness the believer experiences 'knowledge' of Christ within; and through that experiential conformity to the Son, he also finds adoption by the Father. Pentecost celebrates participation in God through refined awareness of the Spirit. Where the reason discovers the Spirit's motions in actual experience, and hence finds the Spirit himself, Donne sets the touchstone for saving knowledge. There believers find themselves 'partakers of his divine nature' (*Sermons*, IX, 248).

To summarize the foregoing commentary on conscience and participation, we need to keep focused sharply on the relationship in Donne's thought between reason and the indwelling Spirit. Conscience in its functions of rational self-scrutiny and considered action sits in judgment on human actions, internalizing principles of divine justice by following the example of Christ, the Incarnate Word. The tribunal of conscience is visited by the indwelling Spirit of Christ, whose witness contributes to conscience's syllogistic deliberations. Conscience's knowledge of law, shared with God, ever dilates beyond mere principle to right behaviour, in which conscience clearly perceives its own and the Spirit's contributions. Also, the full Trinity participates in the human soul through the Spirit's motions; for saving knowledge of Christ that results is proof of man's adoption by the Father. The Spirit's recreative motions, divine repair against sin's erosion, reingraves the likeness between the tripartite soul and tripartite God. Thus, the Spirit's application, the saving knowledge of Christ, enforces the Creator's participation in the human creature. Donne's epistemological and psychological vocabulary enunciates the design of this participation: the broadened experience of human 'knowledge,' that hones natural reason to discern the Spirit's saving presence and to maintain his aid. That such 'knowledge' exceeds reason's powers has inadvertently caused some readers to find scepticism and fideism in Donne: in fact, Donne makes clear that saving 'knowledge' can only outdistance reason by using it. Donne also makes abundantly clear that his notions of conscience and participation view this 'knowledge' from two different, but compatible, directions; the contribution of natural reason can be seen from both.

VII IMPRINT AND SEAL

For Donne, since the 'best' in us is 'our Reason, our Discourse, our Consideration' (*Sermons*, X, 46), the relationship between reason and the Spirit is the centre of man's participation in God; that relationship is both explicit and implicit in the varying spiritual tempos and intonations of the religious experience informing Donne's works. But the terminology of participation is incomplete without the notions of impression and sealing. Predictably, we find further evidence of co-ordination between reason and the Spirit; and, again, we do well to remind ourselves that this co-ordination distinguishes fulfilling life in time. This terminology further characterizes the fulfilment of reason in the saving knowledge whereby man participates in God. Again, the implications for both epistemology and psychology are extensive.

Donne's traditional notion of sealing approaches likeness from two perspectives, God's and man's. The Creator God seals the creature with his image and likeness, bestowing filiation: the human creature in turn must fulfil his engraved likeness, damaged by the Fall, by devoting his human powers to God in rectified being. Only the saving knowledge of Christ again engraves the damaged likeness, erecting the lapsed faculties, returning man to God. Gradual, aided by Grace, fully achieved only in Glory, sealing is necessarily known through the Spirit's 'witness' or 'testimony' to the human spirit. The Spirit is both the seal and the agent of sealing: that is, his presence ratifies the believer as God's heir and contributes to saving knowledge that earns adoption. To 'know' Christ through the Spirit's testimony, or witness, or seal, is to experience the epistemological rudiments of Christian participation in God.

Donne's theology of participation, impressed and sealed form in matter, has broad application to all human knowledge and being. The distinction between imprint and seal bears repeating in reference to the Creational archetype. That is, the Spirit imprints form in creatures after preconceived ideas or forms resident in God's Wisdom or Word, thus sealing or verifying filial likeness between creature and Creator. Impression denotes formal characteristics in creatures; seal in turn denotes the fact of filiation and likeness to the Creator. Just *seal* sometimes encloses both meanings, but *impression* more often preserves its specialized identity. For example, human behaviour causes behavioural changes in other humans: the changed behaviour is both the imprint, accidental form, and the seal of likeness with the human cause. A likeness is sealed, pronouncing the filiative participation of effect in cause. All terrestrial actions repeat the archetypical act of Creation, the Spirit imprinting and sealing form in matter. Either essential form, through impressed likeness to God, or accidental form, through impressed likeness to agent creatures, confers being. Similarly, evil deforms, and God must reform. 'When the devil imprints in a man, a *mortuum me esse non curo*, I care not though I were dead, it were but a candle blown out, and there were an end of all: where the Devil imprints that imagination, God will imprint an *Emori nolo*, a loathness to die, and fearful apprehension at his transmigration' (*Sermons*, VIII, 188). Good battles evil, pitting impressed form against impressed deformity, with the soul's accidental form[56] lying in the balance. The point for Donne's theology of participation is that all being exists according to imprinted and sealed likeness between cause and effect, whether in material forms or human actions.

The epistemological crux is that erected being is knowledge of likeness as the essence of created reality, in impressed form and sealed relationship to informing agent. Thus, erected being must discern, in order to know imprinted form in all events and phenomena; similarly, it must discern the seal of likeness that identifies the cause. Beings and events, physical and spiritual, past and present and future, impressed and sealed by God, established and yet occurring – all must be known by man. Such knowledge, by erecting the tripartite soul, enhances man's likeness to God, and hence his participation in God. Most important, man must recognize God's impressions and seals in his own experience, since God continues in history and human hearts, imprinting and sealing as he did at Creation. For example, he may imprint a 'holy confidence' (Sermons, v, 376) or forms of knowledge; similarly, a discernible grace ratifies or proves his love (Sermons, v, 310). Man must discern not only imprinted psychological effect, the inner event, but also the sealed divine significance. That is, he must interpret what the seal means, that his joy or sorrow is evidence of God's favour or his degree of participation in God. The pattern is familiar: reason must discern, understand, know; the Spirit moves, imprints, seals.

An abundant and manifest God considers man's physical and spiritual needs, engraving with tangible public seals, as well as inner, private ones: 'Home-infusions, and inward inspirations of grace' are the 'Privy seale'; the public Ordinances of the Church are the 'Great seale' (Sermons, v, 310). The sealing Ordinance, 'participation of the helps of the Church,' includes public prayer, preaching, Sacraments, sacramental helps, most significantly the Seal of Baptism, the initiation into Christ's Body, the Church (Sermons, X, 63). Baptism's seal initiates man into the whole Ordinance, the more collective seal, and contracts man to perform conditions covenanted with God. The sealing ordinance accepted, fulfilled, visits the Spirit's inner witness in the human spirit; encouraging bonds of unity through Christ. The Church's public face, its ordinance, manifests God, specifically Christ; its eye is the Spirit that 'lookes upon' and 'foments and cherishes' the individual soul (Sermons, IX, 367). Grace grows in nature; the Ordinance prepares, cultivates, as well as conveys; its custodians, the Church's ministry, work on reason, man's 'best,' aiding and serving him as factors of the Spirit. Sermons illustrate reason and establish faith; prayer is rational, whatever else (Sermons, V, 237); Sacrament as spiritual conveyance assumes understood principles (Sermons, V, 148). Grace grows in this soil, first mysteriously, then apprehended by reason and embraced by faith, followed by the Spirit's witness to the human spirit (Sermons, II, 262–3). The public Ordinance visibly manifests, catechizes, seals participation in Christ's Body; the Spirit's inner witness catechizes and seals participation in Christ's Spirit as well. Thus, instructed in saving knowledge of Christ, the believer renews his divine likeness that guarantees participation in God.

VIII FULLNESS AS GOAL

Saving knowledge of Christ, participation in the Spirit, sealing as evidence – all co-ordinate the central experiential truth of Donne's thought. Continuing intercourse between reason and the Spirit works toward that truth, although Donne's characterization of achieved spiritual life loosens any strict compartments momentarily erected to examine reason. Their walls may extend or contract, but not the clarified sense of reason's pervasive contribution to saving knowledge. Alloyed with faith, not denigrated or sloughed off, reason's indelible contribution melts together the respective identities of epistemology and psychology, engaging the entire soul. Notional and voluntary conviction, rational understanding and loving belief, mutually absorb the Spirit's guiding motions, experiencing gradually the spiritual fullness that is the beginning of heavenly fullness. This fullness of saving knowledge is mid point from the Spirit's initiatory enlightenment of reason and full 'experimentall' (*Sermons*, IV, 87) knowledge of God in Heaven. Donne's conception of reason ripens in this conception of fullness.

The saving knowledge of Christ results from Christ's nature as a receptacle for the informing values of the Godhead, a 'full capacity to all purposes' (*Sermons*, IV, 284). Paul is the source: 'For, it pleased the Father that in him should all fulnesse dwell' (Colossians 1:19). To 'know' experientially Christ's saving patterns is to achieve the conformity that fills man with Christ. Fullness is a progressive reincarnation of Christ in the believer through the Spirit's motions; Christ is born again, comes in the 'fullness of time,' now conceived in the believer's heart and not in Mary's womb. Earthly time is thus filled with divine value when the believer's experience is filled with Christ. Just as fulfilment of prophecy in Christ's life promised future glory, the believer likewise fulfils his own past through Christ and earns future glory, fulfilling Nature through Grace, to achieve Glory. He finds within himself a threefold fullness begotten by God: A 'fulnesse of nature' in the use of natural faculties to 'fill up' God's purpose in him; a 'fulnesse of grace' to help him against temptation; and a 'fulnesse of glory' possible on earth for the believer (*Sermons*, VI, 335). New spiritual abilities, feelings, and thoughts are the measure of this fullness; the internalized model of Christ's life applied by the Spirit is the means. This earthly participation in God, circumscribed by its temporal human residence and hence paradoxically ever fulfilling, will become complete fullness only in glory.

Such fulfilling earthly progress achieves only temporary Sabbaths, degrees of fullness and satisfaction, not an arrested completion that knows both. The goal of Christ's perfection, more insatiably desired as more fully known, expands ever beyond the believer's grasp, though growing righteousness will alleviate sin's burden and quicken the spiritual pace. The legacy of fallen Adam separates fullness from satisfaction. For example, he may be filled with knowledge sufficient for salvation, but not enough to satisfy knowledge of unrevealed mystery. Likewise, he may think that he 'knowes all, when, God knowes, he knowes nothing at all' without knowledge of 'Christ crucified' (*Sermons*, V, 276). Yet a satisfying fullness of Christian belief is possible by knowing and loving God's will manifested in man's Calling (*Sermons*, V, 278). Competence in Vocation after the known pattern of Christ's fullness increasingly gives earthly satisfaction of man's desire for God. Complete fullness and satisfaction, however, are heaven's reward.

Earthly fullness does anticipate heavenly fullness; earthly knowledge of Christ anticipates 'experimentall' knowledge of Christ in Glory; here, the 'face of Christ' manifested in the Gospel (*Sermons*, IV, 124), there, Christ the 'treasure of all knowledge' face to face (*Sermons*, IV, 129). Earthly man participates in the Gospel Christ through the Church and its Ordinance. This participation, founded in 'explicit knowledge of Articles absolutely necessary to salvation' (*Sermons*, V, 276), erected into missionary knowledge how to rectify other souls and into the Christian warrior's religious knowledge, defends against inner and outer threats to the Church (*Sermons*, V, 275). As emphasized earlier, reason lays the foundation and mortars together the edifice of faithful knowledge embodied in thought and deed. Once in Glory, the erected soul is no longer deflected by sin, but turned to God: '*I shall know as I am known*: that glory shall dilate us, enlarge us, give us an inexpressible capacity, and then fill it' (*Sermons*, IV, 129). Knowing as God and angels know, with the full capacity of one's own nature, man will know Christ face to face. The erected reason will know intuitively and directly; and the will shall love the known without perversion, in the co-ordinated fullness of achieved experience.

A great distance separates reason's 'busie proofe' of its own existence from its fulfilled intuitive knowledge face to face with God. Increasingly in Donne's works, the Spirit's motions guide man's way through this great distance, teaching knowledge of Christ crucified, preparing the soul in its progress toward fullness. While the Spirit moves, reason must discern, judge, understand, and know. The same faculty that must pursue the changing rhythms of time in the secular love poetry, seeking to expand the moment, must scrutinize its own changing experience for the imprinted motions of the Spirit's seal in the divine works. Reason's tasks are many, from the humble self-scrutiny in the judgments of conscience, to the knowledge of man and God that teaches wisdom. Above all, reason must constantly sift the soul's own changing experience, in love, joy, assurance, contrite sorrow, changed habit, enlarged comprehension, for evidence of the Spirit's seal. In the gradual fulfilment that describes increased 'knowledge,' reason learns to recognize personal experience of Christ crucified. This knowledge, which outruns reason's own comprehension, depends upon reason's own vigilant guidance and tough-minded applications. As time is fulfilled in the individual soul, in the dilated capacities of reason, memory, and will, it is reason that must sharpen discernment of changes that mark the soul's participation in the indwelling Spirit. In sum, reason's own increase within the sequential movement in time's circle captures Donne's indelible sense of reason's importance. For him, man's 'Form, and Essence' is his 'Reason, and understanding' (*Sermons*, I, 225), essential to his fulfilling participation in God.

3

Bodies

In Donne's thought, knowledge, likeness, participation, and being all express the same truth. Knowledge is understanding of likeness; likeness is participation in being; and gradations of being required varying levels of knowledge. Donne investigates this truth throughout his works; and, although his mature works conduct this investigation with more confidence, his sense of direction always remains the same. His habit of discerning likenesses and establishing comparisons assumes the system of imprinted correspondences that informs created reality, both physical and spiritual. For Donne, all created likenesses and correspondences refer finally to man as the goal of Creation, with pointed emphasis upon the relationship between the human composite of body and soul, and the rest of creation. Few writers keep the eye so keenly trained on the body as he does; few observe with such dissecting intellect its sweaty hands, resident insects, tears and sighs, excretions, lingering illness, decay, and dissolution; few submit their dissections so vigorously to the unflagging control of logical similitudes that refer the body and the details of its experience to the soul, to the material world, or to the social world. Donne's attention to the human body rarely falters: its anatomy, physiology, pathology, and medicinal needs invite his scrutiny. His near equation of knowledge and being necessarily regards knowledge of the body and its experience as intrinsic to being.

However, Donne's conception of the body comprises several dimensions. Similitudes between the body and the physical and social worlds, often crafted with the disciplined logician's hand, define further Donne's attention to the body as an object of knowledge. Just as the natural world is fulfilled in the human body, the body is fulfilled in a human community. Accordingly, by means of the correspondences, the microcosmic body participates through likeness in these macrocosmic worlds. Reversible shifts between microcosm and macrocosm, often too swift for logical formulation, are commonplaces throughout Donne's works. Configuration of the soul's experience in terms of the body's is likewise commonplace. But these commonplaces reveal Donne's deepest assumptions about matter and form, body and soul, in the traditional terms of the microcosm-macrocosm. Predictably, the crux is epistemological: saving knowledge recognizes the body not only as the soul's lieutenant, but also as its primary physical datum, a means to understand not only physical creation, but the soul itself. Therefore, the several correspondences implicating the body must be known. Donne traffics both ways along the correspondences: knowledge of the human body yields knowledge of the 'body' of the physical world, the social Body, or the soul; they, in turn, all yield knowledge of the body.[1] We can approach the complicated epistemological role of the body in Donne's thought through, first, Donne's assumptions about Creation, second, the correspondences between body and soul, and third, those between the individual body and the social Body.

First, Donne's notion of Creation frames his notion of the microcosm. His assertions – that man is an 'abridgement of the whole world' (*Sermons*, IX, 83), that he contains 'The properties, the qualities of every Creature' (*Sermons*, IV, 104), that myriad parallels can be drawn finely between man and the macrocosm – assume that the microcosm is the purpose of Creation. Accordingly, man as the fulfilment of Creation even has 'many pieces, of which the whol world hath no representation' ('4. Meditation,' *Devotions*, p. 19). Quite simply, man 'next to the glory of God' is the 'reason why there is a world' (*Sermons*, VI, 297–8); all creation points to man and God, not to itself. The human body, God's 'Master-piece, amongst mortall things' (*Sermons*, VII, 259), consummates physical creation, to meet in a composite with its 'Angelike spright' ('Holy Sonnet, V'). The intention of Creation was to people Heaven with human bodies: 'The Kingdome of Heaven hath not all that it must have to consummate perfection, till it have bodies too.' To this end the Trinity created 'a materiall world, a corporeall world' (*Sermons*, IV, 47).[2] Thus, the six days of Creation are a 'progresse' running in accumulative steps toward the Sabbath (*Sermons*, IX, 83), and the body is a 'recapitulation' of everything 'said or done, in all the six dayes' (*Sermons*, VII, 272). The progressive stages, being, living, sense, are fulfilled in understanding 'Which understanding and reason, man hath with his Beeing, and Life, and Sense' (*Sermons*, IX, 82). The masterpiece, the human body, subsumes these lower stages in order to perfect them, to be stamped with God's image. All other creatures are *Vestigia Dei*; man is *Imago Dei* (*Sermons*, IX, 83), corresponding in detail to other creatures, while completing the principles of their being. Although man's Fall released destructive and complicating motions of disease, corruption, deformity, disorder and death into the macrocosm, the natural world maintains the imprint of Creational progress in its hierarchy of beings. Mineral forms serve vegetable forms; vegetable serve animal; and animal, human.

If approached through the notion of Creation, the body's epistemological role in Donne's works is more understandable. Its climactic creation not only explains the motive for all physical creation, but also stresses that the body is the central physical element in epistemology. Saving knowledge includes an assessment of the relationship between God and the human composite, the bodily side no less than the spiritual side. Although the macrocosmic Book of Creatures manifests God, Donne's gaze carries through the macrocosm to the microcosm, less interested in what the macrocosm tells directly about God or itself than what it tells about the microcosm. For Augustine the created world enunciated God's glory;[3] and for Calvin, his Wisdom.[4] But Donne's more constricted eye seeks God through illumination of man. Donne's epistemological chain, leading from sense to reason to faith, seems Thomistic, but it takes on another colouration through Donne's continuing search to find imprinted correspondences between the physical world and the human body. Understanding the structure of the macrocosm or its parts is significant primarily for what it tells man about the structure of the microcosm and its parts. Knowledge of both the world and the body serves this self-understanding.

The second important element in the body's epistemological role is that the comparisons between microcosm and macrocosm, throughout Donne's works, express the soul's experience. For example, in 'A Valediction: of Weeping' the comparison between the speaker's tears and the global world reveals the soul's condition; similarly, in *Devotions upon Emergent Occasions* the earthquake, lightning, and thunder of the body's illness reveal sin's corruption. Reversible modulations from world to human body to human soul pronounce another crux in Donne's thought: the correspondences between body and soul that fulfil the correspondences between the microcosm and macrocosm. The body, the masterpiece of physical creation, is fulfilled as the servant of the soul. The soul's bones are its 'strongest powers and faculties' (*Sermons*, V, 353); its blood, the will (*Sermons*, IV, 294); its stomach, the memory (*Sermons*, II, 236); its eyes, the understanding (*Sermons*, VI, 101). Digestion is the work of both memory (*Sermons*, II, 236) and reason (*Sermons*, IX, 274); reason chews, faith swallows (*Sermons*, V, 47). The correspondences between macrocosm and microcosm do not halt at the body, but use it as a middle term between the world and the soul. For example, the notion of the body's corrupted carcass establishes correspondences between the carcass of the world

('The Second Anniversarie,' 55), viewed in terms of its corruption, and the carcass of the sinful soul (*Sermons*, VIII, 188–9). In sum, knowledge of the macrocosm – even more important, knowledge of the body – informs understanding of the soul. Donne's keen interest in the minutiae of contemporary scientific and medical thought becomes more understandable as the knowledge necessary for reading the emblematism of the soul's experience: the more known about the world and the body, the more about the soul. The *Devotions* sharpens the crucial point most succinctly: 'in the state of my *body* ... thou dost *effigiate* my Soule to me' ('22. Expostulation,' p. 119). A final inference is that the correspondences between microcosm and macrocosm provide a further means of clarifying the experience of the soul.

The Creational paradigm, Donne's central figure for regeneration, assumes the correspondences between body and soul that cement a compatible dualism. Significantly, the six-day history of Creation, except for the concluding infusion of the human soul, records physical Creation. However, Donne resolutely characterizes the progress of spiritual regeneration according to this six-day-pattern (*Sermons*, II, 240–3) because successful recreation, like the completed microcosm, subsumes all foregoing stages. Accordingly, any stage in recreation corresponds to a given stage in Creation; and the soul contains all creatures by correspondence, just like the body. In sum, detailed correspondences between body and soul represent a crucial assumption in Donne's unifying notions of the microcosm-macrocosm and of Creation and recreation.

The body's correspondences with the macrocosmic body and with the soul extend centrifugally the body's importance in Donne's epistemology. Reason must ascertain the details of the body, as well as dissect the correspondences and construct the logical forms stating them. Correspondences between the physical body and the social Body – and this is the third crucial element in the body's epistemological role – further the centrifugal extension. This traditional corollary to microcosmic-macrocosmic thought⁵ expresses Donne's troublesome need for community. In a 1608 letter to Henry Goodyere, he laments that yet unsatisfied need. Even the 'greatest persons, are but great wens' if not 'incorporated into the body of the world.'⁶ When Donne says that a person not incorporated is 'nothing,' he is characteristically evoking the polar tension between nothing and creation (*Sermons*, VIII, 177). Donne's traditional assumption conceives the social Body formally according to the shared bodily form of the individuals comprising it. But, predictably, Donne ingeniously discovers the lines of subtler correspondences. Earthly bodies that 'partake of the good of the State' constitute the state. They are 'inanimated with one soule: one vegetative soule, head and members must grow together, one sensitive soule, all must be sensible and compassionate of one anothers miserie; and especially one Immortall soule, one supreame soule, one Religion' (*Sermons*, IV, 47). For Donne, such comparisons always find their power in the immediate bodily realities of human physicality. The Body exists only as a union of flesh and blood members; and man's conception of that union is vivified only through daily intimacies with his own body. For the Christian, especially Donne's contemporary English Protestants,[7] Paul's notion of the Church as Body, with Christ as Head, sustained the conception of community as Body. That Donne's lifelong yearning for incorporation in a community was satisfied in Paul's Body is historically understandable; but the increasing overtness of Paul's notion in Donne's mature religious prose has a special biographical force in light of his earlier exclusion from community. The Pauline notion, appropriately concretized and wittily extended, enriches the sermons. At one point, when nagging about the problems of church unity, Donne underscores the Articles of Faith as the *sine qua non*, 'a skin that covers the whole body' suffering 'concision' when individualized explications forget that rudimentary acceptance is alone sufficient (*Sermons*, X, 113). As an actual, not just a metaphorical Body, the Church can be apprehended through knowledge of the individual human body. Donne's adaptation of the traditional notion of the kingdom's Body and the king its Heart[8] has the additional poignancy of Donne's relationship to King James, who forced Donne's hand to take Orders in the Church. In the *Devotions* Donne's sense of incorporation in both the Church and the kingdom is clearly controlled by that relationship.[9]

Donne's notion of the social Body, especially in its mature formulation, would be incomplete without reference to Creation. On the sixth day God created Adam and Eve, married two in one, essentially social, not singular. First established in Paradise (*Sermons*, III, 241), man's naturally married state was necessary for the ultimate social intention of Creation. Man's 'propagation' was necessary for God's purpose of 'being glorified by man here, in this world, and of glorifying man, in the world to come' (*Sermons*, II, 336–7). Thus, marriage established the actual basis of society by producing its members.[10] In addition, just as the 'marriage' of soul and body (*Sermons*, VIII, 182) predicts by correspondence human fulfilment in the marriage of man and woman, so also the union of Adam and Eve predicts Christ's marriage to his Body[11] that restores mankind. Similarly, Adam and Eve as mutual helpmates establish the pattern of mutual co-ordination within an incorporated community. The essential point is that the created union of man and woman, taken as Man, sets the natural pattern for the social fulfilment of Creation. All social Bodies, including reparative Bodies such as Christ's Church, contribute to this purpose, varyingly following the paradigm of the human body and underlining the importance of marriage. 'Every man is a *naturall* body, every congregation is a *politik* body; The whole world is a *Catholik*, an universall body.' The physical body is sustained and fed by meat; the political Body by industrious members fulfilling their Callings; and the catholic Body by marriage (*Sermons*, VIII, 100). Thus, like other creatures, man furthers the purpose of Creation by fulfilling his own nature, as an individual composed of body and soul and as a participating member in a fruitful Body.

Some implications of the three foregoing elements in the body's epistemological role deserve further consideration. To say that Donne's notion of the body comprises, first, Donne's assumptions about Creation, second, the correspondences between body and soul, and, third, the correspondences between the body and social Bodies, is to suggest a conception of the body both simple and profound: simple in finding the centre of knowledge in the direct and universal experience of bodily life; profound, in using that knowledge to investigate the fuller, parallel realities. The body often operates so automatically in Donne's thought that he need not stop to explain, swiftly passing from correspondence to correspondence, filtering the identities of soul, body, social Body, and physical world through each other. Yet the ground line throughout Donne's works remains the soul's rudimentary experience of the body in a material world.[12] We recognize this rudimentary consciousness throughout Donne's works as one important psychological determinate in his epistemology. That is, Donne's epistemology, in so far as it relates to the body, expresses the mind's pervasive awareness of its natural residence in a physical body.

Explicit epistemological questions relating to the body first surface consistently in *The Anniversaries*, the verse letters, the epicedes and obsequies. 'The First Anniversarie' systematically follows the shifting, protean 'know' and 'world' in examining the problem of knowledge in a corrupt world. Death is the occasion; sin, the cause; and corruption, the subject. The poem dissects, probes, analyses the corruption of bodies: the human body, the collective social 'world,' and the macrocosmic world. But the full anatomy aims at the soul through the system of microcosmic-macrocosmic correspondences. 'The Second Anniversarie' invites the soul, first, to contemplate separation through death from its body, the physical world, and the social world; then, to contemplate its solo progress to reunion with the body amid the assembled heavenly community. Again, Donne's epistemological crux regards the legion implications of the body. Here, the knowledge through contemplation paradoxically draws from other forms of knowing, to follow the soul's changing relationship to the body. Again, an omnipresent but elusive 'know' draws the reader's attention. In the verse letters, and epicedes and obsequies, the problem of community, of social Body, sets Donne's line of vision. Virtuous action is the adhesive holding the Body together. Accordingly, consideration of virtues and the language regarding the constituents of matter and body, instructed by macrocosmic parallels, are corollaries; for only physical action expresses virtue to other men, with virtuous aristocrats as exemplars. The poems examine problems of knowing the Body's components, including even the physical appearance of virtuous members. This knowledge necessarily informs virtuous actions and heals the mortal lesions in the Body and its members.

Although such epistemological considerations enter the foreground more obviously in those works of the middle years, the various elements in Donne's notion of the body are essentially rooted at the beginning. Donne's guiding sense of physical existence in a physical world determined how he viewed the problem of identifying and knowing values. Though by no means the first, 'The Exstasie' is the clearest early example: bodies bring souls together; knowledge of the macrocosm refines understanding of the subtly knotted human composite; and the embodied lovers will affect other humans. The early coherency of Donne's notion, especially as it relates to the community, deserves close attention since it qualifies modern estimates of his sense of isolation. The young Donne's often embittered social criticism, like the antisocial 'égoisme à deux'[13] in some love poems, expresses a frustrated desire to participate in a community. The private mode in the love poetry tends to obscure this desire, although, as we will see later, even there it has important thematic reverberations. Donne's first satire expresses that desire in revealing terms, for this very early poem (c. 1593)[14] of social criticism is evidence that the interrelationships between the physical body, the social Body, and the macrocosm were firmly set in Donne's mind. Thus, the poem will repay a brief examination of the way in which Donne views these interrelationships. Also, the poem points to a continuity extending to the later works. And it points to common assumptions in the love poetry that some critics tend to underplay, in particular the relationship between Donne's bodily consciousness and his desire for incorporation in a community.

Donne bandies the speaker between the lethal dangers of reclusion and the scattering whimsey of the outside world. The 'fondling motley humorist' (1) entices the reluctant speaker from his academic closet. Aware that his 'standing woodden chest' (2) is a 'prison,' a potential coffin (4), the speaker follows his importunate friend into the urban streets. The whimsical friend represents the inconstant world; in turn, the speaker's studious reclusion, with 'constant company' (11) of traditional authors, bespeaks the sober moralist's coherent search for unifying traditional and communal values. Partly, he seeks 'how to tie / The sinewes of a cities mistique bodie' (7–8), recognizing the necessary experiential confirmation of that knowledge; he seeks active participation in a visible community in which bodily action and physical appearance both stress virtuous being. His dissatisfaction with the 'jolly' (7) and the 'Giddie' (10) encourages his reluctant willingness to accompany his friend, a member of the existing Body; for he recognizes friendship as the rudimentary 'sinew.'

But he cannot assimilate the values embodied in the friend, who spastically responds to alluring appearances and seductively greets 'Every fine silken painted foole we meet' (72). Donne's heavy irony throws promiscuous sexuality and love of exteriors against the true vision of the body and its clothing. The hedonistic friend, 'in ranke itchie lust, desire, and love,' enjoys the nakedness and bareness of the 'plumpe muddy whore, or prostitute boy,' not the simple nakedness and bareness of 'vertue' (37–41). The naked body, the soul's only true apparel, corresponds to the truthful simplicity and honesty of the innocently virtuous soul. Contrarily, all clothing emblematizes human sin, although a decent coarseness can express virtuous self-awareness of personal weakness. The members of the 'cities mistique bodie' must learn the true lesson of the naked body; similarly, its members, self-aware in their coarse attire, must be disciplined by virtuous action and co-ordinated through friendship and love, not disruptive lust, or desire, or the 'adultery' (26) of inconstant friendship, or the violent ravishment of lechery (108). However, the 'fondling' friend indiscriminately, ravenously takes either muddy whore or prostitute boy, just as he compulsively yields to the most eye-catching demands on the street. In this world of corrupted action and physical exteriors, perversion also bends the lessons of the macrocosm; the 'gulling weather-Spie, / By drawing forth heavens Scheame' (60) predicts fashions. Appropriately, false values invite false correspondences, corrupting the Body by corrupting its members.

This pessimistic vision allows only tenuous hope for improvement: the poet himself in conference 'with God, and with the Muses' (49); the world's few 'grave' men (79); some traditional knowledge; and perhaps even experiential knowledge of friendship. The friend continually seeks the speaker, perhaps as inconstancy yearning for its opposite; and the speaker, in turn, even 'against my conscience' (66) seeks community through the friend. Yet hope remains slender, characteristically so for Donne's poems of the 1590s. The important point here is that such hope, in expressing physical man's need for a physical community consistent with virtue's demands, draws from a clear notion of true relationships between mircocosmic and macrocosmic bodies. Donne continues to examine the implications of that notion, although the notion itself undergoes little essential change. Its varied treatment, according to occasion and situation, enriches Donne's art.

To sum up briefly, knowledge of the body is richly articulated in Donne's thought by a system of correspondences that mutually implicate the body, the community, and the physical world in the experience of the soul. Fulfilled being requires knowledge of these correspondences. Behind this fully articulated notion of body, which is closely tied to Donne's notion of Creation, lies an elemental bodily consciousness. In the love poetry it is precisely this consciousness that strikes us as one identifying characteristic of Donne's temperament; it is wide-ranging in its effects, and pronounced in its importance. As noted above, Donne's interest in the epistemological questions relating to his notion of the body emerges more forcefully in his middle years, but the same assumptions are present earlier in the love poetry as expressions of his pervasive consciousness of the body. As we will see, this same consciousness, consistent in its demands for a visible community as well as for human exemplars of divine value, later insists on the physicality of the suffering Christ as the centre of belief.

I BODIES, COMMUNITIES, AND ARTIFACTS: THE LOVE POETRY

Donne's absorbed attention to the body characterizes the love poetry. The elegies catalogue the features of woman's body with a microscopic explicitness both unswerving and unabashed. The body's role in love undergoes analysis from several perspectives, so too the experience of the grave, of separation, of change, of social ties, and of subservience to the soul. The reasons for this absorption inevitably have interested critics and occasioned some dispute, particularly regarding the apparent contradictions between libertine and spiritual love. Yet the once strong temptation to identify Donne with the cynically naturalistic attitudes of the libertine poems must give way to a wiser accommodation, since this libertine naturalism[15] runs in an entirely different direction from the traditional moralism of Donne's satires, written about the same time, and from the more spiritualized love poems. The more blatantly naturalistic speakers introduce, through parody or direct defiance, the moral or spiritual standards that censure their narrowly sexual view of the body. The ground line in Donne's notion of the body, the sharpened consciousness of bodily existence, runs through both libertine and spiritual love poems. This consciousness ever includes the physical actualities of other bodies as well. Donne endorses the validity of physical experience, but he is as concerned to investigate both the implications of becoming fixated on the ground line as well as pivoting outward from it. Sexuality most obviously encourages fixation, with profound implications for the community. Yet even for more spiritual lovers, the palpable events of sexuality, physical change, separation, and death threaten spiritual equilibrium. Donne's love poetry asks how to walk the ground line without denying or overindulging the body. Donne answers by reminding his readers that the body's keenly felt experience is the emblematic book for understanding the soul and the social Body, and that the Body must accommodate the needs of both body and soul.

Donne's naturalistic and libertine love poems conspicuously dramatize, both for the individual and the community, the consequences of separating the body's experience from spiritual control. Close attention to the relationship between sexuality and community, between body and Body, blends psychological analysis into social satire, discovering causes of communal abuses in the individual's denial of spirit and the pattern for the denial in the social Body. In the elegies the speakers' compulsion to catalogue the features of woman's body depicts the speakers and their communities, not the woman, who is depersonalized as mere body. The poems do not offer woman's body for the reader's delectation, but examine the speaker's attitudes to it as the centre of his sexual devotions.

In 'Loves Progress' Donne distorts love with excessive Elizabethan interest in sea discovery and world trade, invading private experience with public values. A telling adaptation of the microcosm-macrocosm, woman's body as the world for the speaker's trade routes, poetizes the central issue. Tough-minded, practical, direct, the speaker wants only the 'right true end of love' (2), to sail directly to her 'Centrique part' (36), consciously advertising 'our new Nature, use, the soule of trade' (16). Standards of business efficiency inspire a rudimentary usefulness: 'Preferre / One woman first, and then one thing in her' (1–10). He cautions against shipwreck, the loitering at inessential beauty that would prevent consummation of trade agreements and payment of 'tribute' (93) into the 'exchequer' (94) at the lady's lower purse (92). Nevertheless, his impatience with sightseeing cruises to other parts cannot dissipate altogether his interest in the rest of her body. For example, he praises her 'swelling lips,' those 'Ilands Fortunate' where 'Wee anchor' and 'think our selves at home, / For they seem all' (51–5). Fear of shipwreck, however, encourages more direct routes; rather, 'set out below' (73).

The satire aims less at the speaker's moral abuses than at his self-knowing recommendation of those lethal abuses as the new Nature's standards of value. Such resilient self-awareness blunts the power of reform. Sexual efficiency knowingly shrinks the essential microcosm to the sexual body alone, denying angelic virtue, beauty, even wealth as the essential woman. The speaker bravely advertises that diminished microcosm: 'So we her ayres contemplate, words and hart / And vertues; But we love the Centrique part" (35–6). More implicitly, but more broadly, Donne also points to the macrocosm shrunken by the 'soule of trade' (16). Ironically, Elizabethan exploration and extended trade routes constrict, not widen, the world. Vision turns from the heavens, and their correspondences to the microcosmic soul, down to the earth, which he would use materialistically and not regard as God's creation and adviser of the microcosm. Donne finds two sides of the same coin in sexual and commerical attitudes that guide his society. The nature of the speaker's preoccupation with woman's body expresses Donne's satire, for the manner of that preoccupation characterizes aggressive materialism and spiritual destitution.

In the elegy 'To his Mistris Going to Bed,' a preoccupation with the lady's body depicts the speaker. In neither poem is preoccupation itself the primary satirical target, but the conscious opposition to inherited values. One lifelong tenet of Donne's epistemology, that the body can be read as a language or a book, encourages a careful scrutiny of its experience. In 'Going to Bed' the speaker's conscious parody of that principle, like the knowing constriction of the microcosmic principle in 'Loves Progress,' conveys a conscious sexuality, doubly lethal in its self-awareness, that would strangle traditional values. Here, undressing the body becomes revelation. A religious parody substitutes sexual exhilaration for spiritual vision, offering the woman's nakedness for the soul's intuitive heavenly knowledge. Like 'soules unbodied' bodies must be unclothed in order to 'taste whole joyes' (34–5). Women denuded are 'mystique bookes' (41) to be 'reveal'd' to the Elect, who may 'knowe' (43). Carnal knowledge replaces emblematic knowledge of the soul and spiritual experience offered by the body. The poem's pace, titillation that simulates a ritualistic progress to insight, prolongs the sexual anticipation while insulting a genuine spiritual standard by breathlessly praising an expensive woman of easy virtue.[16] Discovering her is discovering the New World, an achievement of religious insight. This reference to the macrocosm broadens characterization of her sexual person, centring a world of value in her.

The speaker's religious parody carries sexual exhilaration beyond rebellion into a new order that eschews guilt, because of the body's innocence, redefining thereby woman's relationship to man. He undresses first to 'teach' her the new state without 'covering' (47–8). The pun on 'covering' alludes to traditional Pauline denigration that likens woman to man's lower half and covers her head (1 Corinthians 11). And 'covering' develops 'imputed grace' (42) of the Elect, the Reform 'covering' of Christ's merit.[17] Ironically, since

Grace emanates from her, she needs none, especially in this innocent New World where sexual knowledge is truth. The parody blocks access to the old spirituality while pointing to a bogus, naturalistic world that promises freedom (30) through sexual licence, but inadvertently admits that pregnancy could entrap her ('As liberally as to a midwife showe,' 44). The substitution of sexual exhilaration for spiritual freedom deludes the speaker; for naturalistic preoccupation with a body prevents spirituality.

For Donne, pervasive consciousness of the body, characteristic of human psychology, necessarily expresses attitudes of both the individual and his community. The speakers of both elegies share a widespread naturalistic mentality that views the body only as the object of physical pleasure. What is pervasive in all humans gravitates into obsession under the weight of naturalism. Donne's satirical portrait of this mentality denotes its blindness to the consequences of obsession. The singleminded speaker in 'Loves Progress' seeks only one thing, and in one woman, but such naturalistic efficiency does not anticipate that only woman's virtue or her profound ugliness would guarantee her constancy. The speaker of 'Going to Bed,' whose exhilaration requires a direct view of woman's 'beauteous state' (13) manifested in a stagey ritualism, now may find willing partners. But the practical vagaries of competitive supply are only too obvious, except to a naturalism characteristically blinded to its own implications. The paradoxical encomium, 'The Anagram,' mockingly pursues these implications by recommending the repellant physical attractions of an old, ugly woman. Small eyes, large mouth, black teeth, red hair – such details invert a cultural ideal. Formal praise mocks naturalistic obsession with the body, while Donne's satirical probe finds the confusion entangling naturalism: a beast's ethic ineptly applied to humans in both sexuality and commerce ('thee, / Which, forc'd by business, absent oft must bee,' 43–4). On one hand, naturalism releases the beast's greedy desire for easy gratification; but, on the other hand, it cannot satisfy a conflicting human need for order and continued loyalty. In sexual love, only impossibility or absurdity can cut through this problematic confusion, a woman uniquely ugly and undesirable: 'One like none, and lik'd of none, fittest were' (55). The mockery darkly bruises naturalism with its own socially disruptive sexuality, prescribing physical revulsion as the only defence.

Yet in Donne's love poetry, bodily desire establishes one essential basis for human community. This justifiable desire is a necessary corollary of his belief in the body's goodness. Naturalism shakes that basis by referring sexuality back to animal and natural forces in blatant disregard of differences that explain the correspondences between the microcosm and elements in the macrocosm. The glib libertinism of 'Communitie,' 'The Indifferent,' and

'Confined Love' accepts only an inverted community based on the selfish and impermanent mutalities of sexual use. The perverted macrocosmic justification for this libertinism can be found in 'Change.' The lady's momentary protestations of constant devotion are run aground by an argument of correspondency between microcosm and macrocosm that allows neither man nor woman, as part of nature, a capacity for constancy. Man cannot expect woman to be more constant, less libidinous than 'Foxes and goats; all beasts' (11). The argument for freely changing sexual attachments looks backward down the chain of being, justifying man's libertine inconstancy according to lower forms. The macrocosm is ransacked for misleading correspondences, expressing a reductive naturalistic mentality that denies the spirit. The changing river, kissing one bank, then another, is enlisted to defy the permanency of love (31–5), hence the basis of human society. Macrocosmic correspondences are invoked not to confirm human community, but to justify its dissolution.

The breadth and frequency of Donne's attack on naturalism acknowledge its serious dangers to traditional values. Any one of naturalism's assumptions – its materialistic view of nature, its unconcern with the communal Body, its denigration of virtue, its preoccupation with unenlightened sexuality – threatens a crashing domino effect through the interrelated members of Donne's notion of the body. Donne's satirical attack on naturalism particularly resists its scattering effect on the human community. The bravura of mutual love in the *Songs and Sonnets* displays his relieved awareness that substantial spiritual ties are possible even in a hostile social environment. But only in the verse letters does real confidence emerge that a viable social Body exists beyond a painful traditional hope. Yet in the *Songs and Sonnets* a longing for a community that respects the needs of body and soul opposes the debilitating naturalism. In some poems Donne recommends a defensive *égoisme à deux*, but only against a totally hostile world; more characteristically, he believes that this union of lovers is the necessary beginning for a new community. 'The Exstasie' anatomizes love's essential contribution to that community, stating with near-formulaic clarity the relationship between individual bodies and the community.

The poem begins and ends with the lovers' bodies. But here the body serves first the soul, then the human community, not sexual preoccupation. The bodies obediently keep their places in accordance with their ultimate social purposes. The pillow-like 'Pregnant banke' (2) in this spring setting validates the magnetism of sexual attraction according to natural cycles shared sympathetically by microcosm and macrocosm. Temporarily fulfilled as the souls' ushers and immoblized as 'sepulchrall statues' (18), the bodies await the souls' return. Ecstatic knowledge teaches souls the proper response to their bodies: gratitude to necessary intermediaries who will communicate the combined souls to others. Again, macrocosmic correspondences assist microcosmic self-understanding: 'Wee are / Th'intelligences, they the spheare' (52–3). Spiritual insight of pure lovers recognizes the correspondences between relationships, respectively between heaven and earth, soul and body. As heaven 'imprints' air as a physical intermediary between God and man, souls 'may flow' into each other through bodies (57–60). The traffic between heaven and man parallels the traffic between souls. Contrary to a naturalistic perspective, these correspondences are viewed from the soul, not the body.

Yet matter fulfils form, just as bodies fulfil souls; but the body's fulfilment of soul requires a human community. Donne gives two reasons for the soul's willing descent to the body: first, imprisonment in the flesh (68) if it does not, and, second, the soul's responsibility to other men. Spiritual love achieves fruition as embodied example to other humans. Charitable action erects human community after the example of pure love 'reveal'd' by the strong to the weak through the body as the 'booke' (69–72). Charitable action, embodied love, is the physical 'sinew,' to use Donne's figure in the first satire, that knits together the 'mistique bodie' of the community.

The soul as 'Prince' (68) pointedly furthers the progressive linkage of correspondences that runs from macrocosm through microcosm to human community: intelligences are to spheres, as souls to bodies, as princes to states, as pure lovers to 'weake' men. Just as the macrocosm is fulfilled in the microcosm, the microcosm is fulfilled in the community. (A quick reminder of Donne's notion of Creation locates the basis for this progression.) The progression drives to fulfilment in the mystic Body unified by love and expresses Donne's assumption that created form necessarily seeks fulfilment in matter. Intelligences inform spheres; souls, bodies; princes, states; human exemplars, weak men; love, the human community. Donne's notion of community[18] seeks its broadest context in this poem.

In 'The Relique' Donne shifts the perspective, but keeps the reader's eye trained on the relationship between bodies and the community. Donne diffracts two assumptions of 'The Exstasie,' the social value of sexual attraction and the centrality of bodies, to show how they accommodate apparent contradictions in actual experience such as non-sexual love and death's ruptures. In 'The Exstasie' love begins in mutual sexual attraction, but in 'The Relique' a marvellous lady loved only Platonically: 'Our hands ne'r toucht the seales, / Which Nature, injur'd by late law, sets free' (29–30). Donne's point, that sexual love is the most ready social tie, does not reject less passionate, less problematical attachments, as his treatment of friendship in the verse letters demonstrates. Similarly, death's horrors do not refute 'The Exstasie,' where Donne's intentness in building a community of human bodies will not pause to consider the shock of physical death, decayed flesh, and divested bone. Elsewhere, Donne does struggle to diffuse such shock. In 'A Relique' the ironic possibility that her death might strengthen community solves the problems of grief and social continuity.

An almost unwitting meditation on the lovers' continuing relationship to the community is sparked by his intention to be buried with a love token, 'A bracelet of bright haire about the bone' (6). The fiction of disinterment by an idolatrous age makes him realize that he remains very much a part of the community to which he has a desire to reveal the true miracle of their love. Superstition would distort their importance and the later generation would need to be instructed by a poetic tribute to his lady and their love: 'I would that age were by this paper taught / What miracles wee harmlesse lovers wrought' (21–2). The poem affirms the human truth that physical death ruptures physical community only momentarily, that even spiritual presence itself continues, however transformed its material expression. The basically linguistic affirmation of the body as the soul's emblematic 'booke'[19] necessarily allows that any material medium bearing the soul's imprint, such as the union of hair and arm bone or written language, incarnates spirit. The speaker's fanciful disinterment acknowledges that the mode of their material presence could distort the meaning of their union; hence, he offers the poem as clarification. The speaker expresses the wish to keep the lovers' presence sacramentally available for the human community, while explaining the emblemism of his burial.

For some, such as the lady or the refined observers of 'The Exstasie,' less tangible expressions of truth might satisfy. But 'weake' men, like the speaker of 'The Relique,' seek more palpable truths. The bracelet of hair, both touching and bold, assures at least a minimal bodily presence during her lifetime, and after; with him in the grave, it represents his desire for her lost presence. The poem does not disapprove of the speaker's very physical nature. His sexual nature has been redirected by spiritual love; and now, not altogether unwittingly, the speaker offers himself, as well as his lady, as an exemplar to others. They 'lov'd well and faithfully' (23), but within the limits of their respective natures. Her asexual spirituality remained a mystery to him, and she a 'miracle' (33). His wonderment at 'These miracles wee did' (31) carries the stamp of his surprised physical nature, uneasily foregoing sexuality for the sake of spiritual union. Yet he offers his own transformation as an example, not totally conscious how mutual love has bound him to the social Body in his attempt to communicate his experience in a tangible way. Physical in nature, he knows the value of tangible revelation, to which end he instinctively offers the poem.

The exemplarism of true lovers, poetry as sacramental participation, death, and the community's material continuity – these themes explain much in 'The Canonization' as well. A violent opening tears the speaker away from a corrupt outer world, but the poem reveals an inner community with the harassed lovers as exemplars of consummated physical and spiritual love. They exemplify mutual love that not only finds in itself 'Countries, Townes, Courts' (44), but charitably opens their surrogate world to others after death. Their mode of material continuation, in poetry, not 'tombes or hearse' (29) or 'Chronicle' (31), furthers this revolution against the corrupt outer world. These 'hymnes' (35) will canonize them as exemplars and proselytize other lovers through the dramatized events of their 'legend' (30).

Active rebellion leaves them very much *in*, not *of*, the antagonistic outer world. The opening violence suggests a continuing 'rage' (39). That healthy violence, their sexuality, and their desire for a physical commemoration of their love stress their bodily presence in a material world and describe their exemplarism, both while alive and after their deaths, sacramentally through their poetry. As saintly intermediaries between other lovers and God ('Beg from above / A patterne of your love!' 44–5),[20] they will inform a real human community of lovers. Yet they speak from a full sense of their own physicality and the world's.

Their spiritual effect on the actions of others links 'The Canonization' to 'The Relique' and 'The Exstasie.' The questions of relationships between human exemplars and their communities, between artifacts and communities, between dead exemplars and live communities assume certain relationships between form and matter, and form and form. A changing mortality constantly adjusts these relationships. In 'The Relique' the lady dies; her body goes to the grave, her soul, presumably to heaven. Yet a union with the speaker continues, his soul having been imprinted, informed through her influence. That union is emblematized by the bracelet about the bone, and informs the poem. A physical medium bears the spiritual imprint for the willing reader's soul. Similarly, the saints of 'The Canonization,' the pattern of saintly action, imprint the readers through the physical medium of the poem. Donne lays out the foundation of this notion in 'The Exstasie': heaven's 'influence' on man 'first imprints the ayre' just as 'soule into the soule may flow' through the body (57–60). Form affects form through matter. Bodily action stamps the soul's imprint on other souls. Unfortunately, bodily death, change, separation, and decay change the media of communication, requiring material substitutes, often through artifacts, following the paradigmatic relationship between soul and body. Both 'The Relique' and 'The Canonization' examine implications of this substitution.

In both poems Donne accepts artifacts as essential counters in human communication. The problems relating to artifacts are corollaries of the body as a book. The spirit's failure to imprint bodies or artifacts aborts the power of body and matter to express spiritual reality to physical men. The communication line joining soul to soul thereby severs. Donne's dualism stands body and soul in separate dimensions, but hangs their respective fulfilment on mutual use. The human soul pursues fulfilment by imprinting spiritual form in other souls through physical media, primarily the body, then artifacts as surrogates. Human memory can maintain spiritual imprints pressed deeply enough; but composite man, not just through weakness, but more significantly through his essential nature, yearns for the physical embodiment of the spirit.

We have just seen that one of Donne's primary occupations in the love poetry is to examine how consciousness of the body takes shape in human experience. Need for the tangible as a part of fulfilment is a distinctly human demand that guides awareness of the world and other men. Donne was a lyric poet distinctively gifted in showing how this awareness is affected by varying spiritual conditions or by the constants of death, parting, and change. Much in his love poetry combats a selfish naturalistic attempt to free the body from necessary spiritual and social controls that guide the body to higher purposes. Donne's judgment against naturalism is instructed by a coherent sense of the body's place in the fulfilment of Creation and as a book of the soul to guide other men in a shared community. That is, consciousness of the body and of the macrocosmic world ultimately leads to spiritual communication with other humans in a social Body. Poetry as a physical artifact imprinted with spiritual values serves that communication by looking to both physical and spiritual expectations.

II REAL EXEMPLARS: VERSE LETTERS, COMMEMORATIVE POETRY

As noted above, this finely honed physical consciousness enunciates the principles of body, with its correspondences between macrocosm and microcosm, between body and soul, and between individual and social Body. The literary offspring of this consciousness identify clear lines of continuing similarity between the love poetry and other works. These familial ties continue in spite of the varying domains of romantic love, aristocratic patronage, public lament, and church pulpit. In the poetry of verse compliment, the embodiment of exemplary values in social bodies is pushed to the foreground, as the poet Donne steps into an established community; its fate depends on virtuous aristocrats and their poetic advisers, who must jointly consider the physical and spiritual constituents of the community. Epistemological questions, of reading human books for their impressions of spiritual value and of dissecting the necessary ties between knowledge and virtuous action, are the natural accompaniments. In *The Anniversaries*, as we will see below, the more socially circumscribed world of verse compliment dilates into more capacious and inclusive metaphysical considerations inspired by death; and Donne's epistemological considerations dilate accordingly to embrace all the broadest implications of his notion of body. Only the later, religious prose follows these implications more fully, with the broadened authority of mature conviction that can confidently invoke the sights and smells of bodily putrefaction as the necessary way to resurrection. The sermons follow Creation to its ultimate end in the glorified human body entered into Christ's heavenly Body. Donne's maturest thought insists upon physical participation in a unified Body, whether earthly or heavenly. But even in the works written prior to ordination, we find the same essential principles at work.

Donne's longing for visits and letters from close friends reveals a touching personal element in his insistence on the communal Body;[21] and Donne's verse letters to aristocratic friends and patrons, as well as obsequies and epicedes, articulate this principle in the language of verse compliment. The letters to patronesses have begun to receive deserved recognition from modern readers willing to drop older, unfair charges of degrading toadyism, in order to assess the poems fairly as literature. To unexceptionable claims that coherent principles knit together Donne's poems of compliment[22] can be added the claim that a vocabulary referring to the constituents of body and soul, matter and form, macrocosm and microcosm, consistently expresses this unity. Addressed to real subjects, living or recently dead, these poems assume an immediate social Body bonded by the virtuous actions of real human exemplars. Similarly, his belief in the communal importance of artifacts establishes his own role as poet to be his 'part' in the 'body of the world.'[23] Donne's full conception of the body is here concretized in actual subjects as the expressions of earthly value; and his vocabulary leads to the body itself as the book of the soul.

This recurrent vocabulary expresses Donne's notion that virtue cannot be abstracted from its human embodiment in overt action. A verse letter to the Countess of Bedford ('Honour is so sublime perfection') entwines Christian social roles for virtuous aristocratic exemplars with inferiors who '*bestow*' (9) honour. Donne adroitly walks the tightrope between poetic compliment and necessary moral counsel, praising the Countess's virtuous action and religious being while implicitly warning against compartmentalizing them:

> Natures first lesson, so, discretion,
> Must not grudge zeale a place, nor yet keepe none,
> Nor banish it selfe, nor religion. (37–9)

Briefly at the end, Donne appears more openly on the tightrope ('Goe thither stil, goe the same way you went,' 52), skilfully advising the Countess according to her own precedent. Donne justifies his ticklish advisory role with principles of social unity that confirm virtuous actions by their praiseworthy effects on inferiors. Accordingly, only inferiors bestow honour on virtuous actions, hence completing these actions. That her 'radiation' (20) through action expresses her refined inner being emphasizes the essence of embodied virtue. That he has been elevated through this influence is confirmed by his praise and refined advice. Such emphasis upon embodied virtue and responding praise firmly grounds honour and virtue in a concrete social world.

This firm grounding in the world explains the references to material phenomena and material transformation that lead upward to her body as the necessary instrument of virtue. Donne's opening succinctly puts honour within a system of order dating from Creation and including low as well as high, material as well as spiritual. Reference to elemental matter and its transformation for use by higher beings keeps his aristocratic reader attuned to her interdependence with social inferiors in a real world:

> Honour is so sublime perfection,
> And so refinde; that when God was alone
> And creaturelesse at first, himselfe had none;
>
> But as of th'elements, these which wee tread,
> Produce all things with which wee'are joy'd or fed,
> And, those are barren both above our head: (1–6)

Alchemical sublimation defines honour as a recognizable human event, with inferiors bestowing praise on exemplary action. Characterization of praisers as base 'elements' (4) and 'despis'd dung' (12) assumes the Countess's moral and spiritual elevation while keeping her feet on the ground near her inferiors; for distillation by dung wins 'pure parts' (10) from herbs, just as praise by inferiors helps embodied virtue identify its effects. Thus, corresponding processes of physical transformation continue to locate both praise and virtuous actions very much in a real world, as does her body as the necessary instrument for the elevation of others. Donne introduces her body as the actual centre of the poem (22–30). Her body covers her soul as the 'Amber drop enwraps a Bee' (25); it is a latter-day 'specular stone' (29) for showing inner value. Bodily action clearly manifests refined being; and poetic exaggeration invokes physical marvels to depict refinement of bodily matter in fulfilled action. Donne encourages her to continue to manifest her 'quicke Soule' in her bodily 'Covering' (26). Both she and other humans are the beneficiaries.

In the poems of compliment a gravitational pull keeps reminding the reader of real people in a real social world. Values, problems, and concepts are embodied. The language of matter, body, physical transformation, and alchemy follows accordingly. Further, macrocosmic correspondences seek their centre of gravity in the human body in an actual community. Donne's assumptions have undergone no change since those poems discussed above, but a special emphasis has clear literary results. As in the letter to the Countess of Bedford, Donne's special context invites analysis of Christian virtue, which, as Wesley Milgate notes, breaks down into Platonic and Paracelsian elements. The Platonic idea is that virtue is 'one and entire,' not divisible into 'separate virtues.' Donne expresses this notion with 'ideas associated with gold [Plato's figure] and the philosophers' stone by the Paracelsians – the "virtue", "balsam", "tincture", which is the indivisible essence and power of a substance.'[24] This useful observation points to the important relationship between Donne's alchemical notions and his concept of the microcosm-macrocosm. Moral virtue as 'balsam' argues from correspondences between body and soul, substituting physical for moral in order to stress that moral virtue exists only in bodily action. Similarly, Donne's claim to refinement through the Countess's influence ('You have refin'd mee') denotes sharpened social perception as physical transmutation to note concrete behaviour.

Donne's guiding sense of value concretized in a real community furthers his examination of issues investigated earlier in the love poetry. His New Year's Tide letter to Lady Bedford ('This twilight of two yeares') raises questions regarding poetry as a communal artifact, in light of Donne's reputation and current status. Tough-minded practicality rejects a public poem for more indirect advice that speaks to the community through his subject, not through public compliment that would raise cries of his servility and encourage scepticism regarding her value. Donne's depiction of public poetry can be stretched to apply to most of his poetry:

> Verse embalmes vertue;'and Tombs, or Thrones of rimes,
>> Preserve fraile transitory fame, as much
>> As spice doth bodies from corrupt aires touch.   (13–15)

Fame and virtue exist only when embodied; the artifact maintains them in a surrogate body. Not far away are 'The Relique,' 'The Canonization,' and, to be examined later, *The Anniversaries*. High compliment cannot forget tough, practical considerations regarding poetry as a worldly medium. Donne draws out the implications of poetry as a physical medium preserving virtue, first as an embalming agent, then as a body (20) with alchemical and medical limitations. The Countess embodies spiritual values ('the tincture of your name,' 16) amenable to expansion of poetic hyperbole that would threaten poetry as a believable medium ('Kept hot with strong extracts, no bodies last,' 20). His own low station ('One corne of one low anthills dust, and lesse,' 28) would invite cries of toadyism, which, coupled with scepticism toward her, would defeat the whole enterprise. The poetic 'body' necessarily exists in a tangled human world with concrete expectations.

So does the poet Donne. He finds a poetic solution that gives him a concrete role and impresses her exemplary form on the community. He rejects public poetry for private poetic advice that speaks to the community through the Countess's concrete actions. Donne's finely tuned implications advise her by noting problems to be solved with God's help. Milgate detects Donne's 'implied gentle criticism of her indulgence in Court frivolities.'[25] And, in general, the poem provides general lines for her behaviour: 'He will make you speake truths, and credibly, / And make you doubt, that others do not so' (51–2). She will recognize in her own concrete actions evidence for her Election and in that 'private Ghospell' (65) Donne, by implication, will find embodied evidence of his advice and accordingly his own participation in the community. In that recognition Donne will find his own 'New Yeare' (65), a point in place and time for one formerly 'Meteor-like, of stuffe and forme perplext' (3), now informed with a social role by advising her to undertake concrete social actions. Although a Donne would have been only too aware that the necessary refinement of implied advice ironically attenuated the concreteness of his role, the poem speaks his desire to enter a tangible community.

In the poems of compliment, Donne's belief, that concrete bodily actions are essential for the life of social Bodies, must accommodate the problem of death. Much of the solution lies in an intellectually sharpened examination of matter and form, body and soul, and individual and community. His 1625 funeral hymn to the Marquess of Hamilton ('Whether that soule which now comes up to')[26] laments the varying losses to Bodies that once included the Marquess: 'The *Chappell* wants an eare, *Councell* a tongue ... the losse of him / Gangreend all *Orders* here; all lost a limbe' (15–18). Yet the implications of body and soul, examined anew, stretch his notion of earthly and heavenly community. Donne breaks down a rigid understanding of the separation between body and soul at death, by recognizing that fame bears the soul's imprint and the buried body enters heaven by proxy through its form, the glorified soul: 'For, as in his fame, now, his soule is here, / So, in the forme thereof his bodie's there' (29–30). His fame unifies remaining earthly friends, shaping a concrete need for a visible social Body; but it also stretches a spiritual bridge to his human community in heaven as well. The Marquess present in both communities and aware of likeness, between the respective communities of sinners and repentant sinners, can encourage the heavenly community to 'wish' their earthly counterparts 'cleane' (41). That the earthly Body is reunited and a spiritual community envisioned between earthly and heavenly friends, and that man has knowledge that all repentant sinners 'Dy'd scarlet in the blood of that pure Lambe' (34) will be resurrected bodily, give assurance that physical and spiritual needs of community will continue to be met. Readers may judge that Donne's intellectual sutures repairing death's rupture are too finely threaded and tightly drawn here; but his intentions are consistent with his devotion to both body and soul, and to the social Body.

This intellectual sharpness in its relationship to knowledge has prime importance in Donne's commendatory verse. The sharpness assumes that aristocratic readers can make fine intellectual distinctions as part of saving knowledge in a concrete world. The acuity required of Donne's virtuous aristocrats, who must *know* and *dare*,[27] bears its own compliment, as the letter 'To Sir Edward Herbert, at Julyers' reveals. Structurally, the latter is a commonplace definition of man as a microcosm and as an animal fulfilled by rational knowledge and virtue: 'Man is a lumpe, where all beasts kneaded bee, / Wisdome makes him an Arke where all agree' (1–2). Donne's compliment builds toward the climactic affirmation that the virtuous Herbert is an example of the definition. To accept the compliment, however, is to pay the witty price of complicity in Donne's conception of the human composite of body and soul with its justification of physicality. That man contains several beasts may be an ironic allusion to Herbert's Platonism and the Platonists' uneasiness about man's physicality. More important, it assumes that Herbert is one 'Arke' controlling his 'beasts'; through knowledge and wisdom he controls his own physical nature. Donne expects the intellectually acute and knowledgeable Herbert to appreciate the witty implications of the compliment that serve Donne's definition of man.

In complimenting Herbert's knowledge and virtue, Donne cleanly focuses on the links in his thought so crucial in the verse letters, between microcosm-macrocosm, body, knowledge, and Body. Epistemological implications, constituted most fully in *The Anniversaries*, here enjoy an admirable concision. Through wise knowledge man controls his beastly passion and fits into his given place in creation as a virtuous exemplar to other humans. Through knowledge one can rectify nature; and human action is the ultimate object of earthly knowledge, a book for human readers. Donne compliments Edward Herbert as one such book: 'you'have dwelt upon / All worthy bookes, and now are such a one' (47–8). Microcosmic man rectifies and fulfils Nature by both knowing and being known by others. The poem demonstrates the role of knowledge and embodies the solution in Edward Herbert, who subordinates all knowledge to virtuous action.

Like 'The First Anniversarie' this letter distinguishes between kinds of knowledge, *scientia* that satisfies only selfish purposes, or the same knowledge absorbed into *sapientia*; the question is not what is viewed, but how: man's 'businesse' is through proper use of knowledge 'to rectifie / Nature, to what she was' (33–4). He must consume all that his 'faith can swallow,'or reason chaw' (38). Necessary knowledge of the world must be adapted to serve the higher spiritual and intellectual ends of wisdom. *Sapientia* erected nature by teaching man to turn natural knowledge toward humane moral and spiritual ends. Since man is the goal of all nature, knowledge of correspondences between microcosm and macrocosm is necessary for self-understanding. Man contains all beasts – horse, goat, wolf, swine – and must know the beasts to know their similarities in himself. The question is whether or not he controls the known, or submits to it. He belittles himself by not submitting that knowledge to the spiritual direction of wisdom.

Donne's connection between animality and feeding reminds Herbert of his own physical presence in a concrete world and establishes the crucial metaphoric notion, of feeding as knowing, in characterizing Herbert's virtue. Here the witty price of accepting Donne's compliment is at its highest since Donne's praise centres on Herbert's knowledge. That reason chews and faith swallows clarifies how Donne views knowledge as an earthly function; the distinction neatly sums up much of his thought. In a poem that stresses knowledge as a fulfilment of microcosmic man in the social Body, Donne denotes that fulfilling process as a bodily function, pressing forcefully the correspondences between body and soul that reveal man to be a true microcosmic composite of matter and spirit. That knowledge achieves fulfilment in action underlines man's unique position as a spiritual being in a physical world.

The language of feeding, while noting that man is a physiological creature in a material world, also notes the spiritual correspondences to healthy feeding that guide his earthly life. All men must know the world: 'All that is fill'd, and all that which doth fill' (39); but such knowledge must first be digested properly to produce wisdom and then be expressed in virtuous action. And

Edward Herbert, having chewed and swallowed, is filled with such digested knowledge. He has studied the best in man's thought and actions and, similarly, has himself become a worthy book, an embodiment of knowledge for other members of the community. His praiseworthy use of the physical world achieves fulfilment in exemplary actions.

Thus, this letter to Edward Herbert sharply focuses many of the assumptions of Donne's commendatory verse. The image of feeding, which merges epistemology and physiological process, is a figure for Donne's sense of composite man, wittily offered to Herbert. The correspondences between body and soul forcefully require that we know the body and the soul only by reference to each other. Edward Herbert's exemplary virtues, when manifested in his actions, become the active sinew binding together the incorporated community. The poem explicates the epistemological assumption in Donne's poetic commendation and reminds us that virtuous action is a necessary object of knowledge, and that human bodies are the medium for action. In reading human books, in their virtuous actions, man must chew, swallow, and be filled with such virtuous example. Like Edward Hebert, the reader who assimilates this example, in turn, will move others as well. The incorporated community requires the poet's ambidextrous role, not only to encourage, advise, and praise exemplary action as its necessary sinew, but also to embody those actions in poems as surrogate books or bodies. For Donne, fulfilment of both body and soul requires erected actions that inform the community.

III THE SOUL'S DIET: *THE ANNIVERSARIES*

The verse letter to Edward Herbert defines knowledge both as a personal condition and as a necessity of Herbert's exemplarism in the community. The correspondence between feeding and knowing relates to the immediate earthly conditions, the consciousness of the body and its incorporation in community, which are both constants in being. *The Anniversaries* extend the limits of this consciousness to include the cosmos and its relationship to the heavenly state. Yet this metaphysical expansiveness is reined in by awareness that the body's experiences must remain as one ultimate referent for all human knowledge. The fulfilling nourishment promised by the poems, by comparing the respective aliments for body and soul, continues to evoke man's bodily consciousness as a necessary foundation of meaning. The epistemological considerations central to both poems build upon this foundation, as does Donne's crucial assertion that the poems themselves are active contributions to a continuing community.

In the letter to Edward Herbert, the correspondence between eating and knowing applies earthly knowledge to virtuous action; knowledge nourishes the exemplary human book for a community of friends, thus establishing one fixed point in epistemological implications of earthly life. Donne sets this same fixed point in the 'supernaturall food, Religion' (188) in 'The First Anniversarie.' An invitation to epistemological consideration is immediately issued, with recognition of Elizabeth Drury's value as a touchstone for self-knowledge ('that rich soule which to her Heauen is gone, / Whom all they celebrate, who know they'have one,' 1–2). The constant but varied refrain tallies the accumulating knowledge of the world's corruption:

> Shee, shee is dead; shee's dead: when thou knowst this,
> Thou knowst how poore a trifling thing man is.   (183–4)

Similarly, through her death the reader knows the world as an ugly 'monster' (326), a 'Ghost' (370), and dry 'Cinder' (428). To the 'world remaining still' (67) the poem's anatomist urges self-knowledge that recognizes widespread corruption. The epistemological gist follows the first refrain:

> And learn'st thus much by our Anatomee,
> The heart being perish'd, no part can be free.
> And that except thou feed (not banquet) on
> The supernaturall food, Religion,
> Thy better Grouth growes withered, and scant;   (185–9)

Donne's satire replaces one food with another, mocking man's prideful knowledge of a corrupted world, while impressing Elizabeth Drury's pattern of her 'vertue' (76–8). The epistemological diet for this new world includes knowing the 'dangers and diseases' of the old world (88), to control a response to it, and also includes knowing Elizabeth Drury's exemplary pattern. The figure of digestion implicitly carries spiritual knowledge into virtuous action.

In 'The Second Anniversarie' Donne refines the figure in terms of spiritual progress. Shifting his address from Elizabeth Drury to his own soul, he urges it to contemplate death:

> Thirst for that time, O my insatiate soule,
> And serue thy thirst, with Gods safe-sealing Bowle.
> Be thirsty still, and drinke still till thou goe;
> 'Tis th'onely Health, to be Hydroptique so.   (45–8)

This spiritual thirst yearning to become 'Hydroptique' recalls the 'holy thirsty dropsy' ('Holy Sonnet, XVII,' 8), a yearning to be filled even further with Grace. Here, the contemplative soul desires knowledge and love leading to 'essentiall joye,' the heavenly enjoyment of God. This 'full' and 'filling good' is limited to 'Onely who have enjoyd / The sight of God, in fulnesse' (441–5). Elizabeth Drury on earth, 'fild with grace' (465), provides the model; and the very form of the poem follows the speaker's progress in contemplation according to her pattern. The fulfilment of the soul's thirst in joy is the keynote to the poem's complex epistemological statement.

To recall briefly some of Donne's epistemological assumptions emphasizes why this is the case. As noted in Chapter Two, the rational soul is fulfilled through saving knowledge, a progress in the entire soul. In 'The Second Anniversarie' the soul's thirst is the will's desire to enjoy 'The sight of God in, fulnesse' (441), the beatified knowledge and love of God face to face. The poem recommends memory of Elizabeth Drury and ignorance of the world as requisites to the fulfilling progress toward that joy. Given Donne's basic epistemological assumption that love and joy presuppose knowledge, the poem's invitation to fulfilling joy assumes memory's knowledge of Elizabeth Drury and, paradoxically, rational earthly knowledge seemingly eschewed by the poem, but essential to the imagined 'extasee' (321) that envisions the soul's progress to heaven in the manner of Elizabeth Drury. Just as the soul's alimentation recalls the bodily parallel, the poem's paradoxical dependence upon earthly knowledge continues to draw the poem earthward. Donne exploits two working paradoxes: that a poem disavowing the lessons of 'sense, and Fantasy' (292) dwells on Elizabeth Drury's body as necessary for fulfilled knowledge; and that the poem, which forces the soul out of the body in an imagined ecstasy, begins and ends on earth, and consistently dwells on the body. Similarly, the fulfilled experience through the soul's progress returns embodied through the poem to other men. Thus, the poem's keynote, the correspondence between the soul's nourishment and the body's, introduces the complex of physical and spiritual that defines the progress.

Both poems tie knowledge to the body, the first obviously, the second paradoxically. The respective treatments of the body describe the respective epistemological concerns. Barbara Lewalski's description of the first poem as an anatomy of various bodies blows needed fresh air through the increasingly congested criticism of the poem. She finds a dissection of several bodies: the microcosm, the macrocosm, the world's subtlest parts, and the cosmos.[28] Donne's conclusion forcibly stresses this figure: 'But as in cutting up a man that's dead, / The body will not last out to haue read / On every part' (435–6). The poem yields knowledge of various bodies, now infected and dying. Elizabeth Drury's physiological death recalls sin's corruption that runs universally through these bodies related through their system of correspondences; and the many hands of the anatomist encourage self-knowledge of personal responsibility for that corruption. In effect, the corruption in all bodies – microcosm, macrocosm, society – refers by direct and indirect correspondences to the human soul. The refrain strikes its downbeat on the accumulative 'know,' which progressively catalogues corruption and disease while ranging widely along the lines of correspondence between man and other worlds. The poem's rational anatomy contributes to self-knowledge that recognizes Elizabeth Drury's example as an antidote.

The refrain accumulates changing meanings of 'world' through the programmatic dissection. A communal 'world' of men, introduced equivocally, then woven indirectly into the more formal structure, swells that knowledge as well. The initial 'world' (11) protects this ambiguity, at times flavouring it as the physical macrocosm, at times addressing it as a single person. Equivocation prepares for the severalness of 'world' treated more programmatically later; more pointedly, it addresses a community of all men before narrowing that community to the 'new world' of souls regenerated according to Elizabeth Drury's pattern (75–6). The poem addresses this world of new creatures, encouraging self-knowledge ('So thou, sicke world,' 23) that can learn to slough off old ways for new. Yet, appropriately, the more programmatic dissection (beginning at line 91) applies by correspondence to the corrupted communal world, in which all men participate, even those who turn from it. Donne repeatedly weaves in reminders, however, that social bodies lie within his purview. For example, the now lost coherence included 'All just supply, and all Relation: / Prince, Subject, Father, Sonne' (214–15). Donne's anatomy exempts the social world and the soul only from more systematic dissection, not from their share in mortal corruption or the possibility of recreation. However, this more indirect knowledge swells the refrain further.

The anatomist speaks to the regenerate world, pointing to broadened self-knowledge as the means to recreation. He recalls the normative forms of Creation, the interrelationships between macrocosm, microcosm, and social Body, combatting man's sinful thrust to 'bring our selves to nothing backe' (157) with the recreational pattern of Elizabeth Drury. Knowledge leads this fight, but in a form shared by a community reconstituted of actual men. Donne does not counsel an escape from the physical world, but designs a re-entry that protects the physical men who must live there. This knowledge is assimilated in virtuous action that holds the actual community together. Donne's description of the poem simply reaffirms his conception that artifacts are informed by man's composite nature: 'heaven keepes soules, / The grave keeps bodies, verse the fame enroules' (473–4). Donne expresses the same principle found in his New Year's Tide letter to Lady Bedford: here, Elizabeth Drury's 'example, and her vertue' (457) are now embodied in the poem, hence available for use in a real world. Donne's terminology keeps Elizabeth Drury's spiritual example invested in a material world, an important element in the reader's spiritual diet.

Whereas 'The First Anniversarie' works outward from man's basic bodily consciousness and follows the implications of corruption throughout the mortal world, in order to bring man, reinforced, back into that world, 'The Second Anniversarie' looks to final separation from the natural world, the separation of soul from body at death, then their reunion in glory. Yet, by offering Elizabeth Drury as a 'patterne' for 'life, and death' (524), union and separation, Donne parlays consciousness of the body into a much more complicated epistemological statement, accommodating both the movement of spiritual progress upward toward the fullness of heavenly glory, and a gravitational counterforce that keeps the earthly body at the poem's focal centre. Explicit encouragement to escape the world contributes paradoxically to a broader, implicit purpose to describe the continuum from earth to heaven that includes the living and the dead.

Donne's treatment of the body feels this countertension, the ostensible satire against preoccupation with the mortal body paradoxically encouraging a more concentrated attention to it. The poem imagines the deathbed 'unbinding of a packe' (94) against the background of the world's 'fragmentary rubbidge' (82), the world itself reeling like a recently beheaded body. This vision of mortality, unlike that of the first poem, does not look through itself to life, but contemplates the retreat through death, leaving the body to rot (115). Donne's satirical blade thrusts at pretentious estimates of the body's value as the most obvious example of self-defeating worldly attitudes. The soul in the body is like the 'stubborne sullen Anchorit' surrounded by 'his Ordures' (169–72). Similarly, the encouragement to ignorance punctures the ephemeral claims of contemporary medical science, such as the theory of blood circulation: 'Knowst thou how blood, which to the hart doth flow / Doth from one ventricle to th'other go?' (271–2). The satire looks at both bodily impediment and insufficient knowledge of it. Attack on the body seems relentless: it is a prison (249), a 'brittle shell' (250), 'a living Tombe' (252). Elizabeth Drury herself provides the speaker's winning thrust. She was so pure 'That one might almost say, her bodie thought' – but even that body was mortal (241–7). Nonetheless, praise of her beauty tightens the poem's countertension, especially for the reader who remembers the poet's introductory claims to 'embalme, and spice / The world, which else would putrify with vice' (39–40) by praising her. By keeping the reader's eye paradoxically trained on the body, Donne maintains the countertension with familiar claims that she was 'our best, and worthiest booke' (320), carrying upward to a vision of her glorified body that refers backward to her earthly body, so pure that only in heaven could it be made better (501–6). Likeness between her earthly and heavenly bodies explains the countertension without dissipating it, predicting the heavenly reality by means of the earthly; this likeness serves the poem's broadest purpose, to direct earthly readers to heavenly ends through her earthly and heavenly example. Her progress bridged earth and heaven; so must her example for the living.

Likewise, the countertension maintains a consciousness of the body as the necessary vehicle of value while attacking the selfish materialism that obscures the body's real importance and ties it to man like a clog. A striking image depicting death as the connection of earth to heaven expresses how this bodily consciousness necessarily contributes to understanding higher reality:

> As doth the Pith, which, least our Bodies slacke,
> Strings fast the little bones of necke, and backe;
> So by the soule doth death string Heaven and Earth   (211–13)

The image assumes that the human experience of heaven and earth is made understandable through likeness to the human skeleton. In Donne's claim that the Creator intended to people heaven with bodies (*Sermons*, IV, 47), we find the conceptual basis of the image and the belief that the physical body, in itself and as the paradigm for community, constitutes both an earthly and a heavenly reality. Man should not conceive otherwise.

The countertension that holds together the realities of earth and heaven likens Donne's power through the poem to Elizabeth Drury's exemplary influence on the living. Both enjoy God's inspiration that 'gave thee power to doe, me, to say this' (522). His poem embodies her virtue, imprinting readers as she had imprinted others while alive, informing earthly progress with her pattern. Her influence will father his poems of praise, yearly children, embodiments of her example as the motive force in a familial community of virtuous beings. And he asks that these praises may 'embalme, and spice / The world' (39–40). Her poetic children will beget 'great Grand-children of thy praises' (38); these 'progeny' (41), in embalming the world, work toward tangible social ties strengthened by the vision of the spiritual example of her progress, in life and death. His poems can 'say' only because he himself has learned to understand the significance of her pattern and the paradoxical ways it fulfils his hydroptic thirst. Once filled by his participation in her example, he must, like Elizabeth Drury, continue his own influence in the community, even as she does after death.

The sustained interplay between earth and heaven complicates the poem's epistemological statement; the mode of regular accrual in 'The First Anniversarie' here yields to the opposition between varying forms of knowledge, requiring that false be separated from true knowledge in achieving fullness. The repeated 'know' increases in frequency in the second poem; but the steady downbeat of the first yields to more jagged and seemingly contradictory rhythms of the second. Contemporary scientific knowledge produces only ignorance, as the mocking catalogue of scientific uncertainties proves (251–89); the 'Pedantery, / Of being taught by sense, and Fantasy' (291–2) is clearly maligned. Yet the poem reinstates the senses through Elizabeth Drury, who could recognize God's 'face' in 'any naturall Stone, or Tree' (453). Her sensory knowledge was 'fil'd with grace' and sought more 'capacitee' (465–6) when filled, thus providing the model for the speaker's own hydroptique thirst. Such knowledge needs both sense and reason, but likewise needs the 'faithfull confidence' (461), the assurance of the will strengthened by Grace. This knowledge of wisdom can distinguish legitimate from illegitimate subjects, recommending ignorance of one, using knowledge of another. Nor can a soul progressing toward the fullness of joy forget its earthly knowledge, as the poem implicitly admits; for the soul's progress is one piece, linking earth and heaven:

> Know that all lines which circles doe containe,
> For once that they the center touch, do touch
> Twice the circumference; and be thou such.
> Double on Heaven, thy thoughts on Earth emploid;   (436–9)

The earthly comparison enlightens the spiritual progress, filtering out the satirical perspective in order to apply genuinely useful knowledge.

The importance of some earthly knowledge in spiritual progress agrees with the poem's backhanded attention to the body and its social role. Spiritual progress can no more exclude the application of virtuous examples than saving knowledge can dispense with the senses. Elizabeth Drury's example remains to inform the community, just as memory of her pure body is necessary to characterize resurrection and its importance in the heavenly community. The poem leads upward to that community, while concurrently sharpening a sense of responsibility to its earthly precursor. The poem's fleeting attacks on existent social Bodies poisoned even in 'Nailes, Haires, yea excrements' (337) apply Elizabeth Drury both as a contrary pattern and also as a prefiguration of the heavenly community in which her soul now participates. Her exemplary self-control and influence on others 'Made her a soveraigne state' and 'religion / Made her a Church; and these two made her all' (374–5). Thus, she necessarily remains central to the poem's vision of the heavenly communion of saints, both before and after resurrection. Significantly, joy in heavenly communion with patriarchs, prophets, apostles, martyrs, and spiritual virgins (345–58) anticipates joy completed at the resurrection 'When earthly bodies more celestiall / Shalbe, then Angels were, for they could fall' (493–4). Elizabeth Drury's earthly body, in prefiguring the resurrected body, anticipates one essential element in the 'last great Consummation' (491). To underline my point: the poem offers her pure *earthly* body as one measure of fulfilled joy in the heavenly community. A further inference is that her influence on earthly life will end only when the completion in joy begins at the resurrection. Her significance as a 'patterne' for 'life, and death' (524) must embrace this special meeting of time and eternity.

In sum, 'The Second Anniversarie' depicts the paradoxical intercourse between heaven and earth. The countertension that holds the poet on earth, qualifying spiritual escape while he contemplates heavenly joy through participation in Elizabeth Drury, expresses not only the essential interdependence of man's body and his soul, but also his part in a community spanning earth and heaven. Thus, the poem expresses Donne's conviction that the experience of blessed souls looks to earth until the Last Judgment, through the active imprint of virtuous example, or even through the glorified soul's longing for its body. More important, for earthly believers a gravitational pull draws even the contemplative soul into a fulfilment in earthly time that satisfies the implications of man's composite nature without violating his role in Providential history. This downward gravitation is underestimated by many readers, as in Lewalski's analysis of Donne's unfavourable contrast between earthly and heavenly experience.[29] But the soul's epistemological diet must necessarily nourish the paradoxical elements in man's being. Taken together, the *Anniversaries* are spiritual nourishment that enhances understanding of man's status in a corrupt world and encourages the spiritual motions guiding his progress toward heavenly joy. Donne does not let us forget that this knowledge is necessary to assess the body's part.

IV THE INCARNATE CHRIST AND HIS BODY

Donne's sharpened consciousness of the body and his need for visible community gain satisfaction in the years of his priestly Calling. This satisfaction is achieved through a discernibly traditional conformity with the incarnate

Christ, which was responsive to his deepest psychological and epistemological currents. The dramatically realized Christ of the *Holy Sonnets*, the Good Friday poem, and the sermons is presented in physical as well as spiritual terms; he is a tangible model of bodily and spiritual continuity. Donne's so-called 'morbidity,' including his inclination to scrutinize putrefaction and dissolution, is resolved in contemplating resurrection assured by Christ's pattern. Fulfilment in time toward Glory follows the physical statement of Christ's spiritual reality, providing the participatory model for body and soul. In the sermons Donne clearly explicates conformity to the incarnate Christ in terms of the correspondences between man's body and soul. Further, he stresses that participation is fulfilled within Christ's visible Body, the Church.

Increasingly, Donne's theology of participation focuses on conformity with Christ. The Fall subverted the intention of Creation to people heaven, leaving man himself unable to redress the damage or anaesthetize the pain. The Incarnation, accordingly, acknowledges the needs of the full human composite, participating in both the human and the divine to restore the purpose of Creation: 'As our flesh is in him, by his participation thereof, so his flesh is in us, by our communication thereof.' Likewise, humans are 'partakers of his divine nature' through the Spirit's visitation (*Sermons*, IX, 248). The embodiment of Christ's divine nature in Church ordinance offers patterns for human thought and action under the Spirit's guidance. Such patterns redress the body's dislocation from the soul through virtuous action[30] or by informing man's experience of bodily suffering through conformity with Christ's experience. Virtuous action and bodily health manifest spiritual condition, with the likeness between man and Christ enhanced by the indwelling Spirit. Composite man is recreated through a sequential progress that culminates in both physical and spiritual sight of Christ in heaven.

The role of the two resurrections in this progress illustrates how Donne's personal psychology opened congenially into traditional belief. The participating likenesses between the believer and Christ, both in body and spirit, assure that man will be resurrected in the pattern of Christ. More to the point, this traditional Pauline assurance (e.g., Colossians 3:1) of man's resurrection, first, of the soul *In via*, then, the body *In patria* (*Sermons*, VII, 95), is supported by the correspondence between body and soul. For Donne the Resurrection must answer man's deep need to understand the soul in terms of the body. The physical implications of resurrection provide a vocabulary to describe spiritual regeneration while emphasizing dependence on the body.

In Donne's 1626 Easter Day sermon, a programmatic logic compares the resurrections of body and soul, insistently assuming the likenesses that unify their dualistic experience. Donne wittily argues that the body and soul respectively undergo three falls and three resurrections. In the first bodily fall and resurrection, the body separates from the soul at death, but they reunite at the Last Day; the soul falls by neglecting one's Calling, and rises by reassuming its duties. In the second, the body putrefies, then dissolves, until recompacted and informed again; the soul falls into the dissolution of habitual sin, to be renewed when Baptism restores the natural faculties. In the third, the body's dust scatters, until recollected by God; the soul, in turn, scatters into several sins, then recollects itself by examining past behaviour. Donne's systematic comparisons persistently read the body's experience to enlighten understanding of the soul's.

Although the gridwork of logical comparisons contains body and soul in separate dimensions, Donne unaffectedly shifts between sensory and spiritual experience, between bodily action and spiritual condition. Thus, he holds body and soul together in one mutual experience and complements the more rigid truth of comparison with the plasticity of actual experience. Donne depicts the second 'fall' by concentrating initially on putrefaction, inspiring the correspondences between bodily and spiritual smells, in terms of the palpable spirituality of the Song of Songs. The stench of putrefaction describes habitual sin as the 'stinke' of the soul's putrefied 'carcasse' when the original 'Spikenard' of natural faculties is lost (*Sermons*, VII, 108–9). Donne sets the sensory pleasure in the Song of Songs metaphor against sensory disgust. The body's sensory experience provides the terms for censuring the soul. Just as bodily putrefaction indicates the body's loss of soul, spiritual putrefaction indicates the soul's loss of animating Grace (*Sermons*, VII, 109). Spiritual putrefaction worsens at the loss of the 'holy perfume of that oyntment,' Christ's name, with which man was endowed at Baptism, as well as the 'sweet savour of the field' (*Sermons*, VII, 109), those 'degrees of goodnesse, and holinesse' (*Sermons*, VII, 112). The lost sweetness reveals spiritual putrefaction, while it leans toward spiritual redress, defining the principle of spiritual resurrection with terms from sensory life. For Donne this play between sensory and spiritual understanding expresses the essence of human consciousness.

The scattering and recollection of the third fall and resurrection suggest how belief in physical resurrection answers man's sense of threatened identity. Donne's frequent references to dissolution and dispersal, both physical and spiritual, acknowledge this threat. The body falls into separation, then putrefaction, then dissolution into dust, then, finally, dispersion. Similarly, the soul, scattered by sins and progressively weakened, 'baits at every sin that rises, and poures himselfe into every sinfull mold he meets' (*Sermons*, VII, 114–15). Yet belief in Christ's Resurrection assures man's own future bodily resurrection *In patria*, which, in turn, argues by correspondence for the soul's present resurrection from sin *In via*. For Donne the doctrine of resurrection satisfies the deepest need of the individual human composite to maintain its integral wholeness: 'Ego, I, I the same body, and the same soul, shall be recompact again, and be identically, numerically, individually the same man' (*Sermons*, III, 109). Progress towards wholeness, by expressing the active interdependence of corresponding parts of body and soul, articulates the promise of resurrection within the actualities of daily life. The believer dies through sin and is resurrected daily through the thoughts and actions of repentance.

For Donne the essential nexus between resurrection and the correspondences linking body and soul brings to a predictable fruition the realities of consciousness. The sermons exploit these correspondences as a matter of course to recast the doctrinal verity in experiential form. To find the traditional grounds for this essential root in Donne's thought helps to confirm its importance. And the sermons clearly suggest that the influence of Bernard of Clairvaux enriched his conception of these correspondences. Donne adapted the Bernardine characterization of the memory as the stomach (*Sermons*, II, 236)[31] and the will as the blood (*Sermons*, IV, 294)[32] of the soul. Under the surface of these more striking similarities run deep affinities that account for Bernard's influence as one of Donne's closest spiritual and theological masters.

Bernard's conception of the Pauline two resurrections, according to likenesses between body and soul, strikes such deep affinities with Donne. Bernard argues for two deaths and two resurrections, the soul's, then the body's, with one death separating man from God through sin, the other separating the body from its soul through death. Like Donne, Bernard reads the soul's resurrection by the body's. The upright human body has life and sensitivity corresponding to the created soul 'made upright in will, alive in knowledge, sensible in love'; accordingly, the resurrected body 'recovers life and sensitivity' and the erected soul 'recovers ... knowledge and love.'[33] Just as the body manifests the soul, the second resurrection describes the first. Bernard's dissection of correspondences between body and soul, in order to understand the soul's experience, distinctively marked his spirituality, especially his commentary on Song of Songs. Donne's references to Bernardine correspondences demonstrate a deep sympathy with this spirituality restrained only by the character of Donne's own thought. Donne found in Bernard a conception of man congenial to his own belief in a dualism of body and soul made intimate by definable correspondences. Although Donne's essentially physical nature could not follow Bernard's increasingly refined mystical ascent through the will, his own spiritual progress followed a pace like Bernard's in looking to the body to understand the soul.

Similarities in their conceptions of spiritual progress as a form of knowledge bring the Bernardine influences very close to the surface and suggest, if not a direct source for Donne's ideas, at least an identifiable confirmation. The related spiritual notions – thirst, mastication, swallowing, taste, digestion, dilation, fullness, assimilation – all have Bernardine analogues alluded to in Donne's sermons as a means of depicting saving knowledge. Donne's complete notion embraces the processes of spiritual digestion, filling, assimilation: the soul gradually digests knowledge that fills the soul, increasingly assimilating, likening him to God. His desires, that is, his appetite or thirst for saving knowledge, drive his reason to chew, ruminate, masticate and his faith to swallow, that memory may complete the digestive process begun by reason. The soul converts knowledge into blood, that is, the actions of the will, or fills the soul with knowledge and love. The consumer assimilates the object consumed: man is likened to God, in whom man participates with increasing fullness.

For both Donne and Bernard, digestion into fullness describes participation in God through erected human faculties. The will desires, loves what the reason knows, that is, the saving knowledge sensitized by love as wisdom and comprehended in the memory. Speaking about the will's integral role in saving knowledge, Donne explicitly adapts Bernard's notion of the will as appetite fulfilled in love, the sensitivity of the soul. God created humans to be 'partakers of the Divine Nature; *Vivificans ad sentiendum*, So good as that he hath quickned those soules, and made them sensible of having received him.' God gives the soul an 'appetite, and a holy hunger and thirst' for God; then '*Dilatans ad capiendum* ... he hath dilated and enlarged that soule, to take in as much of God as he will' (*Sermons*, VIII, 250). Wisdom as 'taste,' *sapientia* respecting its root *sapere*, knowledge sensitized by love has in its background Bernard's anatomy of love according to the five senses.[34] Again, Donne explicitly borrows Bernard's voice: '*Cui quaeque res sapiunt prout sunt, is sapiens est*, saies he: He that tasts, and apprehends all things in their proper and naturall tast, he that takes all things aright as they are, *Is sapiens est* ...' He that knows and loves the good enjoys the taste of wisdom:

But thus far, S. *Bernard* does but tell us, *Quis sapiens*, who is wise; but then, *Cui ipsa sapientia sapit, prout est, is beatus*, He that tasts this Wisdome it selfe aright, he onely is Blessed. (*Sermons*, VII, 338–9)[35]

Wisdom looks vertically to God and laterally to man. It must be sustained continuously by knowledge, first chewed and digested by reason, then stored and further digested by memory. Digested knowledge nourishes and strengthens the 'blood,' the will, to inspire love of God and charitable action. 'The memory, sayes St. *Bernard*, is the stomach of the soul, it receives and digests, and turns into good blood all its benefits formerly exhibited to the whole Church of God' (*Sermons*, II, 236). Thus, the fullness of wisdom engages the entire soul in charitable actions and spiritual progress that increasingly assimilate man to God.

In both Donne and Bernard, the correspondences between physical and spiritual eating, digestion, and filling regard Christ as the basic staple of all spiritual food.[36] Donne's rich Bernardine endowment strengthens Donne's conception of the epistemological relationships between the believer and the Incarnate Word. Yet this Bernardine parallel to Donne's Christocentrism blends with a Protestant emphasis shared by Donne's contemporaries. For example, Donne notes that Christ the Good Shepherd feeds mankind with himself. He quotes John 6:55: '*His flesh is meat indeed, and his bloud is drink indeed.*' Then, Donne notes that Christ, who fed man earlier with prophecies and promises of his coming, 'feeds us now with actuall performances, with his reall presence, and the exhibition of himself' (*Sermons*, IX, 133). This sense of Christ, visibly manifest through history, now applied in Church ordinance,[37] contributes substantially to Donne's mature epistemology. Nature yields but a breakfast; the Jews, in turn, 'their Law, and Sacrifices, and Types, and Ceremonies,' a dinner; and in the Christian Church a 'plentifull refection' in the Spirit's visitation, the Sacraments, and promise of the '*marriage Supper of the Lambe*' in heaven (*Sermons*, VII, 301). Donne's broadened sense of the Word manifest in Nature, in prophetic types, in the Church ordinance, and also in erected believers as exemplars, extends the scope of Christ as epistemological food or meat. Yet it does not contradict the vivid palpability of the Incarnate Christ in Bernard's thought. Man's 'meat' is to know God's Will (*Sermons*, VII, 303); and the Incarnate Word is its most visible manifestation. But Donne's thought broadens beyond Bernard's mystical commentary on the person of Christ to emphasize varying manifestations of the Word as man's food.

Any summary of Donne's thought needs to account for such a distinctive vocabulary describing spiritual experience in bodily terms. For Donne progressive spiritualization into likeness with God must be understood according to physiological assimilation, the body becoming like the food eaten, the soul like the god known. Similarly, the Grace that progressively fills the believer with knowledge, the mysterious intimacies of the Holy Ghost applying the Word, can be clarified according to physiological filling. The soul's hydroptic thirst, as in 'The Second Anniversarie,' is a desire for Grace to satisfy a wholesome dropsy (*Sermons*, V, 275) that dilates as it fills. Similarly, confession must purge the conscience, like a 'vomit' (*Sermons*, IX, 304) before the soul can be filled. In a word, the complicated participation in God through saving knowledge hinges upon the fulfilment of a rudimentary bodily consciousness along the lines of spiritual correspondences.

As noted, this consciousness perfuses Donne's understanding of the Incarnate Christ's bodily participation in human flesh, and of man's concomitant spiritual participation in God through the embodied pattern applied by the Holy Spirit. This bodily consciousness also distinguishes Donne's understanding of man's resurrection through participation in the merit of Christ's Resurrection, both in body and earlier in soul after the envisioned pattern of the resurrected body. Similarly, personal temperament and orthodox belief converge happily in Donne's conception of the Church as Christ's Body; this satisfaction of his longstanding need for an actual community coherent in shared values embraces communal participation through the Incarnate divine pattern. For Donne, as for Paul, resurrection begins on earth through incorporation in Christ, the Head, as members of his mystical, but very visible, Body. Salvation assumes community; and knowledge of community assumes the body as the paradigm. For Donne, belief in Incarnation, the two resurrections, and the Body become distinguishably, but essentially, fused by the immediacies of bodily consciousness.

The Body's properties stress the humanity shared by Christ and man to characterize the communal relationship within the Church. Not just a likeness, the Church *is* Christ's body, subject to dangers corresponding to the physical dangers of its constituent members. A genuine fear of bodily disintegration, assuaged in Donne himself by the promise of resurrection, describes the equally real threat of the Body's injury or disintegration. Dissension between the Body's members, in denying Christ's unifying Spirit, '*dissolves* Jesus and breakes him in peeces.' Similarly, Christ's Body suffers 'luxations ... dislocations' of worldliness, the 'woundings' of blasphemy, 'maimings' of half-hearted service (*Sermons*, V, 134–5). Significantly, Christ himself is 'wounded' when one member of the Body is 'torne off' and 'withers' through excommunication (*Sermons*, VII, 317). Sharp fear of bodily damage and dismemberment vies with belief in communal salvation; fear anticipates actual physical consequences of refusing salvation, while belief finds in the body's wholeness an assuring model for community.

By the time Donne reaches his maturity in the sermons, his relationship to the social Body has shifted, but not his essential grasp of its importance. The thwarted longing in the first satire, later satisfied partially in minority bodies as in 'The Canonization' or in the strained attempts in the verse letters to define a role for himself in an already established community, becomes the assured priest's role to advise both the Church and kingdom. Fear of exclusion is now forgotten; and fear of dissolution, in turn, is calmed by assurance of established membership in a unified Body. Still, Donne warns against doctrinal hostilities that can sever unity. The eternal Word, embodied in Scripture, informs the Body of believers, just as the derivative Articles of Faith form a 'skin that covers the whole body.' Though obligatory for all, these Articles can tolerate differing explications, that is, 'a skin that covers some particular limbe of the body, and not another,' if preserving the essential Article (*Sermons*, X, 113). Love and knowledge of the Word, in transfusing doctrine and behaviour to make man '*Idem spiritus cum Domino*,' bind together Head and members. Whereas a 'reciprocall embowelling' unites pastor and congregation, many become one in the immediacies of 'holy affections' between the Body's members (*Sermons*, VIII, 169–70).

When such holy affection guides the duties of the believer's Calling, the communal Body of Christ inspirits the whole Christian society. A Whitehall sermon of 1627 ruthlessly boils down Donne's multiform notion of body to Calling, which, if denied, reverses Creation, annihilating being and participation in this world:

this whole world is one intire creature, one body; and he that is nothing may be excremental nailes, to scratch and gripe others, he may be excremental hairs for ornament, or pleasurableness of meeting; but he is no limb of this intire body, no part of Gods universal creature, the world. (*Sermons*, VIII, 177)

Here 'world' conflates macrocosm with the communal Body of Christian society, swallowing all creatures into the fulfilled community of believers. This ruthlessness pursues physical creation to its goal in visible microcosmic action contained in macrocosmic space. In the notion of 'place,' Donne merges the identities of space and action, world and body. Man needs to perform the 'duties of the place in the place' (*Sermons*, VIII, 176). The three meanings of 'place' – physical space, social role, and its defined responsibilities – will not separate Christian duty from the physical and social worlds containing it. And it is the body that performs these duties of place, finding its real existence only in action. Whereas in nature the body 'frames and forms the place,' in grace 'the place makes the body.' By performing the duties of a given 'place,' a person dilates, fills, and extends that place according to its proper 'dimensions' (*Sermons*, VIII, 178).[38] Grace fulfils nature as action fulfils the body in space; and Christian Calling fulfils all of Creation in the Body, according to the pattern of Christ. But the living body remains the tangible centre that not only reveals the power of salvation in erected action, but also portrays the whole in the part, the Body of Christ in the bodily actions of its members. As ever, Donne's vision of truth looks through the actual body itself.

As we have seen, this vision is evident throughout Donne's works. The real thrust is not to make the case for the body, for its legitimacy is assumed, but to know the myriad ways that bodily experience incorporates the principles of being or violates those principles. Donne's God created man, not only for his own Glory, but to include human bodies in the heavenly community. Thus, the body is not only part of the essential man, but is also the essential physical medium of God's earthly influence. These theological principles, clearly set out in Donne's maturest expression, were congenial to a mind sharply aware of man's own bodily properties, and consistently engaged in finding principles that expressed a basic bodily consciousness. The two dimensions of that consciousness, of the self and the community, have not always received equal attention from modern readers. Yet Donne's continuing self-observation by no means stifled his instict to view his body in conjunction with other bodies. That Donne was not immune to the enclosures of self is aptly configured in the first satire, in the speaker's academic closet; but, suggestively, this retreat is a figure for disappointment in the existing Body, not a rejection of the desire for community. For Donne self-scrutiny led just as naturally outward as inward; for consciousness of the body discovered the paradigm for both the soul, and the physical world and social Body. The body thus stood on the boundary between outer and inner, the effigy of both the soul and the outer world. Man necessarily must know the nature of that effigy.

4

Suffering

In a 1629 sermon Donne notes that three of four Biblical names for man signify his misery. Afflicted and calumniated, *Ish* 'cryes, and whines out his time'; *Enosh*, an object of others' affliction and neglect, is 'meer Calamity, misery, depression'; and *Gheber*, though great like Jeremiah, '*hath seen affliction, by the rod of Gods wrath*' (*Sermons*, IX, 62). Affliction, sorrow, lament, mourning, pain, misery – the forms of suffering describe temporal existence. Even Donne's earlier works characterize suffering as the pervasive and inescapable condition of human life. However, in his later works suffering and affliction are divine agents that can reform the heart, freeing it from the constrictions of frustration, hatred, self-protective cynicism, evasive wit, and depression. Increasingly, in the experience of the Cross, Donne finds the model for suffering. His conviction grows that, within this divine discipline of suffering fully understood, the believer can find joy and glory. *Ish, Enosh,* and *Gheber* find their fulfilment in conformity with Christ, *vir dolorum (Sermons,* VIII, 65), in suffering and joy.

The formal shift in *The Anniversaries*, from suffering and lament in the first poem to joy and congratulation in the second, predicts the pattern informing Donne's mature spirituality. Significantly, 'The First Anniversarie' poses epistemological questions that define grief and specify its psychological implications. The poet offers his own intellectualized anatomy of the corrupted world as a model of self-knowledge for the segment of the 'world' still capable of spiritual reform. Grief occasions self-knowledge leading to recognition that sin causes both grief and God's punishing affliction. Such self-knowledge preoccupies Donne's mature Christian art. His fourteen sermons on the Penitential Psalms most conspicuously tread the line from self-awareness of sin to contritional sorrow; but this same line also runs throughout all the other sermons. So, too, does his analysis of God's corrective affliction. Donne's mature Christian piety trains the rational eye of self-knowledge on the events of affliction and grief, scrutinizing psychological experience for evidence of sin, proper humility, genuine remorse, and the Spirit's instructive motions. Similarly, since not all affliction expresses God's punishing wrath, the events of misery require the self-conscious perspective that strains to find personal responsibility for affliction, without unjust self-denigration. Self-knowledge finds joy in suffering, in penitential sorrow for sin and in affliction as evidence of God's favour. Joy does not slough off sorrow, but exists within it. For Donne, this concept of joy is one of the deeply felt lessons of the Incarnate Christ, whose physical and spiritual suffering patterns Donne's finely honed penitential awareness of his composite human self. In this conformity with Christ, we find a later emphasis in his conception of time: the fulfilment of time is the fulfilment of suffering in joy.

The distance between this assured penitential suffering and the early Donne's 'queasie paine / Of being belov'd, and loving' ('The Calme,' 40–1) is shortened by his continuing acknowledgment that misery governs mortal life. In the love poetry suffering is clearly a factor in both idolatrous sexual love and spiritualized mutual love. A wise retrospection in the sermons asserts that grief, however misguided the love object, at least assures a tender capacity for love (*Sermons*, IV, 340). Throughout his works Donne assumes that suffering, whether in love of humans or God, encourages the psychological tenderness necessary for spiritual fullness. However, in the love poetry naturalism, cynicism, and wit stifle the pain of emotional engagement and thereby harden the soul against the possible salutary effects of love's grief. To identify Donne himself too closely with his hardened speakers is to slight the force of moral and spiritual values that censure them. For Donne, spiritual obduration and misplaced, idolatrous love are the serious enemies of the spiritual fulfilment possible in mutual love; but even the grief of idolatrous love at least can maintain the soul's capacity for tenderness. It is only the tenderness of true grief, however, that can prepare the heart for assurance or joy. An overview of all Donne's works makes clear that such joy was a later achievement.

In his middle years only 'The Second Anniversarie' approaches convincingly to the joy celebrated in the sermons, although growing religious conviction recognizes that suffering and affliction rightly understood are the means to embrace God. The 'humorous' contrition ('Holy Sonnet, XIX') of the *Holy Sonnets* – tortured, inconstant, fretful – reveals that later joy was hard won. Self-conscious outbursts express a flawed piety. The voice that asks God to 'Teach mee how to repent' ('Holy Sonnet, VII') also clearly acknowledges the sinful barriers to spiritual satisfaction that must be battered by divine affliction. In this same period Donne's great elegies characterize his human attempt to understand the divine tutelage of grief and death. The standard complaint that Donne's ingeniousness in the Prince Henry elegy betrayed a shallow grief[1] overlooks Donne's working assumption that death and grief pose epistemological questions which the funeral poet must seek to answer for the community through himself. The elegies on Elizabeth Drury, Prince Henry, and Lord Harrington clearly and specifically examine knowledge as consolation. But Donne's funeral poems accept without celebrating; and the varying expostulation against sorrow, death, or the deceased for the most part shares the chafing restiveness of the *Holy Sonnets*.

Assured conformity with the suffering Christ gradually neutralizes the nervous, often rebellious chafing of Donne's temperament. The *Devotions upon Emergent Occasions* humanely allows expostulation against misery, while accepting illness as the punishment for sin that teaches Christlike obedience, patience, and humility in suffering. Throughout the sermons Donne's statement and restatement of Colossians 1:24 not only encapsulate his mature thought, but also mark the culmination of his lifelong development: '*Who now rejoyce in my sufferings for you, and fill up that which is behind of the afflictions of Christ in my flesh, for his bodies sake which is the church*' (*Sermons*, III, 332). Fulfilment in time, participation in God, spiritual joy, achieved community, embodied virtue, responsible Calling – all hinge on the individual's willing likeness to the crucified Christ. In the Cross stands the fulfilment of Donne's thought, but this fulfilment is achieved along a line continuous with his early emphasis upon suffering as one constant in human psychology.

I LOVE'S 'QUEASIE PAINE'

The basic constituents in Donne's mature psychology of suffering engage his attention from the beginning. Although his Pauline emphasis upon exemplary suffering matures only later, his conviction that suffering implicates man in his community often emerges in the love poetry. Whether love suffering is offered as a pattern or encourages defensive hatred or self-conscious shame, it enforces the lover's relationships with others. Individual suffering caused by both bodily and spiritual desires opens the lover to the complementary needs of others. Although love suffering demonstrates human weakness, it can also become the occasion for fulfilment, thus capturing both the limitations and the possibilities of human experience. At best, body and soul respectively find only degrees of earthly satisfaction, since love yields easily to the ruptures of change and to the weakness in human nature and in social habits. Exemplary love suffering is remarkable for withstanding the strategies of idolatry, selfish naturalism, courtly enslavement, or cynicism; it can also adjust to the threat of loss and death. In Donne's love poetry, it is as rare as it is remarkable.

Determining Donne's own attitudes to the varieties of love suffering renews the abiding critical problem in the love poetry. Any strict attempt to merge Donne with his several personae leads into quicksand. Still, Donne identifies his own voice often enough in other secular poems to offer considerable guidance in finding his perspective on specific issues and to control the danger of viewing the love poetry as an enclosed world. Donne's diptych of verse letters, 'The Storme' and 'The Calme,' regards love suffering as one form of misery. Written during the Islands Expedition of 1597, these poems set Donne's personal love experience along with other personal affairs in a more metaphysical ambience. The poems help to point the general direction of Donne's gaze in love poems written contemporaneously. An implicit counterpoint of traditional religious values found in this love poetry invites the consideration that man's control over the pains of his existence can only be shortlived and that some of his motives may be sinful, hence contributory to his misery. These two verse letters wittily invite similar considerations.

Donne views the dramatic weather during the Islands Expedition as events in the familiar *topos* of life as a voyage.[2] He also assumes a tradition of descriptive poetry that emblematizes the sea as fortune.[3] And, as we learn to expect in Donne's works, existential complaint invokes the opposition of Creation and Nothing. Writing to Christopher Brooke in 'The Storme,' Donne wittily claims that he is 'nothing' (1); and in 'The Calme' he pessimistically concludes that man's being approaches to 'Nothing' and that 'wee are for nothing fit' (53). In 'The Storme' the destructive confusion of Donne's fortune is treated as a reversal of Creation that requires a divine reordering. Unless God speaks 'Another *Fiat*,' darkness and 'uniforme deformity' will continue to cover the earth (67–72). Only misery's self-awareness halts utter self-negation by recalling the necessary beginning of being: 'Wee have no will, no power, no sense; I lye, / I should not then thus feele this miserie' ('The Calme,' 55–6). To know life is to know misery.

The imagery of penal suffering and disease, in making us consider that the sufferers are partly responsible for the misery of fate, sets a context for viewing Donne's own presence on the expedition. During the storm some voyagers look out from the ship's cabins like 'sin-burd'ned soules' (47) creeping from graves at Doomsday. And, during the calm, swimmers enter a Hellish 'brimstone Bath' that refreshes them no more than the seeming 'coales' of the ship (30–2). In the storm the ship's mast shakes with an ague; its hold is bloated with a 'salt dropsie' (55); and its bedraggled sails hang like executed corpses. Infernal punishment, implicit judgment, and profound misery are the background for Donne's own welter of motives for accompanying the expedition:

> Whether a rotten state, and hope of gaine,
> Or to disuse mee from the queasie paine
> Of being belov'd, and loving, or the thirst
> Of honour, or faire death, out pusht mee first,
> I lose my end: (39–43)

Whereas uncertainty about his specific motive reveals no clear direction ('I lose my end'), the 'stupid' (2) calm expresses benumbed self-awareness. Donne's complicity with the ship's afflicted community further darkens this spiritual malaise.

Thus, Donne's 'queasie paine' of love shares earthly man's more generalized curse and suggests an important perspective on the early love poetry. In 'The Calme' the macrocosmic sea 'Smooth as thy mistresse glasse, or what shines there' (8) gives back a universalized ambience for the deadening effect of love's pain. The ship itself, emasculated and fallen like Samson (34), suggests that Donne's fellows are similarly goaded toward spiritual annihilation. Further, the traditional sea of fate, depicted as a woman's narcissistic mirror, relates to Samson's idolatry and enslavement. The possibility in Donne's self-judgment of idolatry here gives a thread to follow through many early love poems with their egocentric personae, ostentatiously rejecting traditional values. There, Donne's satirical portraits savour of a self-knowing censure of tendencies encouraged in his society and recognizable in his own immediate experience. Our attempt to find his moral perspective in these love poems should allow for Donne's sympathy with traditional moral expectations guiding his satires,[4] which were written during the same years; likewise, we should remember his confession of sexual guilt and idolatry in the *Holy Sonnets*, later to be recalled in the sermons. Neither the cynical, witty iconoclast found by many twentieth-century readers nor the resolved moralist of N.J.C. Andreasen's informative study[5] adequately accommodates the frustrated conflict in Donne's love poetry between the disturbing realities of loving and deeply imprinted traditional values. Yet Donne keeps recalling the perspective offered by these traditional values.

Donne's conviction of love's necessary suffering remains unchanged in the love poetry, but not his analysis of the reasons. On one hand, the suffering caused by disdain, sexual infidelity, scorn, abjectness, cynicism, and defensive hatred is placed at a stiff arm's length by Donne's satire; on the other hand, Donne's analysis of suffering reveals the conviction that mutual love can design anew the terms of social engagement. Mutuality dissolves the conscious cruelty and blind disregard of selfishness, thereby precluding abjectness, defensiveness, or retaliation. Suffering remains the condition of mortal life; but shared love, freed from the additional weight of self, can find strength and increase in suffering's burden. The defences of self once surrendered, the experience of suffering can discipline the soul toward its fulfilment in love.

Donne's satire in the love poetry, in taking aim at the sources of emotional stunting that prevent this fulfilment, also attends to the role of suffering. In the elegy 'Recusancy' ('Oh, let mee not serve so'), the speaker's disdain and hatred are countermeasures against the hopeless, destructive pain of loving a deceitful and zealously libidinous woman. The satire scores her for selfish sexuality, the speaker for self-constricting retaliation, and their society for the perverted ambience encouraging both responses. The world advocates a mutually demeaning servitude of low to high. The sexually cruel lady expects idolatrous service, but instead encourages the speaker's rebellion against servitude and recusancy against idolatry. The speaker saves his pride through 'disdaine' (38). And he self-consciously resists the ultimate danger of total emotional obduration, the annihilation through 'Carelesse despaire' (36) that scorns all. Nonetheless, the activities of disdain and the competitive shape of his hatred ('My hate shall outgrow thine,' 43) demonstrate that, while fleeing love's pain, he has sidestepped a few spiritual pitfalls only to fall into others. Ironically, by rejecting love's idolatry he has hardened further his rejection of higher spiritual purposes implicit in the poem's parody of religious and ecclesiastical language. His heart, like hers, has lost the softness of wax (14) necessary for receiving love's imprint.

Her faithless cruelty compounds the pain of all earthly love. As even poems of mutual love make clear, complete fulfilment and satisfaction are heavenly, not earthly, states.[6] 'Loves Growth,' in which the sexual and the spiritual interconnect, builds on this assumption. Love's increase follows the biological cycle that includes human sexuality and subjects the speaker to a cycle of pain and suffering: 'this medicine, love, which cures all sorrow / With more ... mixt of all stuffes, paining soule, or sense' (7–9). The biological cycle fuels a spiritual increase that paradoxically can work against the depression following sexual crescendo, or what the embittered speaker in 'Farewell to Love' calls the residual 'sorrowing dulnesse to the mind' (20). Sexual ecstasy devours itself, but not the resulting spiritual increase in mutual lovers. In contrast, a purely sexual love, as offered by the lady in 'Recusancy,' which can give only momentary sexual satisfaction, will be unsettled further by infidelity and cursed with a benumbing pain.

In 'Loves Infiniteness' the desire for 'All,' in struggling against the incompleteness in earthly love, expresses a basic element in Donne's psychology of love. Constant suffering accompanies love's fulfilling growth. The speaker first fears his exhaustion of 'Sighs, teares, and oathes, and letters I have spent' (6), then, that competitors will 'outbid' (17) him. The fearful speaker recognizes that the beloved will need visible proof of his desire; but he also realizes that his suffering visibly expresses his unfulfilled desire for complete union. Love's oaths, in turn, can reassure the beloved's own suffering fears, while love experiences its own reassuring increase.

The sexual implications of 'Loves Growth' emerge in 'Loves Infiniteness' in the speaker's initial conception of 'having' the beloved. Donne's belief that sexual consummation is an instructive correspondence to spiritual union consists with the dualism of body and soul, worked out carefully in 'Loves Growth.' Ecstatic sexual union predicts spiritual union, while declaring its own limitations in its differences. Learning to 'be' and not 'have' is to learn a spiritual truth; but both poems assume a movement upward from the body to the soul. Significantly, the speaker's confident prediction that they 'shall / Be one, and one anothers All' (32–3) reflects the lovers' mutual conviction without actual proof of experiential completion. The speaker has no guarantee against the cycle of sexual suffering and depression depicted in 'Loves Growth' nor against paradoxical and aggrieved incompletion that sparks and accompanies the growing reassurance of mutual love.

Need for completion, fear of incompletion, the necessary inclusion of both body and soul – these are the basis for love suffering. Both sexual desire and the will's desire for love seek the love object; but only the fidelity of mutual love can assure the needs of both body and soul, gratifying sexual desire, at least for the moment, and then engrafting souls in mutual growth. Mutual love accepts fear and suffering as important motor forces. Moreover, while recognizing in love's suffering the tenderness of soul that can merge with others, mutual love follows sexuality upward to recognition that only spiritual union can expand toward fulfilment. Contrarily, libertinism indifferently feeds sexual desire with ready, available sexual confections, but blocks off the soul's suffering with a hardened will.

Fear of incompletion, pulled taut by shock of death, parting, change, or disease, inspires Donne's great poems of grief and suffering. A painful sense of mortality shakes the assurance of mutual love, creating a new awareness of spiritual union in the great valedictory poems. The respective speakers of

'A Valediction: of Weeping' and 'A Valediction: forbidding Mourning' find consolation in the dualism of body and soul that permits a continuing union of souls in spite of separation, thereby relaxing fear. In addressing the necessary grief of physical separation, the two poems confront the danger of overindulged grief that increases, not reduces, the body's unwillingness to allow separation. The struggle is more convulsive in 'A Valediction: of Weeping,' more assured in 'A Valediction: forbidding Mourning,' although even the assured claim that these lovers only 'Care lesse' about the body (20) confesses the grief that must be controlled. Unavoidable suffering must be harnessed so that they may enjoy their spiritual continuity.

Whereas spiritual strength is necessary to manage grief, idolatry weakens spiritual defences against the suffering of existence. The traditional judgment against idolatrously loving the creature and not the Creator is close to the surface in Donne's works, especially when idolatry exacerbates this natural suffering. In 'The Calme' the ship, likened to a weakened Samson, represents a society enervated partially by idolatrous love. In 'Recusancy' the speaker succeeds in a costly revolt against painful, servile idolatry. Here and elsewhere, Donne's satire severally attacks the ladies and their societies. In 'Loves Exchange' rebellion against a courtly romantic pattern, against idolatry to love itself, ironically falls victim to a hopeless, idolatrous passion that serves Love's end. Now loving a 'face' worthy to change the 'Idolatrie' (29–30) of any land, the speaker must suffer denial. Even worse, he pleads for ignorance that others witness his lady's disregard and add 'shame' to his 'woe' (21). Love's demeaning ritual and the speaker's self-pity and defeatism limit our sympathy; in 'Recusancy' Donne's hard scrutiny of emotional hardening as an alternative to idolatry does likewise.

In 'A Nocturnall upon S. Lucies Day' we find Donne's most complicated and moving treatment of idolatry and grief. Love's potential for idolatry reaches it most destructive and touching actuality by perverting mutual love. Excessive suffering, the 'dull privations, and leane emptinesse' (16) of love's incompletion, foretold the speaker's annihilating despair at her death. Lacking the spiritual assurance in 'A Valediction: forbidding Mourning,' these lovers could not look beyond the suffering legacy of all earthly lovers: tear floods annihilated all value, absence was suicide, and mutual idolatry revoked 'Care to ought else,' (26).

Yet Donne sympathetically probes this idolatry in 'A Nocturnall' more ambiguously than in his attacks on the ritual of servility and cruelty elsewhere. Here, a tenderness of spirit, expanded, not benumbed, by suffering, expresses mutual surrender, depth of love, and spiritual capacity absent in other idolaters. The speaker's ambiguous intention to 'prepare' for the dead woman's

'Vigill' (43–44) may continue his idolatry; but, instead, it may suggest that a purgative grief has readied him to understand her spiritual value. His invitation that other lovers study him as an example of love's destitution may suggest both a new spiritual self-criticism and a nascent charity towards 'ought else.' Accordingly, the speaker's desperation might not have extinguished the spiritual potential in all mutual love in spite of idolatry's surrender to human weakness. Together, these lovers lacked the spiritual control painfully achieved in 'A Valediction: of Weeping'; but spiritual possibility may be rediscovered through death's agency. If so, the speaker would have achieved self-knowledge through affliction, hence anticipating an important assumption in the sermons. The poem ends on this ambiguity.

The speaker's grief, as a negative model for others, shows the public face of private misery, a primary concern of Donne in regard to suffering. The exemplary power of personal suffering is one theme throughout his career; it reaches fruition in the sermons in his Pauline refrain from Colossians 1:24, in which members, following Christ's pattern, suffer for the Body. The mutual lovers of 'The Canonization,' phoenix-like (23) in their mysterious love, offer to unify a new community according to their pattern: love's grief has been complicated by the established community's opposition, changing 'peace' to 'rage' (39). In 'The Relique' the speaker's exemplarism is less self-conscious and grief less openly admitted; but his lady's death sharpens a sense of responsibility to inform the community with knowledge of his love. Likewise, in 'A Nocturnall' the individual's suffering can nourish the community. This more ambiguous grief is a warning against love's annihilation, perhaps against the punishment of idolatry. In these poems the lovers, not intentionally, only effectually, suffer for the community. The full Pauline expectation of suffering as fulfilment within the community comes later.

Donne's later thought, in stressing the community's fruition in its members' suffering, turns necessary human suffering into moral virtue. Many earlier poems, however, show less concern with exemplary suffering than with noting, often wittily, how personal grief absurdly implicates man in his community. For example, in 'The Triple Foole' Donne half-playfully toys with the assumptions that poetry can discipline grief and that both poetry and grief have social implications. Now entangled in his own actions, the self-critical speaker laments that his poetry, when repeated, will re-enact his grief. Yet the poem accepts the need to express grief and, thus, to introduce private experience into the public domain that reflects back upon it. 'Loves Exchange' is another example. In a tight Court enclosure, private love becomes public through the ritual of grief and denial played before an audience. First a rebel, then Love's defeated victim, the speaker pleads for ignorance of others' knowledge as a means of self-evasion: 'Let me not know that others know / That she knowes my paine' (19–20). The subtle interplay between individual and communal awareness here unites aggrieved rebel, distant lady, and Court audience satisfied by Love's triumph.

Nonetheless, it is exemplary suffering that engages Donne's fullest attention to lovers' grief. His solution to the speakers' self-conscious absurdity in 'Loves Exchange' and 'The Triple Foole' is not retreat from community and earthly suffering, but enrichment through mutual love and strenuous self-knowledge. Exemplary suffering within a community must find the shared spiritual basis that seeks a new community inimical to Love's institutions. But even that experience can lead to excess. In 'Twicknam Garden' the suffering exemplar, lacking this basis, extends idolatrous love into self-idolatry. In Donne's religious parody love is the serpent (9); the unbending lady, the god of truth; and the speaker, the suffering mediator of truth to other lovers. Bearing crystal vials, other lovers will use the speaker's tears to test their mistresses: 'For all are false, that tast not just like mine' (22). Parody evokes Christ's suffering, a Eucharistic communion of tears, a 'tast' of wisdom that can strengthen the Body of Love's believers with exemplary truth. Donne's parody, in scolding the speaker's self-idolatry, implies that idolatrous love of his lady is rooted in destructive self-concern. The poem's supreme irony, the speaker's inability to differentiate between his lady and tearful ladies capable of feeling, dramatizes the obtuseness of his self-indulgent suffering, offered as a communal touchstone. We need look only to Donne's anatomy of specious martyrdom in *Pseudo Martyr* to find his estimate of this danger.[7]

To review suffering in the love poetry is to look forward to other works, since Donne develops outward along a continuing base. Unremitting conviction of human misery is assimilated into a deepening spiritual growth; suffering is experienced not only as the punishing oppression of temporal life, but also as a way of achieved being. The sense of sin and guilt that discolours some love poems, the evasions of hatred and cynicism, and the satire against destructive forms for love recede together under the influence of mutual love, a pattern not unlike the effect of Grace in the religious works; both encourage a once stunted emotional growth which accepts suffering as its agency. Similarly, the ironies of self-knowledge, the helpless awareness of the pains of entrapment, idolatry, rebellion, or obduracy, are broken down by a will freed by mutual love. The sharp eye of self-knowledge, freed from the soul's misdirection, increasingly serves the needs of mutual love, then divine love, weighing the events of grief for their spiritual significance. In the *Holy Sonnets*, as we will see in Chapter Six, the request for affliction ('Batter my heart') and the nervous attempt to establish the humility of contritional sorrow are functions of self-knowledge of sin and the need for the therapy of suffering. In Donne's more public funeral poetry, this self-scrutiny filters through a communal perspective that develops Donne's conviction, manifested in varying forms in the love poetry, that man is defined by his ties to the community. It is in the funeral poetry that the relationships between knowledge, grief, and communal awareness receive Donne's first explicit and consistent attention.

II EPISTEMOLOGY AND LAMENT

The personal view of public events, which makes the speaker's responses representative of the community, increasingly dominates Donne's literary mode as he nears the pulpit. The devotional cast of the funeral poems[8] predicts the mode of the sermons. The merging of self-knowledge into more broadly 'objective' public knowledge is one epistemological and psychological consequence; the need to understand the shared consequences of publicly disturbing deaths is another. These poems assume that the events of death and grief require immediate understanding by the individual and the community. Such 'timely' disturbances characterize fallen time, to be understood and known as such.

The connection between 'just lamentations' (79) and rational self-knowledge in the Prince Henry elegy is the mainstay of Donne's elegies, for it accepts the inevitability of grief in fallen time while requiring reason as its moderating force. A believer's response to grief reveals his spiritual condition, with the negation of despair on one side, and increased understanding and assurance on the other. Moderate grief teaches knowledge; immoderate grief is sinful; and reason makes the difference. But 'just' lamentation distinguishes between grief and lament, between emotional experience and its linguistic expression, between private experience and public statement. Donne has not only public lament in mind, but also personal statement of grief for which elegy can provide a model. A 'just' lament controlled by reason verifies the existence of reason by verifying its government. The intellectual quality of Donne's funeral poems follows accordingly.

By causing scepticism about given values, the shock of death can strip man down to mere awareness of being. In turn, grief can goad him to a new knowledge that rebuilds assurance. In 'An Anatomy of the World' the public poet Donne reminds his audience how to use that goad, although his recommendation of just lament lacks the personal drama of the Prince Henry elegy. Unlike the 'Sicke world, yea dead, yea putrified' (56), the 'world remaining still' (67) possesses the capacity to follow grief to necessary knowledge of widespread sin shared by the audience. The poem's shifting address, from 'thou, sicke world' (23) to 'thou' (183), separates out the new world from the 'carcasse' (75) of the old. The 'sicke world' had first grieved 'in a common Bath of teares it bled' (12); then 'it joy'd, it mournd' (20), uncertain whether her death was a gain or loss; then, it lapsed into 'speechlesse' (30) ignorance. Contrarily, the new world constitutes those who 'understood' her (72). Still lamenting (174, 360, 401) her loss and goaded by grief, the world will be told the 'dangers and diseases' of the old world, that they may know its 'true worth' (88–90). Given the derivation of the new world from the old, the anatomy recommends a self-knowledge that links sin causally to death and suffering. Grief rationally acknowledges lost value and man's responsibility for the loss. To forget these implications, to ignore the purpose of grief, is to encourage the deathly stupefaction of the old world. Lament acknowledges that reason and knowledge must advise suffering to achieve its end, to see that 'no thing / Is worth our trauaile, griefe, or perishing, / But those rich joyes, which did possesse her hart' (431–3).

In 'Obsequies to the Lord Harrington, brother to the Countesse of Bedford' Donne complicates the necessary relationship between knowledge and grief with a meditation on time and place that portrays how temporal consciousness slows consolation. The speaker expostulates against the premature death of the virtuous Lord Harrington with questions never answered explicitly to his satisfaction, although implicit answers contribute to his unenthusiastic submission to Providence. Here, the speaker's knowledge is less satisfying and comforting than in the Prince Henry elegy, less conclusive than in 'The First Anniversarie,' although it contributes to nascent understanding. A confident assertion that he has by 'goodnesse growne' and can profitably 'studie' the dead Lord Harrington (10), thus making 'This place a map of heav'n, my selfe of thee' (14), lays its own stumbling block by seeking to use the dead man's example to 'discerne by favour of this light, / My selfe, the hardest object of the sight' (29–30). The speaker ends the poem, however, still aggrieved and prepared to bury his Muse with Harrington. He falls far short of the reassuring self-awareness reached in the Prince Henry elegy. His expostulation now bitten off, he has resigned himself partially to the death; but he still fails to understand its necessity or its full effect on himself. Lament does not lead to consolation.

The speaker's seemingly clear understanding of the issues ironically frames his inability to follow his own epistemological implications fully. The same truths that make it possible to determine Harrington's 'epitomee' (78) during his brief lifetime build toward an awareness that 'ev'ry'exemplar man' continues to influence his 'Diocis,' the 'whole world' (225–6). The claim that

Harrington was aided on earth by 'Tutelar Angels' (228) ironically concludes an earlier epistemological discussion that should have consoled the speaker. The argument is that virtue is 'one intireness' (62), however expressed as specific virtues, and is perceived in the manner of angelic cognition and of human reading. Man cannot follow an angel's sequential earthward movement; yet, when he arrives, 'wee know' that he travelled from heaven to earth. Similarly, angels know intuitively by 'quick amassing severall formes of things' (89–90), just as men read without stopping at 'every A, and B' (96). Similarly, in 'short liv'd good men,' their virtue in its entireness, not 'Each severall vertue,' is 'understood' (85–98). Such firm knowledge of virtue and its accessibility ironically exacerbates the speaker's 'reverentiall anger' (237) that jostles even the conclusion that God willed the death.

The speaker's limited expectations about time and place create this irony. He cannot yet accept that a young man could fulfil his earthly purpose by dying early. The speaker is one of those average men, 'pocket-clocks' (131), who need the presence of 'great clocks' (143), the exemplars whose visible 'deeds' (103) fulfil time and place.[9] Ironically, terms used to state the problem express the solution; the basic notion is that time, the soul, and each life are all circular. The circular soul, its 'ends' in birth and death (106), becomes a circular, physical clock in time to be viewed by others. The speaker flatly admits the perfection of Harrington's 'circle' at his death (119), plus the 'intirenesse' of its virtue, affirming a human circularity modelled after God's. But the speaker fails to recognize how Harrington's example still works on him.

That is, he does not see that the 'intirenesse' of Harrington's virtue was based on faith;[10] nor does he see that his own faith holds his 'reverentiall anger' at bay, enabling him to accept that God's 'Prerogative' had 'dispens'd for' Lord Harrington (241). The speaker's own growth in 'goodnesse' (10) results from faith and, by implication, from Harrington's example, demonstrating obliquely how such exemplars guide others. The ironic lag in the speaker's understanding reflects the limitations of temporal consciousness, which feels 'each mismotion and distemper' (132) and, like a slow reader, wants every A and B. Only when understanding supports the conviction of faith can he moderate his grief further.

That a given death raises different epistemological questions denotes not only the individuality of events, but also the several epistemological implications of grief and lament. Similarly, Donne's varied responses to individual deaths articulate a conception of grief clear in its other assumptions and adaptable to given moments. One traditional assumption is the paradoxical clash between grief as sin and as purification. In 'The First Anniversarie' the completion of this paradox distinguishes the somnolent old world from the new world that follows grief to necessary self-knowledge. In 'Elegie on the Lady Marckham' Donne varies this traditional paradox. Ever noting the difficult balance between grief and its ready excess, Donne answers by minimizing death's effect on the virtuous and advancing the deceased as one who 'by teares' (52) climbed the 'common staires of men' (52).

A fully articulated microcosmic conceit ('Man is the World, and death the Ocean,' 1) relates the dualism of body and soul to the paradox of sinful grief and purgative sorrow. Though God sets 'markes, and bounds' (4) that give to death only the body ('the lower parts of man,' 2) and not the soul, man forgets these known terms in his grief. The 'land waters' pollute the 'waters ... above our firmament': that is, 'teares of passion' disturb contritional tears (7–8). The body's afflicted desire for physical presence taints the soul's purgative devotions. Likewise, this desire distorts necessary knowledge of 'what wee are, or what shee' (16), until the penitential example of the deceased again establishes God's set penitential patterns and offers purgation for the sin of excessive grief. Whatever death may 'pretend' (5) to do, it inadvertently refines virtuous bodies and frees the soul for heaven. Death's threat is defused. Virtuous exemplars like Lady Marckham are preserved from sin and enabled by God to repent. Thus, the poem's guiding irony, that sinful grief for the deceased is absolved by her own pattern of penitential sorrow, neatly rehearses the familiar, traditional paradox of grief itself.

In the elegy on Cecelia Boulstred, Donne returns again to the problem of expressing a legitimate funeral grief. The speaker ends his long meditation on grief's potential for either sin or goodness by engaging the problem of excess. This essential indifference of events themselves characterizes the subtleties of temptation. Here, we meet again Donne's resolute conviction, manifest from the love poetry to the sermons, that grief is natural and legitimate, but not its excess. To the principle of grief's indifference, Donne adds the crucial distinction that attitude, not mere quantity, determines sinful excess, 'immoderate griefe'; but man can 'scape that sinne, yet weepe as much' (71), since grief recognizes, as a function of self-knowledge, not only her blessedness, but its own earthly limitation. Yet the quantitative distinction humanely allows 'Some teares' amongst her 'knot of friends,' a chain broken, but 'no linke lost' (73–4).

The relationship between grief and momentarily ruptured community that concludes 'Elegie on Mris Boulstred' is revealingly pursued in 'Elegie upon the Death of Mistress Boulstred' ('Language thou art too narrow, and too weake'). This poem wears down its assertion that language cannot ease grief ('great sorrow cannot speake,' 2) and the truism that sorrow rules life, to conclude with a crucial assumption of Donne's funeral poetry: 'And we her sad glad friends all beare a part / Of griefe, for all would waste a Stoicks heart' (61–2). The poetic strategy that denies language because of grief paradoxically dramatizes the power of language to control grief by sharing it with the community. Donne even hints at the possible sinfulness of containing grief: 'Sad hearts, the lesse they seeme, the more they are, / (So guiltiest men stand mutest at the barre)' (5–6). Belief that the group completes the individual begets the theory of lamentation that resolves just grief linguistically in the community.

This poem clarifies a further principle of Donne's funeral poetry, that lament must be shared with others. The devotional cast of these poems of lament becomes more understandable. The speaker's aggrieved lament brings the community's shared grief into participatory focus. Also, just as the process of rejecting scepticism in the Prince Henry elegy and just as the incomplete process of understanding and assurance in the Lord Harrington poem suggest genuine human responses to grief, the process of reinstating language points to a generic excess caused by death. This excess reveals a subtle idolatry; a refined self-recognition discovers that 'God tooke her hence' (39) in order that some would not abuse her saintliness in idolatrous worship. The speaker, first condemned by excess, then saved by self-recognition, finds with 'sad glad friends' (61) the joy in grief; he now assesses her true value as well as finds joyful evidence of Providential care in her death. Just lamentation, armed with reason and language, wrestles constantly with excess, to find a legitimate place for human grief as a means of understanding man's communal relationship to God more fully.

Thus, the God-given affliction that corrects a subtle idolatry and cultivates joy in sorrow signifies Donne's movement in the funeral poems toward the spirituality of the sermons. The more crudely conceived idolatry of the earthly love poems yields to a finely discriminated self-knowledge that recognizes the potential for sinful love in all human occasions, but likewise observes the patterns of misery more closely for expressions of divine love. Sharpened self-knowledge, although it can be an occasion for sinful self-hatred, finds countervailing evidence that God's punishment can be a sign of his favour. Such punishment, in training the will to love God, establishes the condition for man to gain that favour. In the sermons suffering remains the medium, joy the evidence of favour earned, and community the fulfilment of efforts to enter into union with God. The funeral poems usher us into the sermons.

III FOR THE BODY'S SAKE

Hindsight from the sermons shows Donne's thought seeking its centre in the suffering Christ. In the love poetry, the soul hardened or softened in the experience of love, the struggle for clear-eyed self-recognition, and the active force of suffering all prepare for the fretful interior vision in the *Holy Sonnets*. There, a restive self-scrutiny, unsettled by pride, strains toward conformity with the crucified Christ, while recognizing in its own spiritual tautness the measure of unlikeness. The more public funeral poems modulate this interior cast with a broadened sense of shared public experience: the speaker recognizes in himself the shared suffering for the loss of public exemplars. In the sermons this broader public dimension takes into itself the vivified personal vision of Christ, refusing to separate personal experience of the suffering Head from participation in his Body, the Church. The priest's own voice denotes the border line between the private and shared public conformity with Christ's exemplary pain. The need for human exemplars expressed in Donne's works and the search for mutual love, released from idolatry and joined in community, are satisfied in Paul's joyful fulfilment of Christ's suffering in his own flesh for the Body's sake. Conformity with Christ that leads to loving sacrifice for others imprints the forms for communal love.

For Donne, conformity with the crucified Christ reaches the most intensely personal and the most broadly theological. The realism of torn flesh, moist blood, and tearful grief sets the requirements for man's participation in God. This is the way of likeness, conformity, literally the similarity of form. Donne's most vividly autobiographical works relive the drama of attempted conformity. In the *Holy Sonnets* the self-idolatrous gesture to become Christ on the Cross ('Spit in my face yee Jewes') aborts the necessary humility of conformity; the *Devotions upon Emergent Occasions* follows personal suffering toward a conformity with Christ;[11] and the moving theatricality of *Deaths Duell* offers Donne's own spent body on the threshold of death in visible conformity with the portrait of Christ's suffering that concludes the sermon (*Sermons*, x, 247–8). In this personal '*Conformitas*' (p. 245) with the crucified Christ, Donne's metaphysic of likeness, of assimilation, and the theology of temporal suffering become complete.

We find that this *conformitas* involves several tightly related ideas on suffering. To begin with, Donne argues according to his metaphysic of likeness that the tripartite human Image must conform to the tripartite God by assimilating Christ's suffering; most specifically, he expresses the traditional psychology that conforms the human to the divine will. Donne gives full play, on one hand, to Christ's exemplary physical suffering and to his compassionate tears and, on the other hand, to the human equivalencies through penitential suffering and God's corrective affliction. We also find that this vividly conceived suffering of man in Christ's pattern pervades his notion of the martyr's exemplary suffering for the Christian community. His fondness for Paul's joyful suffering for the Body's sake clearly expresses the Pauline cast to Donne's notion of both Christian martyrdom and of Calling. It also emphasizes that joy is the necessary goal of Donne's mature theology of suffering. Joy arises from conformity with the suffering Christ.

The foundation of this joy must be the restored Image of God in man. The alchemy of Christ's suffering conforms the tripartite human Image to the Trinity, softening and bending the obdurate human will, staking out the patterns of saving knowledge for reason, and stocking the memory with these new patterns. The psychological footing is recognizable from Donne's beginnings and clearly stated later: love is the will's first act and God is its first object (*Sermons*, VI, 361); only the known can be loved; man naturally knows the good and true (*Sermons*, VI, 232); and memory carries these known impressions. Sin perverts, obscures, and defiles, often pulling in opposite directions from the soul's residual goodness, establishing the ironies that inform temporal consciousness. The Incarnate Christ breaks through these ironies. Reason learns God's love through the Christian tradition; the will moves affectively 'in compassion of his passion for thy soule' (*Sermons*, V, 137); and memory records knowledge of enlarging spiritual experience of Christ. Christ's suffering is the divine model of love for man to follow.

In line with Donne's Augustinian disposition, his notion of conformity is a matter of the will, turned away from God by sin, returned through love of the crucified Christ.[12] Conformity requires shock at Christ's bloody suffering and also understanding of its significance. In a 1622 Christmas sermon Donne enumerates Christ's seven-fold shedding of blood (1. circumcision; 2. agony; 3. 'fulfilling of that Prophesie, *genas vellicantibus*'; 4. scourging; 5. crowning; 6. nailing; 7. piercing his side), that graphic pattern for humble, patient obedience to God's will that teaches man. The believer, drawn through such compassionate love, must likewise shed blood, if not literally, then spiritually: by using that 'knife, remorce, compunction' he must 'open a veine' and 'bleed out' his consent to sin. Man must daily 'Poure out' his soul's blood, sacrificing that 'stubborne and rebellious will seaven times too; seaven times, that is, every day' (*Sermons*, IV, 294–5), achieving like Christ the supreme shedding of blood on the Cross by 'crucifying our selves to the world too' (*Sermons*, IV, 297). Shock at seeing Christ's bloody suffering teaches the pattern of obedience. Love advises obedience unto death. Christ's suffering and death teach daily crucifixion; the exemplar Christ, loaded with all man's sin, suffers to the death that mortifies sin. Christ's pattern is imprinted in the loving believer who, with St Paul, must die daily. The believer, by first 'denying himselfe his delights, (which is a dram of Death),' can later suffer the 'tribulations of this world, (which is a greater measure of death),' and then can bear actual death itself more patiently (*Sermons*, VIII, 168). The habit of daily crucifixion attenuates old sinful habits, breaking down those encrustations of the will; consequently, the will can move back to God and the believer conform to the Cross.

Tears also conform man's will to God's; the results are gradual suppling to tenderness, melting to liquefaction, dilating to fullness. Though hardened, bent askew, and dissatisfied, the soul longs to love. It finds in Christ's tears an exemplary human pattern that expresses mutual suffering and infinite loving tenderness. Christ's tenderness inspires love's growth toward its fruition in Christ. A 1622–3 Whitehall sermon on Christ's tears for the dead Lazarus in John 11:35 ('Iesus Wept') anatomizes the three Biblical instances of Christ's tears as an affective model. Conveniently summing up much said above about earlier works, this sermon likewise expresses the richly pervasive emphasis upon contritional sorrow in Donne's sermons. His working assumption is that conformity between man and Christ turns on Christ's willing participation in human nature and on his guiding divinity.

In Christ's response to Lazarus's death, Donne finds a satisfying figure for the problem of expressing compassionate grief. That Christ first wept, then miraculously raised Lazarus, neatly compartmentalizes his human and divine elements. His human tears set a 'clean glasse' (Sermons, IV, 329) for viewing an exemplary, sinless response: 'His friend was dead, and then Jesus wept' with full compassion (Sermons, IV, 325). Donne's emphasis follows from his funeral poetry, justifying the full affectionate reaches of the will, while rejecting self-regarding excess. Sinless, Christ could not know inordinate affection; and his compassionate grief clearly rejected a dehumanizing Stoical reserve; that 'indolencie, absence, emptinesse, privation of affections, makes any man at all times, like stones, like dirt' (Sermons, IV, 330). Legitimate grief follows a clear path of conformity to Christ's natural affection. For regenerate man, a natural love of other believers inspires concern for their distress. Similarly, natural affection turns into moral affection: 'the love of Eminent and Heroicall vertues in any man' as well as 'civill affections, the love of friends' necessarily 'moved in their behalfe' (Sermons, IV, 330). Natural affection controlled by Christ's example broadly informs human ties; more specifically, when humans die, it permits the fearful grief that even in heaven the beloved may never again be known. Christ's tears train human affection to follow its nature to a temperate but tender conclusion.

Christ wept a second time in his prophetical tears for Jerusalem's ultimate destruction. Donne treats this event cursorily as a bridge to the more important pontifical weeping for man's sins, which is the paradigm for contritional sorrow. Nonetheless, these prophetical tears embolden the Christly pattern of tender affection essential in spirituality. This second instance shifts from private grief for the dead Lazarus to 'good affections' (*Sermons*, IV, 336) toward a whole group. Christ's example requires tearful sympathy towards others' miseries as essential to the fellow feeling of charity. Such sympathy assumes understanding of the misery endemic to all mortal beings. Tenderness of the loving soul reaches outward to man as well as upward to God.

The third Biblical instance of Christ's weeping occurred on the Cross when he wept for man's sin. Accordingly, man's compunction for his own sins and his compassion for others are two aspects of the same affectionate condition of the will. Here, in the conformity with the crucified Christ, who is weighted by man's sins, lies the foundation for Donne's notion of contrition. Man must 'lament his own sins,' coming to that 'tendernesse, to that melting, to that thawing, that resolving of the bowels which good soules feele' (*Sermons*, IV, 339). All tears insure the heart's tenderness, but tears that wash away sin perfect the tenderness that unites man's spirit with God. Contrite tears for sin are not a 'damp of melancholy' (*Sermons*, IV, 343), but a way of fulfilment through the will's affectionate movement. The tears of the crucified Christ give the example for contrition.

Previous scholarship has drawn many of the significant lines in Donne's notion of contrition, largely in reference to the *Holy Sonnets* and *Devotions upon Emergent Occasions*. Douglas Peterson accepts Helen Gardner's emphasis upon fear and love; and, further, he suggests that the work expresses Donne's uneasy struggle to find assurance through proper contrition.[13] Patrick Grant finds a native English tradition of Augustinian spirituality that stresses a humble contritional stance and stimulates an effective emotional response to the vividly depicted Christ on the Cross.[14] More broadly, Gerard Cox places Donne's contritional themes in the *Devotions* within an Anglican penitential pattern of contrition, confession, and satisfaction.[15] Furthermore, a vocabulary that links contrition and confession richly informs Donne's sermons while referring to Donne's broadest theological contexts. The keys are metaphorical. Variations on pouring, emptying, and filling distinguish the relationships among humility, holy sorrow, confession, and the fullness that defines conformity with Christ and participation in the indwelling Holy Spirit. Suffering remains the crucial psychological process.

In the sermon on John 11:35 ('*Iesus wept*'), the weeping, contrite soul can 'poure out it self' (*Sermons*, IV, 340), humbling the self further by washing away sins. Humble self-annihilation is the condition for the progress running from contrition through to confession. Clearing himself with the 'physick' of 'humble confession,' the believer can say 'I have emptied my soul by Confession' (*Sermons*, VIII, 206). Donne invokes the audience to '*Poure out thy heart like water before the face of the Lord.*' The sinner requires a new heart because old 'liquors poured out' leave a residual 'taste and a smell' of sin (*Sermons*, IX, 314). The self-annihilation of humility, the cleansing by contrition, and the evacuation through confession are effectively the same experience, however distinguishable in fact. And the crucified Christ remains the pattern of humility.

Donne's metaphors carry much of the doctrinal burden. God emptied himself in the Incarnation, then further in the Crucifixion; his tears and blood palpably instruct mortification and sorrow for sin. The paradoxical 'fulnesse' of Christ's 'emptinesse' keeps the crucified Christ vividly in mind while directing the epistemological and psychological roles of humility in Donne's thought. This 'strange fulnesse ... was all Humiliation, all exinanition [abasement], all evacuation of himselfe, by his obedience to the death of the Crosse' (*Sermons*, IV, 289). This paradox reflects back on man's similarly paradoxical emptying. When man follows Christ in humility and obedience, emptying is the means of dilating, enlarging, then filling the soul.

The paradoxical riddle that emptiness is fullness voices Donne's Pauline belief that all knowledge is of Christ crucified. Herein also lies the epistemological crux that fulfilled suffering includes humble self-knowledge. In Canticles Donne's Christ says to his Spouse that '*If thou know not thy selfe*,' the necessary contemplation of the heavenly state cannot be made. But man's self-knowledge requires a glass that gives out the soul's proper condition: 'we seek no other glasse, to see our selves in, but Christ, nor any other thing in that glasse, but his *Humiliation*' (*Sermons*, VI, 286). To discover one's own rectified suffering is to know Christ crucified[16] experientially within oneself and to experience the fullness of humility, obedience, and patience. The spiritual conformity to Christ crucified is the sum of saving knowledge. The agent is the Holy Ghost, progressively applying Christ and filling the believer's soul with saving knowledge. Man thereby participates in God.

But in Donne's belief that rectified suffering must be furthered by corrective affliction, we find another necessary part of his conception of conformity. An erected believer recognizes the need for this correction. Moved by the indwelling Spirit, the knowing believer discovers in his conformity to Christ the refined torture that he is personally responsible for his Crucifixion. Those who love Christ crucify him most (*Sermons*, VI, 327). Thus, increased spiritual refinement seems contradictorily to widen the gap between the believer and Christ, which only Grace can close. With increasing willingness, the soul recognizes need for corrective affliction to heal the diseased soul. This crucial element in Donne's spirituality makes many modern readers uneasy. Donne's emphasis seems demeaning or pathological, although broadly shared by his English Christian contemporaries as heirs to Paul, Augustine,

Bernard, and Calvin.[17] But Donne's assumptions are unequivocal. Corrective affliction is medicinal therapy that supplements the devotional and religious practices of the Christian believer. God afflicts man to conform him to Christ.

The reason is that affliction mortifies sin. Playing against the Roman Catholic notion of Purgatory, Donne notes that man has a 'generall purging' in Christ's death, a 'neerer application thereof' in the Covenant, and an earthly 'Purgatory' in 'Crosses, Afflictions, and Tribulations' that cauterize 'infectious staines and impressions' of sin, evil habits and fleshly desires. '*God sits as a fire, and with fullers soape*, to wash us, and to burne us cleane with afflictions from his own hand' (*Sermons*, VII, 183). God's afflictions join the battle against man's pride, security, and presumption. God's army includes obvious affliction like sickness (*Sermons*, IX, 409) and more subtle ones like emotional depression. In any event, sin is the cause and affliction is the effect, as the ailing Donne understands clearly in the *Devotions* ('7. Prayer,' pp. 39–40). The Christian believer must understand the connection here between cause and effect.

Donne's claims that affliction is 'our daily bread' (*Sermons*, IX, 331) and that it supples the soul while crucifying sin reveal the distinctive colouration of his epistemology and psychology. Man must not only 'feele' afflictions, but also his reason must 'see' them (*Sermons*, X, 206). When masticated, digested, considered, understood, the daily bread of affliction manifests God's purpose to man (*Sermons*, IX, 291). Whereas reason scrutinizes the experience of pain in order to understand God's message, the will, punished and redirected by physical or spiritual pain, softens under God's punishment. 'Thus my afflictions are truly a crosse, when those afflictions do truely crucifie me, and souple me, and mellow me, and knead me, and roll me out, to a conformity with Christ' (*Sermons*, II, 300). These metaphors express Donne's basic psychology of the will. A soul suppled, not obdurated, by affliction distinguishes the godly from the wicked, whom God's affliction hardens spiritually. The suppleness of the whole soul, through its faculty of the will, shades metaphorically into the liquefaction of contrition, melting a soul 'to poure it out into a new and better form' (*Sermons*, IX, 291). The tender soul is suppled by affliction and moistened by contrition, not desiccated and hardened. Donne's metaphorical progressions shift and converge throughout his mature work, consistently emphasizing how the soul finds salvation in a ruminative self-knowledge and spiritual plasticity that oppose, respectively, ignorance and obduration. Continuing affliction is salvation's agent.

Afflictions as 'medicinall corrections'[18] must be viewed as part of Donne's broader notion of correction. Sin perverts the will, hence the entire soul, thus requiring God's corrections. Forms of correction vary, from the milder remorse (*Sermons*, VI, 57) and the Church's judgment against believers (*Sermons*, VII, 233) to major calamities. However, much correction is affliction. No one escapes, even good men like Job, Jeremiah, and Paul. Donne's Lincoln's Inn sermon on Psalm 38:2 ('For thine arrowes stick fast in me, and thy hand presseth me sore') advances the legitimacy of David's prayer against further correction. Here, David does not share the momentary failure of Moses, Job, Elias, Jeremiah, and Jonah to find in corrective affliction God's purpose for the individual and himself. Rather he recognizes that God's purpose 'to bring a sinner to *himself*, and so to God' through affliction has been achieved in him. With the value of God's correction fulfilled, David can then request mercy. David has found 'nourishment' by the '*daily bread*' of 'stones, and scorpions, tribulations, and afflictions' and also has been purged by this corrective 'physick' (*Sermons*, II, 54). And, more, he has accepted God's treatment without complaint. David's very request that God withhold his arrows confirms his spiritual achievement through medicinal correction.

His request is defined by epidemic human misery, its sinful causes, and its adaptation as divine therapy. The Biblical arrows are the punitive miseries of fallen man: labour, sickness, death, and the pains of conscience. They proceed from sin, which proceeds from temptation; both sin and temptation induce tribulation. God's hand turns these miseries to corrective and catechistical uses. Sinful cause, painful effect, and divine remedy meet in the Biblical figure. The arrows of temptation, as unexpected as they are numerous, stick in helpless man: 'the same sin shoots arrows of *presumption* in God, before it be committed, and of *distrust* and *diffidence* in God after' (*Sermons*, II, 62). These arrows of temptation wound the weakly sinful nature and cause the painful arrows of conscience. Sin causes the tribulation of illness; and man's own attempt to mortify sinful causes simply increases his pain. God's hand shoots the arrows of temptation and tribulation. Each arrow is 'especially from his hand, as it hath a *medicinall nature* in it; for in every *tentation*, and every *tribulation*, there is a *Catechisme*, and *Instruction*' (*Sermons*, II, 68). Man must accompany David in humble self-scrutiny that recognizes both his own responsibility for surrendering weakly to temptation and also the justice of retributive suffering. And he must find the 'light' (*Sermons*, II, 69) of God's arrows, the corrective instruction of temptation and affliction. Justly, he can then echo David's request that God's corrective hand be lightened.

The affliction that both manifests and corrects sin bridges the gap between man and God. Behind David's assured expostulation stands Donne's belief that corrective affliction demonstrates the merciful love and favour of God: 'as long as he corrects us, he loves us.' Here, we touch the hard centre of Donne's mature thought, for by means of corrective affliction man participates in the full Godhead. First, the Father's correction confirms adoption (*'He scourgeth every son whom he receiveth,'* *Sermons*, VII, 188), with the believer participating in the Father as a son. The working guarantee is, second, the participation through conformity with Christ, the Son, whose own exemplary temptation and affliction give the pattern of humility and obedience in crucifying sin. Man the adopted son, through the suffering of affliction, participates in Christ the Son, hence in the Father also. So corrected through affliction, man, third, also participates in the Spirit through his Seal, that is, in the evidence of divine favour and through encouragement to joy.

Thus far we have looked at elements in conformity to Christ as it affects the individual believer; but conformity as the working guarantee of man's participation in God remains incomplete and the absolute centre of Donne's mature thought one step away. Crucifixion with Christ has two sides: the believer must not only crucify his own sins, but do so in a way exemplary for other members of Christ's Body. Donne's fondness for Colossians 1:24 expresses this communal element in his completed notion of conformity: *'Who now rejoyce in my sufferings for you, and fill up that which is behind of the afflictions of Christ in my flesh, for his bodies sake which is the church'* (*Sermons*, III, 332). When others see that the believer's battle against sin conforms to Christ's crucifixion of sin and that he is humbly obedient to medicinal correction, they will be instructed also to mortify their sins. This exemplary penitential suffering combines with the more obvious way of suffering for others, through the self-sacrificial demands of the 'Cross' of the believer's God-given Calling. In both these ways the crucified Head completes his exemplary affliction in his Body through those members erected by suffering and made heroic in affliction; and each believer's suffering is completed by its effect on others. In sum, the root of Donne's notion of conformity – the fulfilment of Christ's suffering in the believer – combines penitential suffering, divine correction, the Cross, and Christian martyrdom. And, as we will increasingly see, from that fullness of suffering arises joy.

But, first, we should look closely at martyrdom. Paradoxically, the public side to conformity with Christ, through Christian martyrdom, is necessarily implicated in the private side, in the mortification of sin. The martyr's effect on other believers derives not from his perfection, but from his imperfection. Even those martyrs suffering for Christ's Body are still inclined to sin. Donne draws a precise line between correction for a specific sin and 'after-afflictions' (*Sermons*, VIII, 215) that follow the assurance that remission has occurred. Like David, the believer must also welcome these corrections against further relapse. The same willingness to recall sins, to 'poure out thy teares from thine eyes, and fulfill the sufferings of Christ in thy selfe' (*Sermons*, VIII, 217), must accept the necessary medicine of after-afflictions against relapse. In David, in Paul, in all exemplars who humbly accept the indelible stains in their own natures, Donne finds the personal fulfilment of Christ's affliction that also has value for the communal Body.

In Christ's injunction that man 'take up' his 'crosse' to follow him, Donne blends penitential suffering with the responsibilities of man's Calling. Significantly, Calling is a form of suffering, a taking up the 'crosse' of 'tentations or tribulations' (*Sermons*, II, 310) in vivid conformity with the crucified Christ.[19] Donne carefully distinguishes that the only afflictions which are 'crosses' are those *whereby the world is crucified to us, and we to the world.* He rejects the bodily weakness caused by the allusively autobiographical 'wantonnesses of my youth' and the poverty caused by 'wastfulnesse of youth.' These are Nature's crosses, not God's. Similarly, he rejects excessive mortification of the flesh. Only the 'way of my Calling,' its temptations and tribulations, can conform him to Christ; here, he and his auditors can find the crosses that fulfil Christ's affliction (*Sermons*, II, 300–1). However, the reminder of private weakness contributes to the humility necessary for public responsibility. Ultimate conformity with Christ demands suffering on behalf of the community; but this conscious exemplarism mines the Christian way with temptations to pride. To take up one's cross is to follow Christ in humble awareness of continuing weakness.

Fulfilled Calling ensures that the supreme conformity is a martyrdom of suffering for others, simultaneously a temptation to pride and an occasion for the greatest earthly joy. Paul's letter to the Colossians recognizes that man's Calling includes sacrificial affliction, *'passio mea'* for others, 'not *pro me*, but *pro aliis*' on Christ's behalf. The suffering is 'mine without any fault of mine' (*Sermons*, III, 344). Here Donne affirms an affliction on others' behalf unconnected with personal sin, while elsewhere he underlines the exemplarism of personal repentance as fulfilment of Christ's suffering. This apparent, perhaps actual, contradiction is not resolved in Donne's use of the Colossians text. Probably, the contradiction is only apparent, a momentary emphasis upon suffering specifically incurred for the Church. In the *Devotions* Donne assumes that man may not know which past sins cause current sufferings ('3. Expostulation,' p. 16); and Donne would have found the example of Paul, whose past sins required little comment, consistent with Donne's repeated emphasis in the sermons on the necessary connection between sin and personal suffering (e.g., *Sermons*, X, 202). In any event, Donne does stress personal instrumentality on behalf of the community. Personal identity sharpened by martyrdom assumes the humility that 'all my sufferings even for Gods glory, are his works' (*Sermons*, III, 345). Donne seeks a clear sense of individual instrumentality that pointedly encourages personal identity without inflating pride. He walks a razor's edge, implicitly distinguishing his own experience in Paul's 'I,' inviting his audience to a similar participation in which to achieve fulfilment in their Callings: 'But *Numquid Paulus crucifixus pro vobis*, was *Paul* crucified for you? is his own question; as he suffered for them here, so we may be bold to say he was crucified for them' (*Sermons*, III, 346). Paul's martyrdom fulfils the sufferings of Christ in his own flesh for the Body's sake. Donne holds out the same possibility of martyrdom to his audience.

Donne expresses that dramatic possibility by merging the privileged excitement of suffering for God with the humility of divine example. 'Gods suffering for man was the Nadir, the lowest point of Gods humiliation, mans suffering for God is the Zenith, the highest point of mans exaltation.' God's suffering answered man's need then, man's serves God's now; in Christ's blood is a cup of salvation, in man's suffering, a 'cup of my blood' given for God (*Sermons*, VIII, 185). Predictably, Donne does not forget the dangers of self-idolatry characterized in 'Twicknam Garden' and the *Holy Sonnets* ('Spit in my face yee Jewes'). The believer, who ever feels God's hand guiding the instrument of personal suffering for the community, imitates the pattern of Christ's humility in his actions. And from Paul and Stephen he can learn charitable suffering for others. Without charity, such suffering is mere 'stubborness' and stupidity, not humiliation compliant with God (*Sermons*, VIII, 187). Humility and charity identify the martyr's suffering for others.

Donne carefully differentiates between man's and Christ's respective suffering for others. Likewise, he distinguishes the extreme martyrdom of a Paul or Stephen, alike in principle with all fulfilled believers, but not in its extreme drama. Like Paul, the believer does fulfil Christ's suffering and is 'offered up for his Church'; the difference lies between 'purchasing' and 'fencing' the Church, between 'satisfaction' and 'example and imitation.' Likewise, most believers cannot experience Stephen's dramatic realities. 'All Martyrdome is not a *Smithfeild* Martyrdome, to burn for religion' (*Sermons*, VIII, 185–6). Most martyrdom is more domesticated: at Court not to revenge the injury of thwarted advantage; in political affairs to resist outer temptations of pówer and inner temptations from affections; in economic matters to be fair and honest; in private life to be chaste. The sum is that 'all victory over the Lords Enemies, in our own bowels, all chearful bearing of Gods Crosses, and all watchful crossing of our own immoderate desires is a Martydrome acceptable to God.' So martyred, if guided by charity, the believer can become a 'true copy of our pattern *Stephen*' (*Sermons*, VIII, 186). This martyrdom, in acknowledging the sinful inclination to immoderate desires, assumes a necessary familial relationship between penitential suffering and exemplarism within the Body, the Church.

In martyrdom lies joy, the natural end to Donne's theology of suffering; and in joy Donne's thought finds its maturity. In rejoicing with Paul that he fulfils Christ's suffering by labouring in his priestly Calling (*Sermons*, III, 347), Donne not only affirms his exemplary conformity with Christ; he also solves the keen problems of suffering advanced in his works. In the limbeck of earthly suffering can be found the joy that is a foretaste of the 'joyes of heaven hereafter' (*Sermons*, III, 340). Donne's anatomy of joy in affliction sums up much in his psychology. He observes three 'degrees' of joy. The first is 'halfe a joy,' actually an 'indolency ... a stupefaction' of the affections that recalls Donne's criticism of Stoical muffling of human feelings. The second and third regard the distinction between penitential and exemplary suffering: the second is assurance in tribulation that 'God will give them the issue with the temptation'; the third is that 'I am counted worthy to suffer rebuke for the name of Christ' (*Sermons*, III, 342–3). Neither of these latter two varieties stifles affliction; both embrace it as the soul's fulfilment in joy. Donne's analysis of the reasons is consistent with his earlier development.

For Donne, not all joy follows sorrow, since temporal blessings can also inspire joy in God's favour. Similarly, not all suffering is joy, since some pain does not clearly reveal God's purposes. Yet rejoicing for our 'crosses and calamities' acknowledges God's favour in his correction for sin. And in contrition for the sins causing God's affliction also lies joy: 'I am very sorry that I have sinned, but yet I am glad that I am sorry.' Man rejoices that God 'opened him a way to mercy' through sorrow for sin (*Sermons*, X, 223). Donne cautions against excessive mortification of the body and against seeking occasions of sorrows. Instead, he recommends strenuously examining existing sorrows as God's corrective guides to one's own sinful condition: 'this is a beam of joy, for I see that he would cure me, though by corosives' (*Sermons*, X, 224). Donne's basic epistemological format controls this joy in suffering. Reason sees God's hand in the correction, which leads reason and memory to search the self for the sin; the will loves and rejoices in God for the correction; likewise, it is softened further by the necessary contritional experience.

Joy in contrition prefaces the joy of martyrdom for the Church, the third 'degree' and highest form of earthly joy. Such 'perfect' joy is a 'fundamentall ... radicall ... viscerall ... gremiall' joy arising from within the tribulation itself. 'It is not that I rejoyce, though I be afflicted, but I rejoyce because I am afflicted.' This ultimate conformity with Christ, suffering for God, who suffered for man, deeply 'fixes' the Spirit's seal (*Sermons*, III, 343). Donne's pointed footnote – that Paul withheld this doctrine until the Colossians had advanced in belief (*Sermons*, III, 337) – acknowledges the potential for self-idolatry in its intoxicating promise of joy. But in that promise lies the earthly goal of Donne's thought, Christ's residence in time and place through the erected believer. The suffering of the perfect God is contradictorily perfected in man: 'there appertaines a joy to such sufferings, which is that the suffering of Christ being yet, not unperfect, but unperfected, Christ having not yet suffered all, which he is to suffer to this purpose, for the gathering of his Church, I fill up that which remaines undone' (*Sermons*, III, 334). Just as Christ's suffering is not completely filled up in time, so also will no one erected believer totally complete the process; yet time can achieve relative fullness through man's participatory martyrdom and, more, joy in that participation.

Anchored in time, this active joy is tied to the effect of sacrificial suffering on others. Those affected, in turn, affect others, who also fill up Christ's suffering; accordingly, the speaker Donne would continue, through his auditors, filling up Christ's suffering. This participatory process extends the Body through time, lasting well beyond any one man's death, but including a given martyrdom indefinitely in the experience of others. The excitement in Donne's joy reveals the importance of this idea and explains why the Colossians text completes his thought. With Paul, his favourite saint,[20] Donne insists on the identity of the self: 'my sufferings ... my flesh.' No stranger to pride, Donne fought to honour the self without encouraging its abuses; and, here, in the humility of conformity that requires personal instrumentality for the community, Donne found a congenial home for the needs of the self.[21] In Paul, whose 'incessant preaching' and 'constant suffering' (*Sermons*, III, 335) in his own flesh unified the Church, Donne found the paradigm for himself and his auditors through him. Like Paul, he recognized his own physical presence as the exemplum of Christ's suffering for his Body, the Church. And, like Paul, in this suffering he found the highest form of earthly joy, a way to fulfil the circle of time in community with others.

Joy is the 'end of our desires' (*Sermons*, x, 214), rest after voluntary motion, assured participation in God. A 'dilatation of the heart' (*Sermons*, x, 223) that fills the soul with God's love, it is 'evidence' (*Sermons*, x, 215) that man is at peace and in favour with God. Its manifestations are both inner and outer: 'Not to feele joy is an argument against religious tendernesse, not to show that joy, is an argument against thankfulnesse of the heart' (*Sermons*, x, 217). Joy has one foot on earth, one in heaven; in both cases its essence, as a fulfilled condition of the will standing on knowledge, remains the same, but not its degrees of fulfilment. Earthly joy that is mingled with grief is a 'meat';

the soul's unimpeded joy in heaven is a 'drink'; and the joy at the resurrection, when both bodies and souls participate, is an 'overflowing' through love of others as oneself and love of God. In heaven joy stands on knowledge of everlasting 'Blessednesse,' but on earth it stands on knowledge of suffering that manifests God's favour and man's weakness. In heaven joy will dilate apace with knowledge; the will shall fill apace with reason. On earth man must settle for the 'earnest' (*Sermons*, X, 228) of joy, the promise of inheritance, the seal of the Spirit in fulfilled suffering. Sorrows outweigh joys, but in sorrow begins the filling completed later.

To conclude, joy that fulfils the soul's powers also fulfils suffering as the condition of temporal life. Conformity with Christ, in weaving anew the various strands in Donne's thought about suffering, reforms this condition. As we have seen in Donne's works from the beginning, understanding of the self is achieved through suffering:

> Wee have no will, no power, no sense: I lye
> I should not then thus feele, this miserie.   ('The Calme,' 55–6)

To identify the self is to know how the 'I' participates in the communal 'wee'; it is also to recognize that the scouring motions of suffering are the condition for this knowledge. Later works stress how erected suffering progressively assimilates man to God through shared experience that finds a new pattern in the essential condition of earthly life. In a Body of mutually likened souls, dilated progressively through knowledge of love and joy, the several members assimilate, in time, to their loving Head. In the shared temporal experience of its constituent selves, responsible in body and soul, the community becomes fulfilled, aware of both its earthly and its heavenly extensions. And the individual 'I' becomes more itself the more it assimilates with others 'in' Christ's suffering and shoulders the Cross of a responsible Calling. 'Since I am bound to take up my crosse, there must be a crosse that is mine to take up; that is, a crosse prepared for me by God, and laid in my way, which is tentations or tribulations in my calling; and I must not go out of my way to seeke a crosse; for, so it is not mine, nor laid for my taking up' (*Sermons*, II, 301). For Donne, even the fulfilled 'I' ever remains the product of suffering.

That suffering provides the measure for the unfulfilled as well as the fulfilled self has continuing thematic significance in Donne's works, as we have seen. The progress toward fulfilment in Donne's own life gives its mirrored reflection thematically in the movement toward the fulfilment of suffering in conformity with Christ. However, suffering as a local condition in earlier works has varying thematic implications, some of which we have examined.

In the chapters that follow in Part Two, respectively on 'A Valediction: of Weeping,' *Holy Sonnets*, 'Goodfriday, 1613. Riding Westward,' and *Devotions upon Emergent Occasions*, our perspective will shift to show in fuller detail how elements in Donne's epistemology and psychology discussed in Part One shape some of his most significant, individual works. These works enunciate, in their varying ways, Donne's conceptions of the rational soul and the physical body as well as his conception of suffering as the prevailing condition of mortal life, both as its ailment and its remedy. Likewise, in the brief conclusion on *Deaths Duell*, itself a proper conclusion to the elements in Donne's thought which we have been examining, we will see how in his final days Donne, at the end of his circle, continues to speak to this prevailing condition.

PART TWO

5

Physical Love, Suffering, and the Emblems of Experience in 'A Valediction: of Weeping'

Donne's conception of time is distinguished by the presence of metaphysical realities in immediate temporal experience. The rational mind has the onerous task of interpreting the events of experience according to these informing realities. Not just the potential of the moment must engage the mind, but the threat of loss as well. In metaphysical terms, this is the tension between Creation and Nothing that is the foundation of Donne's thought. Although the most mature example of such interpretation can be found in the *Devotions upon Emergent Occasions*, it is significant in earlier works also. In 'A Valediction: of Weeping' the speaker, aggrieved by parting, must interpret spiritually the emblems in his own physical experience. Not to do so invites spiritual annihilation, the threat of Nothing. But the conflicting needs of body and soul complicate the speaker's task. In his painful experience of separation can be found many of the problems of temporal experience faced by the human creature composed of body and soul, for whom suffering is the condition of existence.

A crucial factor in Donne's conception of the body is at stake here: there is an essentially compatible dualism between the body and soul, but not without some conflicting purposes. The correspondences between them prove their compatibility. To say, for example, that the will is the 'bloud' of the soul (*Sermons*, IV, 294) and that understanding is its '*eyes*' (*Sermons*, VI, 101) tells us something about both the body and the soul. Similarly, the notion of the body as the 'book' of the soul, in which man can observe an effigy of the soul's condition, underlines the body as a source of spiritual self-knowledge. However, even though the body is the 'Master-piece' of physical creation (*Sermons*, VII, 259) and is essentially compatible with the soul, its distinctive purposes do not always coincide with the soul's in earthly life. The need for sexual gratification, however justifiable, is problematical since, even under favourable conditions, such gratification is shortlived and can cause habitual suffering. When exacerbated by parting, the body's often thwarted desire for physical union causes grief that can destroy spiritual equilibrium

When the speaker in 'A Valediction: of Weeping' faces this problem, he must interpret emblematically the immediate events of his physical experience in order to solve the problem. The tears and sighs of the lovers' anguish exist in two dimensions, as physical events in their sexual relationship and as emblems of a spiritual tendency. The responsibility to interpret these emblems does not immediately reduce the anguish of parting, but first vivifies it. Interpretation is the same self-reflexive experience exploited wittily in 'The Flea' and at great length in the *Devotions*. Whereas the tears and sighs in 'A Valediction' and the events of Donne's illness in the *Devotions* must be examined for their full metaphysical implications, the speaker in 'The Flea' plays with interpretation as a witty seduction play. He uses the flea as an emblem of a sexual relationship that he wishes to establish and justify to her. Like 'A Valediction' this poem places the lovers in close physical proximity, but here interpretation wittily serves illicit sexual desire. Here, in parody form, is Donne's sense that fulfilment of the body's role requires recognizing the emblematism of its experience. In the events of his grief, the speaker in 'A Valediction' finds emblematic evidence that a more spiritual emphasis is necessary to control the destructive grief caused by sexual preoccupation. Just as the body must serve the spirit, sexuality must subserve spiritual love. A failure to interpret the emblems and control the grief denies the godlike power of spiritual creation.

Thus, 'A Valediction' has a special importance in Donne's works by showing us dramatically how that interpreting personal emblematism is a necessary element in Donne's notion of the body and its temporal suffering. The poem is also important for the way that Donne draws ironically upon hermetical materials in developing the tension between creation and annihilation in the lovers' experience. Donne's interest in hermetism, and Paracelsus in particular, is well established in modern scholarship, although the importance of such ideas in 'A Valediction' has not been examined. Here, hermetic materials ironically discolour the lovers' overweening attempts to inform their existence through mere earthly love. More important, the Paracelsian conception of the alchemist as a creator characterizes the lady's failure to fulfil her godlike power of spiritual creation.

Before examining the poem's hermetic materials and their relationship to Donne's conception of the body and its emblematic events, however, we must first examine the poem's opposition between creation and annihilation, to which all other elements must be referred. This basic theme in Donne's thought is forcibly invoked here in the threat of annihilation galvanizing the poem. The speaker, aggrieved by parting, encourages grief openly displayed ('Let me powre forth / My teares,' 1–2), mistakenly assuming that a catharsis in her presence will have the value of easing his grief while reaffirming her lasting importance to him. When he is with her, his tears bear her image ('by this Mintage they are something worth,' 3). But then he recognizes that, like the tear that 'falls' (8), such shortlived value inevitably would be annihilated; the lovers would be 'nothing' (9) when separated on 'divers' shores (9). In stanza two the speaker likewise attempts unsuccessfully to establish the value of catharsis, but his plight again worsens. Not just mintmaster, his lady is now globemaker and the Creator as well:

> On a round ball
> A workeman that hath copies by, can lay
> An Europe, Afrique, and an Asia,
> And quickly make that, which was nothing, *All*,
> So doth each teare,
> Which thee doth weare,
> A globe, yea world by that impression grow,
> Till thy teares mixt with mine doe overflow
> This world, by waters sent from thee, my heaven dissolved so.
>
> (10–18)

But his grief, displayed and joined with hers, is unbearable, whereas her suffering destroys her ability to create a spiritual strength that could permit physical separation. She is tearful, hence has surrendered to her weakness as a mortal, failing to invoke the atemporal spiritual ties that would transcend changes in their physical relationship; her creative powers, and hence her likeness to immortal God who does not suffer, are destroyed thereby. Stanza three ends the poem with the injunction to control grief and its sexual cause. She should not encourage his grief ('O more then Moone, / Draw not up seas to drowne me in thy sphaere,' 19–20) and should stop her own grieving when near him: 'Weepe me not dead, in thine arms, but forbeare / To teach the sea, what it may doe too soone' (21–2). To encourage excessive grief is to confess an annihilating dependence on the body, on the mortal.

The poem's most serious death threat is not the annihilation of separation, but of spiritual death through indulgence in the suffering of sexual love. His injunction, that she not 'teach the sea' and not let the wind 'Example finde' (22–4), signals the achieved awareness that such self-indulgence leads to drowning, to being overwhelmed destructively by their experience. Their earlier absorption in sexual love overlooked that this love is subject to physical change, hence to necessary mortal limitations. However, now they have found that sexual love, dramatized by Donne in their embrace ('in thine armes,' 21) cannot accommodate parting. The speaker now sees that such suffering, although it is the necessary legacy of mortality, must be moderated and transcended, in his case by turning the sexual direction of their love. The poem's warning about the spiritual entrapment in mortality, implicit at the beginning, grows increasingly explicit, first expressed in the tear's 'fall,' the emblem of suffering humanity, then in the lady's failure to create value and, finally, in the injunction against excessive grief. Surrendering to mortal limitations is spiritual annihilation, a denial of creation.

The competition between creation and annihilation advances in the treatment of the lady first as failed creator, then destroyer. Having failed in their mutual assumption that physical love will be sufficient, she becomes the occasion for possible spiritual annihilation. Yet she can evoke her spiritual potential, expressed in the Petrarchan characterization 'more then Moone,' by curbing the tears induced by physical love. Like Laura's, her supralunar power expresses her spiritual capacity which, if properly evoked, might erect her failed powers as a creator. But she must follow his advice to stay their self-indulgence in physical love.

The poem's threat of annihilation can be measured by turning to the closely related *Essays in Divinity* and 'A Nocturnall upon S. Lucies Day.' The *Essays* has a close thematic kinship to 'A Valediction' despite obvious differences in form and intention, whereas 'A Nocturnall' and 'A Valediction' can be viewed almost as companion poems, as we will see in even greater detail later. The *Essays*, written when Donne was considering the priesthood, embodies his deepest fears and hopes. The threat of Nothing receives here a more complete explication than in 'A Valediction':

For to be Nothing, is so deep a curse, and high degree of punishment, that Hell and the prisoners there, not only have it not, but cannot wish so great a loss to themselves, nor such a frustrating of Gods purposes.

In comparison to nothingness, all the worst miseries 'laid upon mankind,' even if distilled and thrown upon one soul, 'would not equall the torment of so much time as you sound one syllable' (pp. 30–1). But the horror of Nothing is refuted by the possibility represented by Creation. The ultimate Being, God, created the world, conferring being on the creatures. Moreover, the principle of Creation continues when God converts a soul and when souls themselves create by realizing with God's help their Godlike capacities for spiritual being. In the *Essays* Donne prays that with God's help his soul might 'now produce Creatures, thoughts, words, and deeds agreeable to thee' (p. 37). The idea of Creation expresses the possibility of being, which Nothing denies.

This possibility appears to be lost by the devastated speaker in 'A Nocturnall.' A painful love has transmuted him even beyond the accursed state of nothingness described in the *Essays*; the lady's death has turned him into the 'Elixer' of the 'first nothing' (29). But not only her death invokes the devastation of Nothing; for even before she died, the excesses of mutual absorption did 'expresse' in the speaker 'A quintessence even from nothingnesse' (14–15). The experience in 'A Valediction' stands to that in 'A Nocturnall' as does a fearful threat to a fully realized horror. The lovers of 'A Valediction,' if they do not control their physical self-absorption and its grief, can become like the suffering lovers of 'A Nocturnall,' for whom 'absences' even before the lady's real death 'Withdrew our soules, and made us carcasses' (26–7). Then, if the speaker should drown during his voyage, his lady would face the devastation depicted in 'A Nocturnall.' Likewise, the annihilation threatened in 'A Valediction' carries the full danger of annihilated being, of denied Creation, and of the lost possibility of being. It is this possibility that is being enjoined on the lady in 'A Valediction' so that she in turn can inspire the speaker.

Thus, these works give affecting examples of the conflict between creation and annihilation that expressed the ultimate problem of being for Donne. Whereas the prose *Essays* sets forth this conflict according to the individual soul's direct relationship to its Creator, the two lyrics set forth the conflict as it includes love for a fellow creature. But the conflict is the same, and in each case the possibility of spiritual creation requires both the individual's awareness of his spiritual condition and also his voluntary action. Proper use of human powers, including the task of interpreting the emblems of experience, must be worked out according to that conflict so central to 'A Valediction'; and, as we will see, Donne draws ironically from hermetical notions in suggesting what is proper.

The key to this hermetical background can be found by looking further at the filial relationship between 'A Valediction' and 'A Nocturnall.' The similarities make a compelling case for considering the two lyrics together: mutual concern with Being and non-Being, nothingness, annihilation through inundation, failed creation, grief. Their shared interest in Paracelsus is less obvious, but no less informative. Like Donne's 'Loves Alchymie' the lyric 'A Nocturnall' directly confesses Donne's interest in alchemical notions since love is characterized as an alchemist; also, the poem's imagery exploits alchemical terminology, and Paracelsus in particular.[1] W.A. Murray notes that in 'A Nocturnall,' Donne's depiction of the lovers drowning in their own tears as 'two Chaosses' is a nearly verbatim translation ('Ideo Chaos duo sunt') from a Paracelsian treatise on the generation of water.[2] Murray's discovery gives us the direction to follow in 'A Valediction' as well, since those lovers also drown in their own tears and since Donne has the Paracelsian background in mind here also. This imagistic kinship has interested some readers,[3] but the Paracelsian basis remains to be examined. In general, Donne uses Paracelsian details in 'A Valediction' to discredit the lovers' limited earthly attempts to understand and control their mortal experience.

Donne's attitude to Paracelsus was mixed. On one hand, Paracelsus occupies one of Hell's highest places in *Ignatius his Conclave* for fathering a new medical theory, and hence unsettling established order. In 'Loves Alchymie' Paracelsian alchemy ('chymique,' 7) and metallurgy ('loves Myne,' 1) express a futile attempt to find spirituality through sex (" 'tis imposture all,' 6). On the other hand, in 'The Crosse,' a poem with close ties to 'A Valediction: of Weeping,' Paracelsian iatrochemistry is a figure for tribulation that purifies the spirit (25–30). *Biathanatos* mixes negative and positive attitudes. Although commending that 'excellent Chirurgian,' Donne criticizes Paracelsian advocacy of certain techniques of hermetical medicine, then zigzags to suggest their possible legitimacy under special circumstances.[4] Thus, Donne was both interested and sceptical, but in any event was willing to use Paracelsian ideas freely for local purposes. In 'A Valediction' and 'A Nocturnall,' Paracelsian borrowings are used to depict a debilitating love that turns toward Nothing, away from Creation.

The root notion in 'A Valediction' as in 'A Nocturnall' is Paracelsus's comparison between God and the alchemist as creators, a comparison used invidiously in 'A Valediction' to characterize the lady's limitations. Interest in Creation distinguishes Paracelsus and his followers.[5] Paracelsus hinges his alchemical theory on the comparison between the alchemist and the 'supreme Creator,' God. In forming compounds, in separating or transmuting metals, the alchemist learns from the 'body of the metals' bestowed in the earth 'from the beginning of Creation' to instruct man.[6] Likewise, Creation is a model for alchemical proceedings: the alchemist acts on rude matter, 'chaos,' just as God acted on the chaotic Deep. The comparison between the alchemist and the Creator is pivotal in both 'A Nocturnall' and 'A Valediction,' in which Donne allows doubts about alchemy to depict the failures of mere earthly love. In 'A Nocturnall' the punning 'two Chaosses' recalls the alchemist's chaos, the bi-level aerial 'chaos' enveloping and stabilizing the earthly 'globe,'[7] and the unformed Deep of Genesis.[8] Just as the lovers' physical love has reversed the alchemical process, transmuting them to the 'chaos' of unspiritualized rude matter, this love has destroyed their spiritual universe, drowning their 'world,' turning them into the insubstantial 'two Chaosses' of the sky and into primal Chaos, and finally uncreating the speaker altogether into 'None.' In 'A Valediction' the comparison is most obviously expressed in the lady as a failed Creator.

The other leg of the comparison, the lady as specious alchemist, is expressed in a splendidly complicated coinage image. The tainted reputation of corrupt alchemists stands behind Donne's characterizations of the lady. Alchemical charlatans, promising to help coin money, compromised the public's attitude to alchemy. Paracelsus himself nervously attacked alchemists who sold bogus materials, thus transforming 'goldsmiths and mint-masters' into 'false coiners.'[9] Similarly, Donne in 'The Crosse' links alchemists and coinage in order to characterize pride's distortions: 'But, as oft Alchimists doe coyners prove, / So may a selfe-dispising, get selfe-love' (37–8). The difference between alchemy's failures and the successfully created world and firmament was clearly in Donne's mind. The important point is that Donne's connection between alchemy and coinage is an undercutting device: in 'A Valediction' the lady is mintmaster, hence specious alchemist, and her mintage ultimately stamps no substantial coin, only tears that fall.

The coinage imagery, ever complicated by the twists and turns of Donne's wit, constantly cuts back to the Paracelsian alchemist as creator. Each element – earth, water, fire, and air – is metaphorically a tree able to bear 'fruit,' since God through nature brings forth fruit, like the alchemist during his proceedings. According to Paracelsus, one fruit of water is metal.[10] The stamped tears of Donne's speaker are 'Fruits of much griefe' (7) through anticipated parting from the lady. She coins, turns to metal of 'worth' (4), the speaker's watery tears; but she is the unsuccessful alchemist and Creator, since each tear as a coin bearing her image, ultimately 'falls' (8). Unlike God in Genesis (1:9–11) she cannot successfully bring forth 'fruit' from the water. And, unlike Paracelsus's comparison between alchemist and Creator, Donne's comparison between the lady and God undermines regard for mortal powers.

The reason why Donne undercuts the lady by an invidious comparison with the alchemist is expressed in the central image of the poem, the flooding. This image ties 'A Valediction' closely to 'A Nocturnall' and its Paracelsian basis. The Renaissance identification of woman with moisture, as in Iago's sexual reference to Desdemona's moist hand,[11] was commonplace in alchemical proceedings. Jay Levine's reading of Donne's 'The Dissolution,' as referring to unsuccessful sexual congress, notes the alchemist's fear of flooding, that is, of excess female element in such proceedings.[12] Levine argues that in 'The

Dissolution' the woman climaxes, dissolves, before the speaker, figuratively flooding their 'sexual experiment.'[13] In 'A Valediction' inundation also refers to orgasm, as well as crying; Donne pointedly tells us that the speaker is couched tearfully in a sexual embrace, 'in thine armes' (21), and that his 'heaven' is 'dissolved' (18). The lady's alchemy, expressed earlier in the coinage imagery, is emphasized in the word 'dissolved,' which refers also to a stage in the alchemical procedure.[14] Donne's point is that the lovers' grief and the lady's specious alchemy are both caused by excessive sexuality.

This central image of flooding, standing for the excessive importance of sexuality in their love, illuminates other sexual connotations: the image of pregnancy and the suggestion of androgynous confusion in the speaker. His 'Pregnant' (6) tears 'beare' the 'stampe' (3) of the lady's image and are 'fruits' (7) of suffering. That is, the male speaker's tears are wombs, pregnant by the lady's reflected image, rendering him feminine and the lady masculine. The dubiety of the androgyne, of hermaphroditic confusion,[15] shows how much her influence has inundated the speaker. He has surrendered part of his masculine control to her feminine influence. Significantly, their momentary offspring, the abortive, womblike tear bearing her impression, falls and is destroyed. The speaker must recognize the sexual basis of his problem, stop the flooding, and reassert his masculine control.

By suggesting that they control their grief, and hence its basis in sexual excess, the speaker is appealing to his lady to use her human powers properly, while he does the same. The Petrarchan 'more then Moone' speaks to the godlikeness in man and to the inherent human ability to give meaning to temporal existence. The poem's central irony is that the lady can be either the abortive alchemist-creator or she can be like God and give order to their existence. That is, the poet's real concern is proper use of our created human powers. This concern accounts, in general, for the use of alchemical and hermetical notions in the poem. The attempt of the magus to use astral powers and to manipulate matter sharply focused the question of man's microcosmic role on the boundary between physical and spiritual worlds. Donne's dubious view of Paracelsus, as well as alchemists in general, lies immediately behind the characterization of the speaker and his lady in 'A Valediction.' That characterization evaluates her use of her powers, while suggesting at the same time how she can change. We need only recall the spiritual devastation in 'A Nocturnall' and the cynicism in 'Loves Alchymie' to weigh the consequences of love that misuses human powers.

The importance given to their proper use explains the issue of emblems in the poem and brings us full circle back to a consideration beginning this chapter. The speaker's tears as 'emblemes' (7) of additional grief allude to the emblematic nature of human experience and the responsibility to interpret it. Similarly, the minted sovereign's image emblematizes his power; and the round ball laid with 'copies' (11) emblematizes the actual globe. That Donne is introducing emblem as an issue is confirmed by the same issue in the closely related 'The Crosse.' There Donne affixes the word 'Crosse' as the poem's pivot, then repeatedly discovers the cross emblematized throughout the physical world: from the birds on 'crossed wings,' to 'Meridians crossing Parallels' of the globe, to the swimmer with outstretched arms, to the 'Mast and yard' (17–26). Likewise, the right kind of tribulation contains spiritual crosses, and all mortal activities need such 'crossing.' The believer's task is to interpret the emblematic dimension of events.

The speaker's interpretive task in the love lyric, culminating in his injunction that his lady stop her crying, is defined by a further ironic hermetical parallel. In Donne's time astrological science assumed that astral influence was recorded in physical signs; a wise man had to interpret these signs according to the intentions of nature or God. Various branches of astrological science had to interpret different signs. For example, Paracelsus argues that hydromancy reads certain natural events ('waves, inundations ... new floods, etc.')[16] as signs of certain stars' intentions. The wise man must interpret such signs so that, unlike the brute, he can control his physical experience. In 'A Valediction' Donne draws an ironical parallel between this astrological notion, necessary for controlling one's physical existence, and the speaker's need to interpret the emblems of his experience for the sake of his spiritual existence. The command not to 'teach the sea' or give the 'winde / Example' (22–4) follows from the recognition that the lovers must control and not be controlled by their physical experience. They must stay their tears, so that his death at sea would not find the speaker and his lady spiritually unprepared.

The speaker determines that his tears emblematize the lovers' participation in the continuing possibility of the Fall, the Flood, and the Creation. His androgynous tears are 'Fruits of much griefe' and 'emblemes of more,' signifying not only anticipated suffering, but since she 'falls' when the tears bearing her image fall, participation in the primal Fall as well. Their flood of tears, caused by excessive sexuality, whereby his 'heaven' is 'dissolved,' introduces the Flood as the Christian emblem for sin and its punishment. William Empson is right that the lovers' tears suggest 'such a flood as descended upon the wickedness of the antedeluvians.'[17] And, as implied earlier, his tears as aborted globes emblematize the failure to re-enact the Creation. The speaker's concluding advice that she stop crying reveals how clearly he understands the business of interpreting his experience.

Interpretation of emblem completes the poem's examination of human powers: of the lady's failed spiritual powers, which the speaker is trying to revive; and of his understanding, earlier crippled, now regenerating. He now ventures to teach her, readied by the active intellectual process of interpreting his experience emblematically. With his passive dependence ended and active responsibility accepted, he can place her limitations in perspective. The poem cuts as much against the speaker as against his lady. His masculinity inundated by femininity, he can be faulted as much as she. The poem walks the razor's edge between puncturing his earlier overblown assumption about her value, without unfair attack on her, and tracing out the proper dimensions of human powers. She fails as a creator because the lovers have been too earthly, too sexual. Yet she is still 'more then Moone' and has a power that the moon, which by nature must 'Draw ... up seas' (20) in affecting the tides, does not have. Instead, she is astral like Laura and hence capable of controlling her tear floods and affecting him spiritually; but her godlike influence on him, her spiritual 'impression,' must be effected in spiritual terms. Thus, understanding the 'emblemes' of his experience, recognizing her continuing astral powers, and advising her are all related to her realization of her highest capacities. For these lovers use of human powers is a mutual task. Proper use can tip the balance toward creation, away from annihilation.

A concluding word can usefully remind us that the poem dramatizes the very human grief of parting. The lovers' tears – whatever else they become in the poem – express a recognizable anguish. The poem no more rejects this simple human reality than it offers a kind of Pauline valediction to physical love. A further human reality very touchingly conveyed in the poem is how such emotional ruptures can enforce a new perspective on our experience. Donne's great poems of parting express a clear sense that few other human experiences hold up the mirror so demandingly to how the body and soul are together engaged in the events of time. Parting forces these lovers to recognize the danger of not keeping the body in its place as the servant of the soul; that is, sexual love, ironically characterized with alchemical terminology, cannot do what alchemy claims to do – transform matter into a higher form. But parting also reminds the speaker that his grief, however natural for an earthly creature, must be interpreted in spiritual terms as well. What we can regard as principles of Donne's thought – the compatible dualism of body and soul with its occasional conflicts, the inevitable grief of sexual love, the body's emblematism of spiritual experience, the mind's task of interpretation – are clearly realities of being in time. The poem's hermetic materials, particularly the ironic Paracelsian comparison between the alchemist and the Creator, express an attempt to find terms from Donne's immediate, temporal world to accommodate these realities.

6

Love and Repentance in the *Holy Sonnets*

In the *Holy Sonnets*, no less than in lyrics like 'A Valediction: of Weeping,' suffering is the measure of love. Penitential mourning, guided by the affecting image of the crucified Christ, works to nullify the sinful grief of idolatry, reforming one love with another. In writing a collection of love sonnets, Donne indicates that his broadest context is love; and we find him bringing together his former profane mistresses, his wife, God the Creator, God the Redeemer, and his Spouse the Church. Only the marriage between the re-formed soul and God can satisfy his soul's frustrated thirst for God, whetted by an admired wife, shared by participants in the true church, and purified by a penitential suffering that continually acknowledges human debility. The spiritual frustration recorded in the *Holy Sonnets* lies not in ignorance that divine love is the goal, but in the failure to reach that goal through repentance. Holy mourning falls short of joy and love falls short of fullness.

A bold comparison between profane and divine love threads together these love sonnets. As we will see, Donne uses his Petrarchan forms to express his personal need for a penitential change from one kind of love to another. Also, we will see reason's varied role in this penitential experience. But, to begin with, it is useful to draw out somewhat further than in previous chapters some lines in Donne's conception of the will. In the *Holy Sonnets* he looks directly at the relationship between love and repentance, and the motions of the will are fundamental.

For Donne the will's role in repentance assumes both the tenacity of sinful perversion and the importance of human individuality. In the *Holy Sonnets* the striking obtrusion of sexual sins, long past, confesses not only residual sexual guilt, but also the will's continuing debility. It is misguided love, not love itself, that debilitates the will; by nature, the will loves. Donne's sermons, as early as 1617, repeat Aquinas's '*Amor est primus actus voluntatis*' (*Sermons,*

1, 242). But the will is coloured by its own individuality; and spiritual love, in reforming the will according to new habits, preserves that individuality. Donne's keen guilt acknowledges the imprint of past habits pulling athwart the new. This imprint, consistent with Donne's tough-minded understanding that the given shape of each human nature is ineradicable, ensures in his own case the continuity of a passionate nature, but guards against its recurrent abuses. Accordingly, divine habits that superimpose the profane necessarily must accommodate to the character of the individual will. The 'covetous person,' once he is converted, will have a 'spiritual covetousness,' a desire to have 'all' of God; in a similar vein Solomon, whose love of women was 'excessive,' later expressed his 'amorous' disposition in his 'old phrase and language' in loving God (*Sermons*, 1, 236–7). Donne found a similar pattern of love in his own experience. The memory of past sins emphasizes the disposition of his passionate nature.

In the *Holy Sonnets* the respective roles of memory and will reveal further contours of Donne's Augustinian legacy.[1] Explicit borrowings from the *Confessions* in the *Essays in Divinity* (pp. 15ff.) and in early sermons (e.g., *Sermons*, V, 237) indicate the importance to Donne of Augustine's experience. The competition in the *Confessions* between divine love and profane love of the creature, plus the power of remembered sins and tenacious habit – the analogues in the *Holy Sonnets* are compelling. Prior to Augustine's dramatic conversion, growing spiritual love competed with idolatrous sexual love; and only Grace decided the conflict. For Augustine the force of habit maintained the past in the present; the memory harboured 'images of such things, as my ill custom there fixed.'[2] Donne's paraphrase of Job's statement expresses his fundamental empathy with that notion: 'my best actions, now in mine age, have some taste, some tincture from the habit, or some sinfull memory of the acts of sin in my youth' (*Sermons*, V, 358). For both Augustine and Donne, only experience of reformed life can superimpose to reshape such imprints, just as new experience habituates the will anew. Donne's youthful sexual sins do not continue; but the idolatry informing them must be reformed by new habits and new memories.

Donne's 'idolatrie' of his 'profane mistresses' (XIII) reveals further traditional features in the will's experience of love. As he says in a sermon, any 'inordinate love' of the creature is idolatry (*Sermons*, II, 132–3), characterized in the *Holy Sonnets* as a betrothal to Satan (XIV), a spiritual fornication or adultery. We need go no further than the Bible for Donne's frequent equation of idolatry and spiritual fornication.[3] But the presence of this equation in Elizabeth's ordained homilies attests to the wide currency of the notion in Donne's time: 'the bond of love betweene man and him [God is] as much broken by Idolatry, which is spirituall fornication, as is the knot and bond of marriage broken by carnall fornication.'[4] Not beside the point is that Augustine's *Confessions* characterizes actual fornication as merely one species of spiritual fornication, of perverted love,[5] a substitution of the creature for the Creator.

In the *Holy Sonnets* the will's desire to be drawn away from these idolatrous perversions to experience holy love establishes the central principle of coherence in the work. Donne's Petrarchan form follows accordingly. His excerpt from a Petrarch *canzone* inscribed on the title pages in his personal library indicates how directly that the pervasive tradition established by the *Canzonieri* had reached Donne.[6] Obvious differences between the *Canzonieri* and the *Holy Sonnets* need not obscure fundamental similarities linked to shared Augustinian assumptions.[7] Like Augustine's *Confessions*, both sonnet collections assume the human will in conflict between idolatrous love of the creature and holy love of the Creator. Likewise, the *Canzonieri*, under lifetime revision, commemorates the abiding imprint of past experience that we have seen to be so important for both Augustine and Donne.

The strongest thematic affinity between Donne and Petrarch is the love conflict. Petrarch never works free from the contradiction that idolatrous sexual desire for the innocent Laura magnetically held him so that he could view her virtuous example. Abiding desire for the complete Laura, body and soul, continues to jar against repentance for that lustful desire. In the conflict between Petrarch's physical attraction to Laura's beauty and his guilt for sexual passion, we find an analogue for Donne's own remembered attraction to the 'beauty' of his 'profane mistresses.' Petrarch's 'blind desire' (LVI)[8] suggests an autonomy of bodily appetite and passion that would have struck a kindred note in Donne's experience. We have just seen in Chapter Five, on 'A Valediction: of Weeping,' that the body had its own independent needs which often work against the soul. Also, much in Donne's early love poetry is directed against the encouragement of naturalism to satisfy the body without paying heed to spiritual requirements. The guilt expressed in the *Holy Sonnets* may admit the degree to which Donne felt that he had surrendered to physical passion.

It is the pivotal connection in the *Canzonieri* between love and repentance that has the profoundest implication for the *Holy Sonnets*. Petrarch's tenacious commitment to the earthly Laura vied with his religion. A forcefully asserted penitential pattern censures his early love for having hindered his love of God. The penitential keynote, strategically placed in Sonnet I and confessing 'shame,' sets our response to Petrarch's commemoration of the Good Friday when he claims to have fallen in love with Laura (III). Loving her resembles killing Christ – hyperbole thus emboldens a point not easily submerged in later ambivalence toward that love, especially since a later Good Friday poem ruefully commemorates eleven years of love suffering (LXII). Petrarch's concluding hymn to the Virgin affirms Laura's virtue, yet pointedly moves her aside as Petrarch's centre of value. The virgin, 'ever-fixed star' (CCCLXVI) and love object, must preside over his repentance for having loved Laura. Thus, the *Canzonieri* begins and ends with penitential statements.

Donne's *Holy Sonnets* makes a similar connection between repentance and love that became commonplace in the Western European devotional lyric of the sixteenth and seventeenth centuries. Widespread adaptation of the Petrarchan sonnet for devotional uses lengthened further a Christian tradition that, by intersecting the vocabularies of secular and divine love, adapted easily to repentance. Ever more popular, the devotional sonnet established its own currency as a separate form in which the degree of indebtedness to Petrarch varied, but which commonly tied repentance to divine love.[9] It is useful to look in passing at one French example of this commonplace tie, in the sonnets of Antoine Favre, for it suggests the immediate Continental background for viewing the *Holy Sonnets*.

His 1595 title states the commonplace:[10] *Centurie premiere de sonets spirituels de l'amour divin et de la pénitence.*[11] The invidious comparison between profane and divine love is established with Favre's first breath in Sonnet I. And renunciation stresses a very Petrarchan opposition between Cupid and God,[12] warmed predictably by lovers' conventional flames. New spiritual love, while accepting Grace as mistress, offers vows exclusively to God as master (VI). To clarify renunciation, Favre loosens the more delimiting sexual denotation of love to include all worldly preoccupation; yet he maintains the lover's conventional traits such as suffering. Throughout the work, Favre recasts his Petrarchan conventions in order to sharpen the edge of his comparison between the two kinds of love. For example, he chides lovers for their claims of constancy: they pursue beauty, but get 'legereté,' not the 'constans' assured only in God (XIIII). The comparison between the conflicting kinds of love cuts most deeply when penitential sighs and tears, as repayment for love suffering, converge with Christ's agony as a model, and when love's fires recede or transform before God's fiery love and punishment.

Favre's Christ excites both fear and love. Implicit judgment against Christ's sinful murderer, muted by the Cross's dramatic statement of love, emerges stridently in Favre's bold threats of Doomsday and Hell Fire. Repentance must convert worldly love in order that man may escape just punishment. Penitential tears extinguish sinful love's flames, and God's love warms the heart anew: 'Courez au feu du ciel pour y ardre tout-vifz / Du feu, mourant par feu, on sauve ainsi sa vie' (L). But only conformity to the Cross can bring together the demands of both love and justice. Throughout the *Centurie* affective piety vividly accents man's guilt and God's love. The penitent must be crucified with both the world and Christ, mortifying worldly sin and dying with Christ to live. He must live the bitter and the sweet of Christ's nails: hatred of sin and love freely given, fear and love of Christ (LXVIII). However varied its expression, the voice of God's love necessarily speaks most clearly in the Cross, drawing the penitent away from service to Cupid.

Favre's use of the Petrarchan sonnet for devotional purposes had its parallels in England, where both devotional sonnets and sacred parody merged in the late sixteenth century. By the end of the 1590s Henry Lok, Barnabe Barnes, Henry Constable, and William Alabaster had written devotional sonnets. The influential Robert Southwell, in encouraging that poetry of profane love be transposed to divine ends, expressed assumptions congenial to Donne's: 'Passions I allow, and loves I approve, onely I would wishe that men would alter their object and better their intent.'[13] Frequent editions of Southwell's works between 1591 and 1636 disseminated his comparison between secular and divine loves.[14] By 1609, Helen Gardner's date for all but three *Holy Sonnets*,[15] the devotional sonnet and sacred parody had English as well as Continental roots. Thus, Donne's penitential conversion of profane to divine love in the *Holy Sonnets* clearly reveals a consciousness attuned to current potentialities of sonnet form.

Donne's penitential thrust, which any interpretation of Donne's sonnets must take into account, is a case in point. Guilt and fear of judgment inspire the penitential dialectic informing man's effort with God's aid: 'Yet grace, if thou repent, thou canst not lacke: / But who shall give thee that grace to beginne?' (IV). The self counsels penitential 'holy mourning blacke' and a compunctious shame 'red with blushing' as a necessary prelude. The desired aid implies an active tutelage by Grace: 'Teach mee how to repent; for that's as good / As if thou'hadst seal'd my pardon, with thy blood' (VII). Achieved repentance, in conformity with Christ's grief, would assure the pardon of the Cross, the 'strange love' of the humiliated God whose pardon, unlike a king's pardon, 'bore our punishment' (XI). Yet frequent attention to penitential tears suggests varying degrees of achievement that do not reach complete repentance, which is constricted by the remaining sense of sin and human weakness. Varied requests for divine aid restate that same condition ('Batter my heart'; 'burne me ô Lord, with a fiery zeale'; 'repair me now'). The need for holy mourning and these requests for aid form a thematic ground line through the sonnets.

Douglas Peterson contributes much to our understanding this ground line. For him, holy sorrow for sin is Donne's goal: 'The *Holy Sonnets* represent a series of efforts to experience those states of feeling that either precede or are concomitant with contrition.'[16] Unlike Catholic attrition, which accepts sorrow inspired by fear of punishment as evidence of salvation,[17] the more demanding Anglican contrition requires hatred of sin and love of God that fulfil that fear. Contrite sorrow requires Grace; hence contrition, properly achieved, denotes a state of Grace and assures salvation. Seeking contrition, the penitent believer necessarily contemplates the expression of God's love as his inspiration. For Peterson, Donne's search to experience and maintain contrition establishes coherent relationships between those sections of the *Holy Sonnets* ascertained by Gardner: fear (1–6) fulfilled in love (7–12) that works to maintain a proper state of contrition (penitential sonnets 1–4); occasional sonnets (1–3). In the Gardner components, Peterson finds a progressive structure founded on Anglican doctrine, with a beginning, a middle, and an open end.

Peterson's argument does present some problems, however. The structural and thematic singlemindedness perceived by Peterson suggests the careful direction of set intention that would work against the flexibility of actual experience. And we do well to heed the spirit of J.B. Leishman's and A.J. Smith's reservations about an overly schematic description of the *Holy Sonnets* as a possible barrier to understanding the force of individual sonnets.[18] Also, Anglican contrition, as described by Peterson's source Richard Hooker, forms the first step in repentance, following on to confession, then satisfaction: three parts in a penitential whole.[19] Contrition looks not to itself, but beyond to changed behaviour. Peterson's argument stresses love as the means to contrition, not contrition as a means to higher ends.

And the larger penitential design is asserted in Donne's sonnets. For example, the penitential sonnet (v: 'I am a little world made cunningly') asks for a stronger medicine than just contrition to heal a sinful will. The same *topos* as in 'A Valediction: of Weeping,' the world annihilated by tears, leads to a request for God's infused zeal. Betrayed by his own sin, Donne wittily seeks new models for penitential tears, to 'Drowne' the 'world' of sin and to replace the lost world: first, the self-annihilation through humility, then, purification. But this world bears a sinful imprint, through fires of 'lust and envie,' that resists contritional tears. Such imprints require a powerful cautery. The traditional opposition, between the fires of earthly and heavenly love, varies Donne's own continuing thematic opposition between profane and divine love. The fire of lust and envy must surrender to 'fiery zeale / Of thee'and thy house.' This request for holy fire recalls the even more strenuous invitation for afflicting Grace in the sonnets, 'burn and make me new' (XIV), and in the Good Friday poem, 'Burne off my rusts.' Here, also, punishing affliction need burn away sin from the will; but 'fiery zeale,' now God's, then possibly Donne's, speaks severally, throwing the possible meanings of 'fire' as ardour, anger, or love into the possibilities of 'zeale': jealousy, wrath, ardent pursuit, devotion, or love. God's powerful love must reform Donne's love – punishment, just anger, and reformation are included in the same act of love that likens the human will to the divine will.

The important point is that neither contrition nor corrective affliction is an end in itself, but each is a form of love between God and man, engaging the natures of both. Donne's attempt to maintain a proper contritional stance is important to the *Holy Sonnets*, but it reveals a special emphasis when seen as one mode of love between God and man. The crux is Donne's request that God 'Teach mee how to repent' for it assumes a shared effort consistent with Donne's assertion elsewhere that God's contribution demonstrates his love (*Sermons*, v, 319). Similarly, just as God's nature and actions inspire the love basic to sorrow for sin, so too does the Grace that effects achieved contrition demonstrate God's love further. To enunciate my point: the *Holy Sonnets* offers a perspective on repentance as one experience of love.

The approach to repentance and Grace in terms of love agrees with Donne's Augustinianism, particularly the drama of the suffering Christ as a penitential model. Patrick Grant has traced out some Franciscan elements in the Augustinian tradition that undergirds the *Holy Sonnets*. He notes that the Franciscans 'make of contrition the moving and profound emotional experience of conversion that it was for Augustine himself.' Man's Original Sin and Christ's reparative suffering are central to repentance, which 'by moving men to love properly' prepares toward the Eucharistic feast of love; that is, repentance points toward the fuller experience of love.[20] The suffering Christ, as both the pattern for that penitential movement and its object, is both the way and the end.

The theological assumptions framing that conformity[21] have pointed application to Donne's choice of the love sonnet as a devotional genre. The agony of the Cross dramatizes God's love, not only by demonstrating the divine gift to man, but also by offering that very suffering as a pattern for returning love to God. Hence, Christ's suffering pays sin's debt, and repentance does likewise; it also follows that the pattern of love conveys the pattern of just payment. Not an end, but a means, repentance is nonetheless part of love's growth into conformity with Christ. Thus, to save man, God's love encourages man's love to return to God himself. In the *Holy Sonnets* a similar view of repentance reinforces Donne's larger impulse to refer all intercourse between God and man to the experience of divine love. Donne's basic source of dramatic energy remains the turning from profane to divine love, with the corollary turning from idolatrous grief to penitential suffering; that drama suffuses even though it may not exhaust all forms of love depicted in the *Holy Sonnets*.

In making this change from profane to divine love, the tripartite human soul must respond to those varying manifestations of God's nature assisting the change. Accordingly, this change, itself an expression of love, has a multifariousness and a breadth that give to individual sonnets their momentary separateness while including them in a larger experience. Donne's sense of spiritual experience – incomplete, exploratory, frustrated – qualifies the *Holy Sonnets* as an accomplished whole. He tentatively suggests in individual sonnets how that completion might be achieved. At the same time he pointedly reveals many of the same impulses that characterize his mature thought. The *Holy Sonnets* shows Donne moving toward his mature theology of suffering, with penitential grief and affliction as complements in conformity to Christ. Also, consistent with attention to reason elsewhere, Donne closely observes reason's role in the soul's drama of love. On one hand, he notes how 'Reason your viceroy' can be infected by sin; but, on the other hand, he invites it to 'digest' a 'wholsome meditation' and inspire the will to love God. In the following discussion we will see how the thematic lines tying reason and suffering are integral in Donne's uneasy attempt to contemplate the ways that love mediates between man and God.

To begin with, we can see in Donne's meditation on Christ of the Last Judgment (XIII: 'What if this present were the worlds last night?') the problematic attempt to follow the right pattern of suffering and divine love in order to control the impulse to idolatrous love. Donne depicts his sense of sin according to remembered idolatry, evoking from love-sonnet conventions a statement of his own potentially ambiguous, hence possibly idolatrous, love of Christ. Old patterns of sinful idolatry compulsively struggle to emerge. The question posed in the octave ('And can that tongue adjudge thee unto hell, / Which pray'd forgivenesse for his foes fierce spight?') is answered negatively in the sestet by the soul's regard for Christ's beauty ('This beauteous forme assures a pitious minde'). The soul's dialectic involves an explicit comparison between former 'profane mistresses' and Christ: both are judges who grant or reject Donne's suit for mercy; both are attractive for their beauty. The comparison replaces the Petrarchan lady with Christ as the centre of value, presumably redirecting idolatrous love, noting likenesses to embolden the differences. The ritualized Petrarchan distance between mistress and aggrieved lover is contracted by Christ's suffering for man in a radically different expression of love that offers to man a new pattern of love suffering.

But the soul's ready comparison, perhaps too facile, too quick, may compromise ambiguously the shift to divine love, hinting at traces of remaining idolatrous love that blinds the soul to the fullness of the differences. The too obvious distinction between Christ's spiritual beauty ('Which pray'd forgivenesse for his foes fierce spight') and his mistresses' physical beauty blunts the argument that both, by analogy, assure pity and suggests instead the tenacity of old, sinful patterns in describing new realities. After all, the argument for 'pity' is a seducer's logic. For Donne, well-schooled in the sinful soul's evasive dodges and turns, a spirituality that stimulated love of the suffering Christ could set its own pitfalls by fixing on physical realities at the expense of spiritual. This damnable idolatry would have its ironic likeness to the worship of feminine beauty, and the divine pattern of suffering would have been perverted. Yet this possible idolatry qualifies without denying the presence of spiritual love of Christ, just as abiding sinfulness weakens assurance without dissipating hope.

Recognition of sin's fine subtlety, even in the face of 'Christ crucified,' proves the will's dubiety and promotes the request for divine aid. The urgency with which the full Trinity is invoked in 'Batter my heart, three person'd God' (XIV) suggests the special importance of this poem in the *Holy Sonnets*. Christ's suffering, as a model of love, is not in itself enough to turn the sinful will; instead, it must be supplemented by the suffering of affliction. Donne can love God 'dearely,' but not without perversion, which only the Trinity's assembled power can convert. Here, as when looking specifically at the sonnet on the Last Judgment, we find that basic sonnet constructs articulate further the conflict between loves; we also find expressed the notion so basic to Donne's religious thought that only the power of God's affliction can break that conflict. In this sonnet Donne's variations played on love's militarism suggest how God's loving affliction can bend further the hardened will made tender by Christ's love. Cupid's assault on the lover's heart,[22] the lover's attack on the woman's fortress, spiritual warfare, the heart as an adulterous female town besieged by God – familiar Petrarchist, devotional, and Biblical *topoi* extend further the comparison, galvanized by sexual violence, between profane and divine love.

The poem's arresting sexual language is pivotal. Allusions to love's battery, sexual entrance ('Labour to'admit you'), embrace ('Take mee to you'), the 'heart' as vagina,[23] sexual renewal ('make me new')[24] – all accentuate the sexual dimension of ravishment and the feminine soul as a besieged fortress. This sexual diction blatantly asserts the pivotal spiritual problem of the *Holy Sonnets*: on one hand, it crudely suggests the stubbornness of profane love and the impulse in Donne's nature, like Petrarch's, to concentrate upon physical realities; and, on the other hand, it suggests the radically incomprehensible expression of divine love that alone can redirect the will's stubborn inclination. Passionate love of God ('Yet dearely'I love you, and would be lov'd faine'), even when enkindled by the vision of the crucified Christ, can be rescued from idolatrous entrapment only by an incomprehensible divine rape.

The schizoid will, fully Pauline and Augustinian in its divided loves, invites the divine attack suggested elsewhere in the sonnet collection (11). It is now that God must rise to win back the 'usurpt towne,' crashing one system of spiritual law onto another. In Donne's hands the spiritual combat *topos* pointedly stresses not the soul's independent field movements against the enemy Satan,[25] but God's liberating force against the sinful soul itself. A passage from a Donne sermon is informative: 'But he hath petrified his heart in sin, and then he hath immur'd it, wall'd it with a delight in sin, and fortified it with a justifying of his sin, and adds daily more and more out-works, by more and more daily sins' (*Sermons*, I, 193). The powerful and destructive 'three person'd God' besieges, through affliction, the heart hardened by sin.

Spiritual warfare merges easily with the common prophetic *topos* of the soul as an adulterous female town.[26] Calvin's commentary on Jeremiah, which is especially instructive given Donne's similar interest that led to translating the Lamentations, points to popular interpretive associations immediately available for Donne's poem. Commonly, the prophets compared the people to sinful believers in search of idols, like 'wanton women, who labour to gain the hearts of adulterers' and who break the pledge of faithfulness and mutual 'chastity.'[27] City as woman, tainted by her sex and lust – Donne's own translation of the Lamentations serves best: 'Jerusalem hath sinn'd, therefore is shee / Remov'd, as women in uncleannesse bee' (29–30). Shifting metaphors merge adulterous women, the city, its architecture, applicable to a whole group or the individual heart. A God wrathful at human sin, judging, punishing, now as a powerful enemy attacks in fires of affliction, breaking down the sin-hardened walls of the heart (117–22). Sin, the call to humility and repentance, fear of angry divine judgment and punishment, a call to accept his chastisement and correction, the affliction of punishment and amendment – these emphases made Jeremiah and the Lamentations, along with other prophetic literature, central Christian penitential texts.

Viewed in this context, the emphases in Donne's sonnet become more clear. God must afflict, 'o'erthrow' the walls of the hardened heart, 'burn' to purify. The request for a broken heart wittily invokes the negative secular meaning of a broken heart, in order to define the search for a 'broken and contrite heart' (Psalm 51:17), humbled and penitential. Yet Donne's sonnet looks toward the love bond, not just the bar of justice. His adulterous female town strains not idolatrously to multiply lovers; perhaps only betrothed and not married to Satan, Donne seeks full return to God's love. Unlike Calvin, Donne seeks penitential affliction as the fire of love, not just anger alone.

Such affliction, in bending the sinful will, can free reason, which is debilitated by the will's perversion. And, in investigating the role of reason in this sonnet, we find a direct debt to Bernard of Clairvaux that gives us one side to reason's many-sided role in the *Holy Sonnets*. Donne's 'Reason your viceroy in mee,' God's ruler in the 'usurpt towne,' unfortunately 'captiv'd' and demonstrably 'weake or untrue,' is indebted to Bernard's *The Steps of Humility*, a source explicitly influential in Donne's later thought as well (e.g., *Sermons*, v, 346). Sensitive to the spirit though by no means subservient to the letter of Bernard's discussion, Donne's sonnet also connects humility as rational self-knowledge to love and to divine ravishment. Bernard's anagogic path, from humility to love to purity, respectively assisted by the Son, the Spirit, and the Father, similarly leads from rational self-knowledge of sin to mystical marriage. One function of reason, prevented by Grace, is self-examination; the result is an invidious comparison of man's own pride to Christ's humiliation that renders man 'contemptible in his own sight':[28]

when the Son of God, who is the Word and wisdom of the Father, finds that faculty of our soul called reason [ratio] weighed down by the flesh, captive [captivam] to sin, blinded by ignorance, and given over to external things; he gently lifts it up, powerfully strengthens it, prudently instructs it, and turns it to internal things. Miraculously making the reason his vicar [vicaria], as it were, he appoints it judge of itself, so that, out of reverence for the Word to which it is joined, prosecutor and witness and judge of itself, it performs the office of Truth against itself. From this first conjunction of the Word and reason is born humility.

The strengthened reason advises the infirm will, readied thereby to be 'kindled with the fire of love' by the Spirit;[29] and the soul thus humbled, loving, thereby purified, is united to the Father as a 'glorious bride' in a longed-for embrace. This lover's embrace of the chaste married soul is enacted when the soul is 'caught up' (rapitur)[30] by the Father's power. How far along this anagogic path to mystical contemplation itself Donne either desired or was able to go will remain an open question. It is possible that the poem's Bernardine cast reveals Donne's desire for mystical ravishment with its suggestive comparability to Ann Donne's soul 'early' into heaven ravished' by death

(XVII). But, clearly, he found in the traditional language of spiritual embrace and marriage powerful goads to his own unsatisfied need for divine love: and, clearly, his contradictory sense of sin, reminiscent of Paul's 'captivity' to the rival 'law of sin in my members' (Romans 7:23), prevents spiritual completion without diminishing his need. He breaks through Bernard's more programmatic anagogy, actively, directly, urgently, to request God's power in purifying his reason and will.

Donne's similar connections between humility, the broken heart, and 'viceroy' reason's agency in self-knowledge contribute substantially to understanding Donne's conception of reason's role in the struggle to experience holy love. The *Holy Sonnets* make no case for rational scepticism, but portray reason's share in the debility from sin while granting its essential contribution in erecting the soul through repentance. It is sin that makes reason 'untrue.' Louis Martz notes that Donne's 'besetting sin of intellectual pride' leads him to attempt to lay a logical trap for God:[31]

> If poysonous mineralls, and if that tree
> Whose fruit threw death on else immortall us,
> If lecherous goats, if serpents envious
> Cannot be damn'd; Alas; why should I bee?   (IX)

The argument in the octet brazenly ignores the difference between man and lower creatures until reason itself in the sestet, by censuring such misguided 'dispute' and demolishing its own untrue constructs, ironically dramatizes that difference. The sonnet features the contradiction of reason's sinful weakness and its necessary strength. The later request for the battered heart addresses this weakness, referring reason's contradictory plight to the traditional Petrarchan attention to reason's status in love. In both Donne and Sidney, Petrarch's conflict between will and reason[32] metamorphoses into reason's inner conflict. Astrophel's Reason, on one hand captivated by Stella's beauty, 'kneel'dst, and offeredst straight to prove / By reason good, good reason her to love' (X); on the other hand, Reason submits Astrophel to a stringent 'audite' that declares his given talents 'banckrout' through love (XVIII).[33] For Donne, only Grace can shatter the contradiction, freeing reason from the imprisonment of perverting love to conduct the penitential self-scrutiny that humbles the soul and prepares it for purified divine love. Reasoning is the necessary constant.

This rational dissection of sin is not reason's only task in the *Holy Sonnets* for, as Martz makes clear, rational analysis was inherent in religious devotions. Formal meditation stimulated the soul's tripartite powers – memory, reason, will – and led in those poets influenced by it to a 'deliberate evolution of the threefold structure of composition (memory), analysis (understanding), and colloquy (affections, will),'[34] thus renewing man's tripartite image of God. The issue is not *if* reason is engaged, but *how*. By no means schematic or complete in individual works, this structure left its identifiable imprints and, in the case of reason in the *Holy Sonnets*, several traces are noteworthy. Martz's analysis of the *Holy Sonnets* stresses how parts of the formal meditations are abbreviated, conflated, excerpted to serve the poet's ends, and how the individual powers of the soul may combine their efforts. Martz works from the firm assumption that the power of reasoning is a given element in Donne's meditative form and that it is revealed diversely in different sonnets.

Martz considers 'Wilt thou love God, as he thee!' (xv) to be purely rational in form, 'analysis only, understanding.' The revealing similarity that he finds to St Ignatius's 'Contemplation for obtaining love'[35] has particular applicability to reason's part in the *Holy Sonnets* as love sonnets: like Ignatius, Donne contemplates God's benefits as a goad to love. The soul is invited to 'digest' a series of paradoxes in this 'wholsome meditation.' For example, the Father who has 'begot a Sonne most blest' is, contradictorily, 'still begetting'; and the 'Sonne of glory,' who created man, was slain. The immediacy of Donne's connection between love and meditation, and his notion of 'digestion' as a rational process, as noted in Chapter Three, leave little room to question his intentions or to argue that the poem's diet of paradoxes is indigestible to reason.[36] To recognize these paradoxes is to gain a necessary measure of understanding God's wondrous love. A special feature of the Jesuit meditation described by Martz is finely wrought intellectual examination of Christ's paradoxical nature; the understanding, so fed, stimulates the soul to love and wonder.[37] A related ascent through reasoning to wonder at Christ's paradoxical nature as Creator and Sacrifice occurs in Donne's meditation on Creation (xii: 'Why are wee by all creatures waited on?'). The reasoning process takes the form of prolonged questioning that opposes man's dignity as fulfilment of the created world to his sinful guilt; these questions preface the 'wonder at a greater wonder' that the Creator died for his enemies. Douglas Peterson observes that in this poem reason is 'treated as the gift that enables man to rule the natural world and second only to the Atonement as an indication of God's love.'[38]

That gift of reason necessarily continues throughout the *Holy Sonnets* in the search to enjoy God's love, although the perspective keeps shifting in given devotional moments: fumbling half-truths, conscious bewilderment, traps laid then dismantled, principles manifesting God's love recognized and digested. As we see in Sonnet viii ('If faithfull soules be alike glorifi'd'), the ways in which reason is caught in the continuing tug of war between God and Satan are often subtle. Reason discovers that even in times of 'white truth,' with the soul's sinful blackness temporarily pushed into the corner of the mind's eye and with the assured Donne 'valiantly' astraddle 'hels wide mouth,' it must bridle its wayward curiosity. Assurance recalls likeness between purified sinners and glorified souls and, again, sparks Donne's inquisitive interest in the tie lines between earthly and heavenly members of Christ's Body. He wonders if those glorified members can accurately distinguish his devotion and its 'true griefe' from the false devotion and suffering of others. Curiosity thereby pursues the unessential, encouraged by the potential pride in social recognition. It is reason's necessary task to discern the soul's true penitential grief as God's gift to his labouring soul. Whether or not glorified souls see Donne's new purity misses the point that God, the only true end of love, worship, and devotion, can be found in the true repentance that empowers them.

Donne's close attention to reason's behaviour follows from a devotional love that calls forth varied traits in both himself and God. Fretful, uneven, the many pulses in Donne's spiritual experience express degrees of assurance and a changing need for Grace. The faces of Donne's God – warrior, judge, creator, father, lamb, husband, lover, king, punisher, scourge, ravisher – often more desired than fully known, reflect back the altering shape of Donne's experience. Donne viewed his progress in divine love with a hard clarity that recognized the exaggeration in his own singular nature. Yet his strenuous reason, usually sharp-eyed and penitential, measures the range of the soul's stances, from yearning helplessness to free responsibility and wonder.

To sum up the *Holy Sonnets* is to keep our attention focused on the variousness of God's love and on the variousness of psychological experience encouraged by Donne's Petrarchan form, with its collection of separate but related sonnets. Donne finds in God's several faces the expressions of divine love that guide the human struggle to reform idolatrous love in accordance with divine pattern. This penitential struggle in love remains central throughout the *Holy Sonnets*. To ignore this spiritual centre and its expression in sonnet form, as does Barbara Lewalski in her attempt to apply a 'Protestant paradigm of salvation,'[39] is to lose much. The Petrarchan sonnet, shaped as it was by the conflicting motions of Petrarch's own experience of love and repentance, provided Donne with a form for scrutinizing the varying motions of the penitential soul. As we have seen, reason's part in this self-scrutiny accommodates to the varying demands of Donne's love experience; in general, it meets the need to understand the patterns of therapeutic suffering that reform the sinful will and relieve the suffering and guilt of idolatrous love.

Thus, the variousness of the Petrarchan form is happily congenial to both the dramatization of Donne's spiritual experience and to the characterization of God.

It is the need for a multiple expression of God's love that points to Donne's incompletion and explains why the parts govern the whole in the *Holy Sonnets*, following a direction without reaching an end. By contrast, Donne's other sonnet group *La Corona* and the long prose *Devotions upon Emergent Occasions* achieve an architectural wholeness that is conclusive and dominating. The *Holy Sonnets* falls between the genuine conviction of his inherited faith in *La Corona* and the later, more personal assurance of that belief in the *Devotions*. In the *Holy Sonnets* it is fitting that we do not know if the last sonnet we read (XIX: 'Oh, to vex me, contraryes meete in one') was intended to come last, or was written last. Equally fitting is that this sonnet laments the paradoxically constant 'Inconstancy' of Donne's devotion. He knows the roots of his 'humorous' contrition to be implicated in the oxymoronic suffering of profane love; and Donne cleverly plays the Petrarchan convention against the devotional convention of inconstancy in divine love, which parodies it. As many readers have found, Donne's assurance was not easily achieved; and there is much to suggest that it came when his earnest request for the punishment of God's corrective affliction was answered. Much in the corrective illness of the *Devotions* answers the heartfelt request in the Good Friday poem, that God burn off his sinful rusts. In the *Holy Sonnets* Donne reveals a clear sense that the ways of divine love are many, but the shape of old loves unsettles the assurance that would fulfil his experience of that love. What appears to be an unresolved structural whole in the *Holy Sonnets* is itself a figure for the incompletion of his love. Intentional or not, the 'true feare of his rod' (XIX) points the way of fulfilment, through God's affliction.

7

Conversion Psychology in the
Good Friday Poem

Donne's need for corrective affliction leaves deep marks in his spirituality. In the *Holy Sonnets* his world must be burnt, his heart battered; in 'Goodfriday, 1613. Riding Westward,' God must punish, to correct, to 'Burne off' Donne's sinful 'rusts.' With sin resisting a strenuous desire for purity, Donnenecessarily requests the violence of corrective affliction so that he can 'turne' to God. Then, Donne can 'dare' to face the crucified God, hence reach the spiritual goal awaiting after his death. Turning is a life's work. No less convinced of personal sin than in the *Holy Sonnets*, Donne here reveals a conception of spiritual progress as perpetual conversion dependent on affliction. The poem does not encourage the sudden drama of Paul's conversion, but it does welcome affliction as the agency of Grace. Donne can conclude his lifelong turning only when standing face to face with God, when he will know as he is known. He expects to reach Paul's end, but accepts the revised means of corrective affliction and rides at a different temporal pace. Donne's connection between affliction and lifelong turning expresses a principle of Christian psychology necessary for the fulfilment of earthly time.

The paradoxical westward movement, the figure for Donne's sin and also the means of purification, will not end in his desire to turn eastward to Christ. At first, his movement seems like a conscious perversion of his Good Friday devotion; he is 'carryed towards the West' by 'Pleasure or businesse,' while his 'Soules forme bends toward the East' (7–10). Reluctance to face the crucified Christ acknowledges a personal responsibility for that 'spectacle of too much weight' and tightens his sinner's fear of punishment for looking into 'Gods face' (16–17). Finally, he discovers the paradox that his sinful westward movement will purify him.[1] His actual movement continues unchanged, not his attitude toward it, which moves him to invite, then welcome,

God's corrections with his back turned to God. This is the exercise that will contribute to his turning eastward, to complete his circle at death:

> I turne my backe to thee, but to receive
> Corrections, till thy mercies bid thee leave.
> O thinke mee worth thine anger, punish mee.
> Burne off my rusts, and my deformity,
> Restore thine Image, so much, by thy grace,
> That thou may'st know mee, and I'll turne my face.   (37–42)

As a sinful killer of Christ, who does 'Crucifie him daily' ('Holy Sonnet, XI'), he requires a lifelong conversion.

The pervasive language of conversion in Donne's age expressed a spiritual emphasis[2] that lends to Donne's climactic weight on turning a special force for any contemporary reader. But Donne's primary interest is not in the sudden conversion of Paul,[3] but in the more protracted kind of conversion, with its centre in repentance, that fulfils time. Every believer, misdirected by fallen selfishness, repeatedly turns away from God, then repeatedly is turned back by repentance: 'In one word, (one word will not do it, but in two words) it [repentance] is *Aversio*, and *Conversio*; it is a turning from our sins, and a returning to our God' (*Sermons*, VII, 162). Repentance enacts a yet larger notion of conversion that returns the believer to God through the Church: 'And this guiding us with his eye, manifests it selfe in these two great effects; conversion to him, and union with him. First, his eye works upon ours; His eye turnes ours to looke upon him' (*Sermons*, IX, 367). Conversion so conceived is not domesticated to unimportance, since every sinner is Christ's daily killer and must be punished. Obligatory daily conversion thus shares the drama, but not the singular momentousness, of Paul's change en route to Damascus. Donne's statement that he will 'turne' his back plays with the notion of turning, since he is not actually proposing to turn away from Christ, but to accept willingly his penitential correction as the means. Donne asks for God's necessary help so that he can make his own answering effort to face eastward. Donne offers his back to receive the rod of God's wrath and corrective affliction as a continuing impetus to repentance (*Sermons*, X, 195).

As I have shown in some detail elsewhere,[4] this broader conception of conversion was widespread in English Protestantism, ranging from William Perkins to Jeremy Taylor. Calvin was one primary source. Like Paul, Calvin experienced a specific moment of conversion;[5] yet, as François Wendel notes,

Calvin's works describe conversion in broader terms applicable to Donne's notion:

Conversion is a turning back of the will, which frees us from the grip of original sin, but does so little by little, in such sort that it cannot be regarded as complete so long as our earthly existence endures.[6]

While claiming with Ezekiel that man's conversion is the 'creation of a new spirit and a new heart,'[7] Calvin pointedly explicates why 'repentance' and 'conversion' can be interchanged, noting a general tendency, to him a just one, to understand the 'whole of conversion (conversionem) to God' as ' "repentance." ' Calvin's justification for doing so constitutes his definition of repentance as 'the true turning (conversionem) of our life to God, a turning that arises from a pure and earnest fear of him; and it consists in the mortification of our flesh and of the old man, and in the vivification of the Spirit.'[8] The assumption that the penitential turning to God is lifelong has ties of similarity to many English Protestants, including Donne, thus informing our understanding of 'Goodfriday.'

Yet this Reform context cannot explain turning in the poem without reference to its foundation in Augustinian psychology. Calvin's claim that conversion begins in the will[9] furthers an Augustinian conception of conversion as essentially the experience of the will affecting the entire soul. For Donne turning is the will's natural activity: 'the will of man cannot be idle ... till it love something, prefer and chuse something, till it would have something, it is not a Will; neither can it turn upon any object, before God' (*Sermons*, VI, 361). The Augustinian character of Donne's psychology of turning is boldly traced in his definition of sin: 'It is one of Saint *Augustines* definitions of sinne, *Conversio ad creaturam*, that it is a turning, a withdrawing of man to the creature' (*Sermons*, II, 132). The Biblical opposition between *aversio* and *conversio*, played throughout Donne's sermons, is inspired further by Augustine's thought, in which it matured into a central metaphysical principle confirmed by his own personal experience.

Augustine's notion pivots on a psychology of the will turned from God to the world through sin, needing to return to God through Grace. The *Confessions* follows the sinful, wandering Augustine 'turned from' (aversus) God.[10] Shortly before his climactic conversion, his will was divided painfully between old sinful habits and a nascent belief in God. 'Thus did my two wills [duae voluntates meae], one new, and the other old, one carnal, the other spiritual, struggle within me; and by their discord, undid my soul.'[11] Then his climactic reading of Paul established his conviction in faith, turning the will through God's aid: 'For Thou convertedst me unto Thyself' (Convertisti enim ad te).[12] This connection between *voluntas* and *conversio* cuts deeply through Augustine's works. Man must be taught to 'condemn and restrain' that movement 'whereby the will [voluntas] turns away from [avertitur] the unchangeable to the changeable good'; rather the will must be converted to enjoy the 'eternal good.'[13] In 'Goodfriday' this connection between will and conversion articulates with several related notions that have an Augustinian colouring: the bent and deformed soul, correction, and spiritual sight.

Augustine's influence not only passed through contemporary thought to Donne, but also directly, as the *Essays in Divinity* and the sermons make obvious. The profound influence of Bernard of Clairvaux on Donne entered through similar avenues. Donne scholarship, having progressively assessed Donne's deep borrowing from Augustine, supports the possibility of immediate Augustinian influences in this devotional poem. Donald M. Friedman has made a convincing case for the poem's Augustinian conception of memory.[14] Bernard's role as an influential spiritual and devotional guide, though not so well established in Donne scholarship, frequently asserts itself. In 'Goodfriday' Donne uses an Augustinian vocabulary shared by many contemporaries and explicated in the sermons according to Augustinian and Bernardine texts. We can leave open the question about the degree of direct influence in the poem, while nonetheless confidently asserting its Augustinian and Bernardine character.

Augustine and Bernard share a psychology of the soul or will 'bent' by Original Sin, needing to 'turn' from the world back to God. Augustine commands the believer, 'converte cor tuum.'[15] The 'heart' or the soul, and alternately the will, are bent (distorta; curva), unlike God's will. 'Distortus tu es, ille rectus es.'[16] Conversion conforms man's bent will to God's straight will. According to Bernard, the soul before returning to God is 'blind, bent' (curvam) earthwards.[17] Its return is a *conversio* that establishes a conformity between the divine and human wills.[18] For both Augustine and Bernard this turning to God is the process of erecting the bent soul or, more particularly, the bent will. This notion, bearing primarily Augustine's paternity and tutored further by Bernard and others like Calvin,[19] significantly influenced Donne as the 'turne' in 'Goodfriday' attests. The soul bent westward by sin while its 'forme,' its devotion, 'bends toward the East' (10) further reveals its Augustinian and Bernardine background. That same background supports the 'bent' soul needing to become erect in the *Holy Sonnets* (XIV: 'Batter my heart'), where Donne requests 'That I may rise, and stand, o'erthrow mee,'and bend.'[20] Later, he explicates Augustine's definition of sin, *conversio ad creaturam*, with Augustine's own terms: the burden of his sins 'bend down my soule, created streight, to an incurvation, to a crookednesse' (*Sermons*, II, 133).

Turning the bent soul is the Augustinian-Bernardine centre in 'Good-friday,' but correction is the necessary corollary. In the soul turned from sin by divine correction can be found the psychological basis for the principle of medicinal affliction discussed in Chapter Three. God's correcting anger turns the soul, burning off its 'rusts' and 'deformity' through affliction. Donne's request for such anger parallels his frequent sermon references to Bernard's 'Sermon XLII' on the Song of Songs, as in this assertion of the corrective importance of affliction:

and with S. *Bernard* [he shall] desire, *Irascaris mihi Domine*, O Lord be angry with me, for if thou chidest me not, thou considerest me not, if I taste no bitternesse, I have no Physick; if you correct me not, I am not thy son ... (*Sermons*, II, 362)

Here, in one of Donne's favourite passages,[21] Bernard says: 'I desire that Thou wouldst be angry with me, O Father of mercies [Volo irascaris mihi. Pater misericordiarum]; but with that anger wherewith Thou dost correct one who wanders from the way, not that with which Thou dost exclude such an one from it.'[22] Bernard offers corrective anger as evidence of God's love, and Donne characteristically repeats such emphasis. The sermons reveal the Bernardine debt going still deeper. Like Bernard he characterizes God's anger as fire.[23] While depicting corrective affliction as anger and again recalling Bernard's request for anger, he speaks of an earthly purgatory of 'Crosses, Afflictions, and Tribulations' that God sends 'to wash us, and to burne us cleane':

Let no man think himselfe sufficiently purified, that he hath not passed this Purgatory; *Irascaris mihi Domine*, saith S. *Bernard*, Lord let me see that thou art angry with me. (*Sermons*, VII, 183)

Donne's own characteristic emphasis – that God's anger expresses corrective affliction ('Mans suffering is Gods anger,' *Sermons*, III, 324) – is allied here with Bernard's notion that God's anger is corrective 'fire.' Donne's weight on the affliction and tribulations of correction is undergirded, as we will see, by Bernard's similar notion of correction. Donne's insistence on such corrective suffering demonstrates its importance in his theology and spirituality, and explicates the 'Corrections' that 'punish' in the Good Friday poem.

In both Augustine and Bernard correction establishes conformity between man's will and God's, and Bernard is Augustine's theological follower in this regard. Augustine says, 'Wish not to bend the will of God to thy will, but rather correct thy will to His.' God's will is a rule by which the bent or crooked soul becomes straight or erect. 'As long as the rule is straight, thou hast whither to turn thyself, and straighten thy perversity; thou hast a means of correcting what is crooked in thee.'[24] Bernard characteristically gives special importance to God's agency in correction and tribulation. He invites his auditors to 'hope for a ... blessing from on high ... for correction' whereby believers are 'exercised by trials and tribulations.'[25] In Donne's sermons the force of tribulation, as God-given correction to conform man's will to God's, receives strong support from Bernard.

This support marks Donne's personal expression of corrective affliction, a notion widespread in the spirituality of his time. For example, in the widely circulated *Christian Warfare*, John Downame speaks in a language similar to that in 'Goodfriday,' while pointing to God's 'rods of chastisement' taken up anew 'to correct our new sins with new affliction.'[26] The 'fire of affliction' inflames devotion and makes sinners 'break off their sinns by unfeigned repentance,' and 'turne unto the Lord.'[27] The popular Richard Sibbes uses the same language. The 'crooked' and 'perverse' soul must come to God's ordinance to become 'right and straight.'[28] A loving and just God mixes 'crosses and favours, corrections and mercies.'[29] Afflictions given first as punishment by an angry God, then as corrections by a loving Father, turn the believer. This spirituality of affliction, shared by such widely heeded divines as Donne, Downame, Sibbes, clearly identifies a commonly held cultural inheritance. Nonetheless, these writers do not speak in unison, but with voices pitched after their respective spiritual and theological natures. As Donne's sermons show us, precise Augustinian terms contribute to his conception of this shared spiritual experience of his age. The specifically Bernardine elements in his characterization of affliction in the sermons are similarly informative for our understanding of 'Goodfriday.' In any event, Donne's contemporary readers would have heard a familiar strain in Donne's request for corrective suffering as the means of turning the sinful soul.

His readers would also have recognized the complex drama of sinfulness in his reluctance before he makes that request for conversion. At first, Donne's toughening reluctance to face the crucified Christ threatens to crossbias the soul's turning movement toward Christ, especially since it is only Christ's punishing corrections that can break down this reluctance entirely. Yet Donne must bend his sinful soul to request these corrections. Donne's Christ, vividly 'present' to the 'memory' (34), shares a long literary history with the palpably vivid Christ of the meditative tradition. In Donne's engraftment of human and divine elements, a shocking mixture of blood, Golgothan soil, and cruel lacerations strikingly counterpoises the 'endlesse height which is / Zenith to us, and to'our Antipodes' (23–4). The theme is repeated in Christ's punctured hands that improbably 'span the Poles' (21). The speaker's shock at Christ's blood heightens his awareness of his own troubling response to Christ's mixed nature. As we will see, the degree of his shock is the measure of the 'deformity' of sinful 'rusts' on his tripartite 'Image' (41) of God. With his rusts taken off by God's punishing flames, he can turn to 'see' (11) the crucified Christ, the incarnate Word who would 'know' (42) the converted Donne. The poem's drama progressively blends the personal into the metaphysical, with the shocked soul growing desirous to conform to the crucified God who, just as he creates and turns the 'Spheare' (1) of the tripartite human soul, also creates and turns the astronomical spheres as well. By pursuing the implications of the tripartite soul's conversion in terms of the metaphysical ambience that contains it, we increasingly find reference to the agonized God.

Many sides to Donne's Trinitarian psychology have become understood gradually by modern scholarship. The Medieval-Renaissance meditative tradition sustaining Donne's works viewed man's tripartite soul, composed of memory, reason, and will, as a creation in the image and likeness of a Trinitarian God. It follows that the techniques of this tradition appeal to all three faculties in re-assimilating the soul to God. Donne's request that God 'Restore thine Image' alerts us that, having already mentioned the memory, he may be addressing implicitly the function of the soul's other two members as well. Friedman notes that Donnian memory, schooled by its Augustinian background, 'insists, in its own subverbal, unargumentative way, on the remembered image of God in each man, and man's responsibility for obscuring or defacing the image.'[30] Friedman's argument leads even further, to the actions of the will and the reason also. The 'rusts' to be burned off by the fire of God's correcting anger encrust the will, and the sight of Christ, the ultimate goal of the poem's movement, is reason's act. This is not to suggest a clumsy Trinitarian scheme, but instead to point to implications of Donne's figurative language and, in characterizing the interaction of the soul's three faculties in conversion, to advance our earlier examination of reason's motions. We recall that in Donne's Augustinian and Bernardine sources the whole sinful soul and, more exclusively, the will, are 'bent.' Donne's sermons verify that *bent* and *rust* refer finally to the will and that spiritual 'sight' is an experience of reason.

The climactic request to 'Burne off my rusts, and my deformity' assumes the bent soul conceived figuratively as metal and the stamped human Image of God made 'rusty' with sin. Donne characterizes both the soul and the will as metal. We find the 'rusty copper' of God's Image in the human soul

(*Sermons*, III, 250) and the allied 'Leaden and iron wills' ('Resurrection, imperfect,' 15).[31] The 'rust of our hearts,' that is, 'old habits' (*Sermons*, I, 199) or perversions, corrode and deform the will, to be 'burnt off' (*Sermons*, II, 146), or filed off. In a sermon Donne acknowledges specific support from Augustine and Bernard for notions enjoying longevity after them:

Uri potest, non exuri [Bernard]; The Devil hath this Image in him, and it cannot be burnt out in hell; for it is imprinted in the very naturall faculties of the soule. But if we consider how many waters beat upon us in this world to wash off this Image, how many rusty and habituall sins gnaw upon us, to eat out this Image, how many files over our souls in calamities, and affliction, in which though God have a purpose, *Resculpere imaginem* [Augustine] to re-engrave, to refresh, to polish this Image in us, by those corrections ... (*Sermons*, X, 46)

For Donne the 'rust'[32] to be burnt off by God's anger, God's affliction in 'Goodfriday,' is sin's selfishness deforming the tripartite human Image. But, to underline more specifically, Donne's reference to 'old habits,' traditionally the domain of the will, and the figurative characterization of the will as iron (*Sermons*, VI, 321) put sin first on the will, then on the whole soul through necessary participation.

The rusted Image is thus the human soul perverted, turned askew, bent by its fallen will. In the close interaction among the faculties of the soul lie the reasons for speaking synecdochically about the entire soul and a given faculty. Never independent, any faculty necessarily includes the remaining faculties in its actions. To restore the human Image, God must afflict Donne so that his will, acting through its close relationships with the other two faculties, can be turned. Such affliction holds the line with traditional Augustinian psychology in blaming the will for the Fall.

Singling out the will as Donne's primary target for afflictions accounts for another member of the tripartite Image, since Donne specifically mentions the memory as the inner stage for the Passion. Only reason remains to be accounted for. Friedman argues that Donne's beginning analogy between man's soul and a sphere is evidence of reason's prideful posturing.[33] Taken further, Friedman's analysis can lead to evidence of the erected reason, since reason begins to achieve its end when the will begins to heal. Herein lies the significance of 'sight.' Winfried Schleiner's argument, that the 'eyes of the soul' in Donne's sermons is 'the central metaphor of a field of imagery in which the act of understanding is represented in terms of visual perception,'[34] can apply to 'Good Friday' as well. In the sermons Donne habitually equates sight with understanding, the 'spiritual eye' with understanding, and seeing with knowing, plus any number of related variations.

While riding westward on Good Friday and voluntarily bending his meditating soul eastward to the Passion, the speaker Donne finds that, though he 'should see a Sunne, by rising set' (11), he does not 'see / That spectacle' (15–16). Yet his denial of sight gets entangled in contradiction, since the vivid dramatization, strengthened by the latter assertion that the Crucifixion events are 'present yet unto my memory, / For that looks toward them' (34–5), refutes total blindness. In sum, the speaker Donne 'looks' but does not 'see'; only the memory now 'sees.' The sinner Donne voluntarily recalls the events and principles of the Passion, originally submitted to reason, then stored in the memory to be dramatized again at will. A partially turned will enables a recall of previously understood events. Full 'sight' hangs on the meaning of the events being assimilated into the speaker's experience. He can 'turne' the 'face' of his soul only after corrections burn off his rusts. Full understanding of the crucified Christ and the sorrowing Mary can follow only when the corrected will humbly turns from love of the world to embrace God's love expressed in the humiliated Christ. Rational 'sight' needs a healthy will.

A sermon on Job 36:25 (*'Every man may see it, man may behold it afar* off') elucidates this understanding with reference to three kinds of 'sight.' The first is rational 'knowledge' of God from his creatures. The second is rational knowledge of Christ gained from actual Christian experience: 'it is a *seeing of God*, not as before, in his *works* abroad, but in his *working* upon himself, at home.' Such rational 'sight' through personal experience is achieved by affliction according to the pattern of suffering Christ; and it necessarily precedes the third kind of sight, the beatified 'sight' of God in glory with the 'eyes' of the soul. 'Eternall life hereafter is *Visio Dei*, the sight of God, and the way to that here, is to *see God* here: and the *eye-salve* for that is, to be crossed in our desires in this world, by the hand of God' (*Sermons*, IV, 173). Thus, affliction is the means of earthly 'seeing' – and we can build strong parallels with 'Goodfriday' – for through the misery of affliction, the believer becomes like Christ, hence able to 'see,' to understand rationally while embracing the love embodied in the painfully humiliated, self-sacrificial Christ. He will possess the knowledge of Christ crucified, without which he knows nothing. Visited with 'a cloud of medicinall afflictions, and wholsome corrections,' the believer 'shall see God; and then *he will see God*, his will shall be inclined and disposed to it' (*Sermons*, IV, 174). In 'Goodfriday' in asking that his rusts be removed through corrective affliction, the speaker Donne is asking for humility in Christ's pattern, that he can turn to 'see' Christ, to understand experientially the meaning of the crucified Christ. Albeit a co-ordination of the entire soul, such 'sight' is most explicitly reason's.

Although we can separate out the distinctive functions of reason, memory, and will, it is co-ordination of these faculties in relation to the crucified Christ that describes the events of conversion. Donne firmly fixes the incarnate Christ at the poem's centre as the object of the soul's efforts to turn. The soul's progressive reformation requires that Christ act in both his functions, of love and judgment. One assumption standing directly behind the poem is that the first step in bending or turning the sinful soul is preliminary 'vision' of the humiliated Christ: the facts of Christ's life and Passion embody the principles of his divine love, first given to reason, then passed on to memory. Only then is love that turns the will possible as a step toward complete rational sight through experience of Christ. Unfortunately, knowledge through reason and memory is not enough to turn a recalcitrant will, and only Christ's punishing corrections can bend the will and permit reason's fuller sight. The deformed soul's rust and blindness call forth both the loving Sufferer and the punishing Judge.

The powerful dramatization of Christ in his humanity and divinity reminds us again how, for Donne, moments in time are expanded by metaphysical dimensions. It also advances crucial elements of conversion psychology that explain the believer's perception of time. The dramatization of the suffering Christ increases unbearably the speaker's guilt; Mary's plight likewise gives more evidence of his violation of Christ. Relief that he cannot see Christ gives no true respite, for he must face a similar reluctance to contemplate the 'miserable mother' (30). Stunned by his sinful awareness, the reluctant speaker Donne must confront his responsibility for Christ's and Mary's agony. Any habitual sinner who crucifies Christ daily would be damned by his sin if now forced to face Christ at the Last Judgment. His horror at this 'spectacle of too much weight' (16) expands uncontrollably when he senses the cosmic scope of his daily crime for killing a God whose hands 'span the Poles.' Personal guilt for cosmic violation also guides Donne's sketch of Mary. She is 'Gods partner here,' who 'furnish'd thus / Halfe of that Sacrifice' (31–2), housed infinity in her body as did the lacerated body of Jesus. The shock generated in the characterization of Christ and Mary damns Donne's sinful deformity and justifies the urgent request for corrections in time that alone can assuage the cosmic dimensions of his guilt.

But Donne's reasons for fixing Christ at the poem's centre do not end with characterizing the speaker according to the means and end of his own conversion. It is more striking that Christ, in restoring the speaker's deformed

Image, 'may'st know' him and thus benefit from the conversion. Such knowledge is recognition of something previously known but later deformed; and
it registers a Bernardine rhythm that contributes to the poem's profoundest
sense of *conversio*. In this Christ that 'may'st know mee,' we can trace elements
of the native Augustinian tradition found in the *Holy Sonnets* and indebted
to Franciscan spirituality with its high-pitched affective response to the Passion.[35] Donne's concluding lines in 'Goodfriday' give us a latter-day cognate
for the Franciscan Jacopone da Todi's cry in *De Passione Domini*, a work once
attributed to Bernard himself:[36] 'in hac tua passione / me agnosce, pastor
bone.'[37] Bernard's thoroughgoing influence on the Franciscan tradition[38] leads
to the theological assumptions of *agnosce me*,[39] which Donne would also have
encountered through his broad acquaintance with Bernard's works. In these
assumptions are a rich suggestiveness for Donne's intentions in 'Goodfriday.'

In *Sermons on the Song of Songs*, Bernard's explication of 'knowing' or
'recognizing' the Image leads to the broader stretches of his thought. His
commentary on this mystical text describes God's relationship to the human
soul in his chronicle of the marriage between the Bride soul and the Bridegroom Word. By turning to wander away, its Image of God now defaced,
its conformity with God's will destroyed, the sinful soul substitutes deformity
for its created likeness to God.[40] Donne's accents co-ordinate broadly with
Bernard's: Christ at the centre, the sinner wandering in the distance, having
admitted worldly competition from 'Pleasure or businesse' (7) or, as Bernard
also has it, 'taken captive by the allurements of sinful pleasure' (captam il-
lecebris) or 'absorbed in businesse' (distentam negotiis).[41] To love the incarnate Word in this suffering model of humility, perceived first by reason then
recalled by memory, is to reform the deformed and bent will and restore the
lost likeness to God. Wandering from God, like John Donne westward riding
in 'Goodfriday,' the soul must 'turn' to efface the soul's deformity, to redis-
cover the likeness to him, man's Creator. Purification rebuilds conformity
between man's will and God's. From Etienne Gilson's rendering of Bernard's
notion, we can adapt our own parallels to Donne's use of the notion in
'Goodfriday.' Through purification the soul recovers 'its lost likeness.' God
can now 'recognize Himself in it once more' and 'dwell on it with compla-
cence.' Just as he loves himself, he loves his 'image and likeness,' which is,
'as it were, another self.'[42] The Word can recognize again God's Image in the
human soul, made according to God's real Image, the Word itself. Like will
'know' like. The Bridegroom shall 'rejoice over the Bride, because knowledge
and love are reciprocal between them.'[43] As Donne says to Christ, 'thou may'st
know mee.'

In 'Goodfriday' Christ's recognition of the restored Image agrees with another ingredient in Bernard's understanding of 'know,' which bonds Christ's suffering to the invited corrective affliction of the speaker. The sinner John Donne can be known only when suffering, and here we touch the poem's emotional and thematic heart. In Bernard's *The Steps of Humility*, a work influential in both the *Holy Sonnets*, as we have seen in Chapter Six, and the sermons (*Sermons*, V, 346), Bernard offers one divine motive for Incarnation in that God, knowing human misery only 'by nature from eternity,' had to learn it 'in time by experience.'[44] Likeness works two directions. To become like man, Christ needed human flesh for the experience of misery, that man would become more like him. In suffering is expressed the right form for human existence: 'From the things which he suffered, therefore, we learn how we who are mere men ought to suffer patiently for the sake of obedience, for which he who was also God did not hesitate to die.'[45] In 'Goodfriday,' Christ can 'know' and teach only suffering man, namely John Donne reminded by affliction of his necessary suffering. An implicit irony rides with Donne away from Christ in his evasion of misery consequent to his sin. He needs God's reminder through more suffering. The suffering as a condition of mortal life to be understood experientially by any who would understand mortality becomes the instrument that bends the selfish will. Mutual suffering in the same pattern, the man 'humbled' like the God (25), violated in flesh and blood, remakes the likeness between the human Image and the Word, when both man and Christ are both knower and known. And the 'backe' turned willingly for the punishing rod includes the physical as well as the spiritual self.

The drama of the suffering Word, who 'turns' the averted sinner, sounds the poem's metaphysical depth. For suffering, as means to turn the soul, expresses not just a psychological or a penitential principle, but also a metaphysical principle of turning likewise expressed in the Christ whose hands 'turne all spheares' (22).[46] The notion of turning holds together the forces of repentance, redemption, and creation; and there is a rich Christian tradition of the God who turns the human soul as well as the universe. To annotate this God who turns the spheres in 'Goodfriday,' A.J. Smith points to medieval graphic art, in particular a Pisan fresco depicting the universe as concentric circles in a series: 'God appears at the top as First Mover, with his arms spread wide to encompass the whole and his hands clearly gripping the entire system of spheres at either side. His attitude is just that of Christ on the Cross.'[47] Donne's poem in joining these same two divine functions, the suffering Person and the creating and sustaining Power, to a third, the Judge who corrects, purifies and absolves, gives detail to 'turning' as one aspect of God's nature. In Old Testament penitential texts lies the basis from which Donne, like his Protestant contemporaries, evokes turning as an activity assimilating human and divine motions.[48] A Donne sermon on Psalm 6:4–5 ('*Returne, O Lord; Deliver my soule*, etc.') counterpoints the turning motions respectively of God and man:

So that this Returning of the Lord, is an Operative, an Effectual returning, that turnes our hearts, and eyes, and hands, and feet to the wayes of God, and produces in us Repentance, and Obedience. (*Sermons*, v, 369)

For man the turning is penitential conversion; for God it is the return through mercy that ends just anger and parallels God's return to man through the Sacrament: 'he returnes to us in this place, as often as he maketh us partakers of his flesh, and his bloud, in the blessed Sacrament' (*Sermons*, v, 368). In this same sermon the astronomical correspondence, the sun's daily return, is fitted to the standard divine pun called forth in 'Goodfriday' ('a Sunne, by rising set,' 11):

... This son fils him, and fits him, compasses him, and disposes him, does all the offices of the Sun, seasonably, opportunely, maturely, for the nourishing of his soule, according to the severall necessities thereof. And this is Gods returning to us, in a generall apprehension; After he hath made us, and blest us in our nature, and by his naturall meanes, he returnes to make us againe, to make us better, first by his pre-venting grace, and then by a succession of his particular graces. (*Sermons*, v, 367)

The incarnate Word, the human soul, and the sun all have turning movements that follow rhythms in God's own nature, with the suffering God-man as the bond of likeness that, through a pattern for penitential turning, conforms man to God. Like movements harmonize the rhythms of Creator, Redeemer, and believer. Thus, penitential turning fulfils the believer's life in time in accordance with metaphysical principle.

Another possible resonance in the metaphysical notion of turning that strengthens the poem is notably consistent with the poem's Augustinian character. For Augustine *conversio* is the integral movement of Creation, the Fall, and Redemption. The kernel is that Creation itself involved *conversio*; the Fall, subsequently, *aversio*; and the Crucifixion, the re-establishment of the individual soul's *conversio* back to God. Interest in the literal and spiritual meanings of Creation distinguishes Augustine's works. In *De Genesi Ad Lit-teram* he sets out his metaphysical notion of *conversio*, giving two crucial stages in the Genesis account of Creation: first, creation of unformed matter, both spiritual and physical ('In the beginning God created the heaven and the earth') and, second, information of both kinds calling them to himself that they be 'turned' to him. To receive form, *conversio*, is to receive illumination. When God said, 'Let there be light,' he was turning the unformed matter to himself for informing: 'cum dictum est, *In principio fecit Deus coelum et terram*: ut quod *dixit Deus, Fiat lux; et facta est lux*, eam revocante ad se Creatore, conversio ejus facta atque illuminata intelligatur.'[49] The informing light – 'Fiat lux' – is the Logos, the eternal Word, the Son. Any creature when formed, spiritual or physical, becomes like the Word: but this resemblance disappears when the creature turns away from the Word:

In qua conversione et formatione, quia pro suo modo imitatur Deum Verbum, hoc est Dei Filium semper Patri cohaerentem, plena similitudine et essentia pari, qua ipse et Pater unum sunt (Joan. x, 30); non autem imitatur hanc Verbi formam, si aversa a Creatore, informis et imperfecta remaneat ...[50]

The important point: *conversio* fulfils Creation, *aversio* reverses it. The Fall rejects the basic metaphysical principle of Creation, *conversio*, and in this *aversio*, this turning away from God, all Creation, angelic, human, subhuman, was affected. Only through the Word again, this time through the Incarnate Christ, can the very principle of creation, of *conversio*, be reaffirmed.

Rough parallels in the background inspirit Donne's poem without binding him to the Augustinian letter. The hands that 'turne all spheares' are the Creator's hands, the illuminating Logos that informs and sustains existence. Likewise, these same hands would repair the damage caused by *aversio*, the cracked 'footstool' (20) of Nature, the winking sun, any damage to the heavenly spheres, as well as damage to the 'Spheare' (1) of the human soul. Donne's Christ, a turner of spheres, resembles Augustine's illuminating Logos, that 'Sunne' (11) who forms the world in Creation, who sustains it as the principle of order, and who reforms it by his death and resurrection: 'There I should see a Sunne, by rising set, / And by that setting endlesse day beget' (11–12). Donne's Christ as a turner of spheres stretches Donne's context to include his own personal turning, while riding into Wales on Good Friday, within a cosmic principle of *conversio* that joins Creation and Redemption.

Thus, the poem dramatizes Donne's participation in the continuing principle of conversion. His physical movement westward for pleasure or business, by opposing the eastward movement of the soul, establishes the tension between *aversio* and *conversio* that characterizes the fallen believer. He must continually seek a penitential conversion ever incomplete in a mortal world; for, although his westward movement will reach the East at his death, it expresses paradoxically the *aversio* in this life toward the nothingness of sin.

Donne's request for punishing corrections, to be humbled in the pattern of the suffering Christ, is the ultimate means of dissolving this tension between *aversio* and *conversio*. Yet the tension must remain until death, a live principle of Christian penitential psychology that determines the interplay between the members of the tripartite soul. To sum up the effect of the poem is to concentrate upon the desired likeness in suffering between the believer and Christ that will reform those faculties in conformity with the very principles of being. The penitential suffering of affliction is the way of turning, and turning is the way of fulfilling life in time.

8

Considering the Moment:
Devotions upon Emergent Occasions

The virulent illness in *Devotions upon Emergent Occasions* answers Donne's earlier requests that God enter the circle of time to batter and burn through affliction. Nowhere in Donne's works does he express so explicitly his understanding that time is the medium of salvation and that suffering is its temporal mode. And nowhere does he examine at such length the temporal motions of rational consciousness in response to bodily experience. The events of the illness excite reason's bright attention to 'consider' the events of bodily affliction as God's catechistical correction. However, each moment in time suffers from the perplexities caused by man's composite nature of body and soul and by his relationship to the communal Body. The considerate soul must find in the body's experience not only the evidence of its own sin and God's favour, but also the immediate implications of his participation in the Body. The assurance with which Donne concludes the *Devotions* is achieved when he comprehends how his affliction in time, by enhancing his conformity with Christ, is an essential tie to both God and other men.

This understanding is not achieved easily, owing to the motions of time itself; and much in the *Devotions* is concerned with finding the principles of temporal order in his immediate experience. The basic premise in his consideration of time is the traditional conception that time is the measure of motion.[1] Unfortunately, time's weltering crosscurrents and unexpected events disturb the struggle to find lines of continuity. The psychosomatic complications, the 'cold Melancholy' attending his 'hote fever,' reflect the confusions of time by unexpectedly accelerating the illness: 'O perplex'd discomposition, O ridling distemper, O miserable condition of Man' ('1. Meditation,' p. 8). Likewise, the differing orders of body and soul, encouraging different temporal paces, tangle that perplexity further. The swift vicissitudes of bodily illness not only contradict the constant tempos of both heavenly and earthly motions, but also follow motions starkly counterpointed to the soul's as well: 'My *body* falls downe without pushing, my *Soule* does not go up without pulling: *Ascension* is my *Soules* pace & measure, but *precipitation* my *bodies*' ('2. Meditation,' p. 11). And then there is the swift change in his bodily movements that violates his human desire for comprehensible order in the motions of body and soul. Discerning God's motive in that swiftness perplexes Donne further. The same God responsible for these changes waited one hundred and twenty years before flooding Noah's generation, but then comes hard upon Donne in an instant.

At first, Donne does not tame his shock by finding in time itself the orderly principles that can bestow governance over temporal motions or even cure his human vulnerability to further shock; rather, he perceives in the very perplexities of shock certain reference points to special events of divine intervention, such as resurrection, that make his experience less alarming. God's hand in Donne's swift illness approximates the divine power which will be manifested even more mysteriously at the resurrection in the 'hast, & dispatch, which my *God* shal use, in recollecting, reuniting this *dust* againe at the *Resurrection*' ('2. Expostulation,' p. 13). Paradoxically, this greater mystery assures him of God's attending power and ends his shock. But it is not swiftness as a comprehensible measure of time which reassures him, but recognition that God, for man's benefit, can ignore human expectations to intervene in time. In short, temporal motions continue to perplex his human comprehension.

Nonetheless, a desire remains to find the principles of order and continuity in God's tempos which move the human composite, that '*Watch*' with 'many various wheels in the faculties of the Soule, and in the organs of the body' ('1. Expostulation,' p. 9). The watch, by definition a means to measure comprehensible motions, must find God moving its wheels, 'proceeding' ('2. Prayer,' p. 13) in time according to established paradigms. For example, God reveals himself in the corrected believer, just as he revealed himself to Moses in the burning bush and later in the Incarnation ('2. Prayer,' p. 14), to be perceived in the mind's consideration. Similarly, Donne in attempting to understand the onset of this sickness, requests that God aid him in a backward look, to consider his mercy in Donne's various 'beginnings,' his election and his membership in the church; these beginnings are the model for a 'holy consideration' of God's mercy in the beginning of all Donne's actions here, and for Donne's desire to heed God's voice at the beginning of all sinfulness ('1. Prayer,' p. 10). To consider the immediate pattern of God's intervention is to insure the proper function of the human 'watch.'

Finding these patterns can be problematical. One reason is that the soul's consideration makes all events in time vivid. Shocking collisions between the expected and the unexpected are not inherently more immediate and vivid than orderly events, although they may cause considerably more tension. Another reason is that temporal motion and man's perception of it are deranged by unruliness in nature, caused by effects of the Fall or divine miracle, and by unexpectedness in the realm of Grace, owing to the darkness of God's motives. Yet another reason is that the experience of shock does not guarantee an actual violation of order, since the lineaments of order may remain undiscovered by the considering soul. The soul's inability to accommodate easily all temporal motions contradicts neither the Providential hand that Donne finds directing his illness nor the traces of Providential order framing all temporal events.

Yet the soul's struggle to find these abiding patterns that penetrate the immediate moment is obligatory. In fact, the whole of time, with its beginning, middle, and end, can be found in the given moment. That assumption explains Donne's interpretation of the pivotal 'criticall dayes' in the fourteenth devotion. In response to his physicians' determinations that his illness has reached its critical days, he first questions the substantiality of time. With supporting echoes from Augustine's examination of time in the *Confessions*,[2] he wittily argues that time is nothing:

but if we consider *Tyme* to be but the *Measure of Motion*, and howsoever it may seeme to have three *stations*, *past*, *present* and *future*, yet the *first* and *last* of these *are* not (one is not, now, & the other is not yet) And that which you call *present*, is not *now* the same that it was ...

Nonetheless, he acknowledges that this '*Nothing*, *Tyme*' is the medium of value which '*inanimates*, and *informes*' it ('14. Meditation,' pp. 71–2). That every value has its critical day, its time of fruition, excites the urgency of time, creating this 'Nothing' into something. Donne fulfils his discussion in the expostulation by locating the full seven days of Creation, the basic paradigm for historical time, in any 'criticall day' in time. That is, he has repeated *creatio ex nihilo*, in accordance with the original temporal pattern of seven days, by considering the dimensions of the immediate moment.

The elastic term 'criticall dayes,' in taking into itself the full week of Creation, expresses Donne's conception of Providential time. In requesting that God inspire a '*Crisis*, a *Judgement*' in this critical day, Donne stretches the categories of time to include God's and man's respective relationships to time: 'Since *a day is as a thousand yeres with thee*, Let, O Lord, a *day*, be as a *weeke* to me; and in this one, let me consider *seven daies*, seven *critical daies*, and *judge my selfe, that I be not judged by thee*' ('14. Expostulation,' pp. 74–5). God will help him consider how this immediate event, this moment in his illness, dilates in meaning beyond itself, first to mean the illness itself, then his whole life,[3] then providential history as a new week of Creation. Consideration can find in the present both the past and also the future events that guarantee Donne's salvation: 1 / 'thy *visitation* by sicknes'; 2 / 'light, and testimony of my *Conscience*'; 3 / 'preparing, & fitting my selfe for a more especial *receiving* of thy *Sonne* in his institution of the *Sacrament*'; 4 / 'my *dissolution* & *transmigration* from hence'; 5 / 'my *Resurrection*'; 6 / '*The day of Judgement*'; 7 / 'my *Everlasting Saboth* in thy rest, thy glory, thy joy, thy sight, thy selfe' ('14. Expostulation,' pp. 75–6). The beginning of the illness, like any event in time, even when recalled later, begins a consideration how personal time is absorbed into the saving rhythms of Providential time, which orders the experience of all men.

Thus, as Donne extends the possible meaning of 'criticall dayes,' we glimpse further rooms in his conception of temporal consciousness and, hence, the temporal form of the *Devotions*. Just as the fulfilled moment can express a whole life and its potential, the fourteenth devotion, in its week of seven critical days, enunciates the temporal format for the whole work. Through consideration, these seven 'days' literally recreate this moment according to the paradigm of Creation; thus, if God should exercise his fearful prerogative to end Donne's life at this moment, his act of recreation promises that his life, in fact, would conform to that very pattern. Gerard Cox argues that the clearly enumerated seven critical days in the fourteenth devotion are by no means discrete; rather, they recapitulate Donne's progress in the *Devotions* thus far and, Cox contends, preview the emphases extending through the eighteenth devotion. Consideration of the first three critical days has already occurred: first, the 'visitation' of the disease; second, the 'testimony' of the conscience; third, the physicians' remedies or cordials, that remind Donne of the cordial, the Sacrament ('11. Devotion,' pp. 56–61). The remaining four 'days' follow the fourteenth devotion: the fourth in the seventeenth devotion, when the death bells remind Donne of his own death; fifth, in the eighteenth devotion to Donne's prayer that the dead man and other believers meet at the resurrection, to be followed, sixth, by Christ's performing his 'office' as judge, after which, seventh, time will end and man will enjoy rest in God's glory.[4]

Cox discovers a crucial principle of coherence in the *Devotions*, although his argument needs teasing further since the seven 'critical days' inform the larger work less programmatically and more pervasively than he indicates.

For example, a suggestive difference separates Donne's renditions of the third critical day: in the fourteenth expostulation Donne speaks directly about the Sacrament; but in the eleventh meditation the actual event is the physicians' ministrations. Clearly, our approach there must be figurative, not literal. On the other hand, Cox ignores Donne's figurative rendition of the fifth critical day, the resurrection, in the twenty-first expostulation when the convalescent Donne rises from his bed: 'This *Resurrection* of my *body*, shewes me the *Resurrection* of my *soule*; and both *here* severally, of both together hereafter' ('21. Expostulation,' p. 112). Similarly, in the nineteenth devotion Donne's anticipation of restitution admits its figurative relationship to the eternal sabbath of rest, joy, and glory: 'yet since thou hast now of thy goodnesse afforded that, which affords us some hope, if that bee still *the way* of thy *glory*, proceed in *that way*, and perfit *that worke*, and establish me in a *Sabbath*, and *rest* in *thee*, by this thy *seale* of *bodily restitution*.' This promised sabbath, Donne tells us, will conclude his illness, hence paralleling the 'Creation of this *world*,' when God 'continuedst *day* to *day*' until perfecting his work and establishing the rest and Sabbath in God ('19. Prayer,' p. 103).

Clearly, the seven-day *schema* in the fourteenth expostulation informs but does not impose a heavy hand on the whole *Devotions*. It is the salvational design for every Christian believer, to be realized in time with God's help and concluded in eternity. To find God's hand actively imprinting one's experience, both literally and figuratively according to this saving pattern, is to have grown enough spiritually to participate in it. Accordingly, to consider that the body's resurrection from illness prefigures resurrection to glory is to achieve the assurance that deserves that reward. It is fitting, and no doubt intentional, that Donne explicitly distils this recreational format in the middle of the *Devotions*, although, as Cox notes, he has yet to address specifically all seven critical days. The present must contain the past and the future; it must distil the whole generic pattern in the moment. But the present is personal as well as generic; and the *Devotions* follows the events of Donne's illness, leaving Donne, as an exercise in his own salvation, to scrutinize how each event exists within the generic pattern.

In a word, God set the original pattern during Creation and now inspires the events that enable believers to complete it. This closely Providential sense of time and history co-ordinates the Protestant typological arteries in Donne's thought described by Barbara Lewalski.[5] Just as New Testament fulfilment of Old Testament types is recapitulated in the individual believer in time, his own immediate experience now prefigures his fulfilment in Glory, through God's help. Such pervasive Providential control plays an active role throughout personal and universal history. Donne's conception of typology invests time with a crucial importance that incarnates all value, past, present, and future, in the immediate moment within the believer.

There are two legs that hold up Donne's typological conception of divine history. First, the soul necessarily must consider its participation in typological development. Proper human action in time assumes both the 'watch' and the motions of Grace. Man can recapitulate types of salvational history and prefigure his own fulfilment in glory only if he consciously recognizes this salvational design in his own experience. Second, the typological arteries reestablish history according to the original Creational pattern, hence are contained by it. Progressive revelation of God in the burning bush, then the Incarnate Word in Mary's womb, then in the heart of the believer recreates a fallen order. For his part, the believer must strive against *utter darknesse, ignorance of thee*, or *inconsideration of my selfe* as his part in recreation; he must consider the Spirit's *overshadowing* in order to illuminate his darkness ('14. Prayer,' pp. 76–7).

At this point we need to look more closely at Donne's notion of consideration, for its role in recreating historical time underlines its central importance in the *Devotions*. As a process of reason,[6] Donne's 'consideration' reveals its kinship to Protestant meditational practices recognized as a context for the *Devotions*. Misdirected efforts to find Ignatian parallels for Donne's *Devotions* have been cleaned away by recognition that the individual devotions do not begin with the *compositio loci* by the imagination, either a replay of remembered Biblical events or a fictive dramatization featuring the sinner himself; rather, each devotion begins with a sharp-eyed rational scrutiny of immediate physical events as a basis for stimulating the affections. Moreover, Barbara Lewalski has noted areas of contact between the *Devotions* and two forms of contemporary Protestant meditation, combined for the first time in the *Devotions*: first, the set piece, ' "deliberate" meditation upon doctrines and religious topics' and, second ' "extemporall" meditation upon occasions offered by the natural world.'[7] U. Milo Kaufmann finds the source of such meditational forms in the works of Bishop Joseph Hall, whom Lewalski suggests as a probable influence on Donne. Kaufmann notes that Hall's carefully plotted rational forms, sharply focused by importing the 'heads of argumentation' ('description, division, causes, fruits and effects, the subject wherein or whereabout it is, appendances and qualities, contraries, comparisons and similitudes, titles and names, testimonies') detailed Hall's desire for a 'thorough examination of the topic at hand' before stimulating the affections.[8] Hall's titles for these sections (e.g., 'Chap. xxi.-4. The consideration of the fruits and effects'; 'Chap. xxii.-5. Consideration of the subject wherein or whereabout it is')[9] clearly put consideration in reason's domain and establish one context for understanding the frequency of 'consideration' in the *Devotions*.

Although Donne could agree with Hall's emphasis on rational consideration as the ground swell of religious devotion, Donne's *Devotions* lacks both Hall's analytical architecture and his compartmentalization of reason and the affections. Nonetheless, Donne's first prayer clearly assumes consideration's role in man's conversation with God. Donne invokes the aid of God:

> enable me by thy *grace*, to looke forward to mine end, and to looke backward to, to the considerations of thy mercies afforded mee from the beginning; that so by that practise of considering thy mercy, in my beginning in this world; ... I may come to a holy consideration of thy *mercy*, in the beginning of all my actions here ...

Such considerations strengthens him for his concluding request, that God deliver him from vain fears about the beginnings of illness and every 'offer of Sin' ('1. Prayer,' p. 9). By no means restrained by the more categorical role described by Hall, this rational cogitation necessarily operates throughout meditation, expostulation, and prayer.

Donne's notion becomes more clear if we examine the relationship of consideration to expostulation, also conceived as a rational process. By formalizing expostulation, Donne reveals his willingness to tailor devotional form to fit his own temperament. Though expostulation was not uncommon in Christian devotion, often in the strains of Job, Jeremiah, Jonah, and the crucified Christ, Donne's bold formal innovation sets our responses to the whole work. Biblical precedent notwithstanding, Donne confesses the risks: expostulation can easily drift into murmuring that denies God's will ('10. Meditation,' p. 52). Yet these 'Expostulations, and Debatements with God,' as Donne's title page calls them, necessarily bring man and God into communion, on one hand honouring the vast gulf between human and divine comprehension that encourages human complaint, and, on the other hand, inciting precisely such a desire to comprehend God's motivations.

Expostulation is quite natural in a belief that views medicinal affliction as a primary means of divine statement. Illness aggrieves; its events require explication; and the 'debatement' of the aggrieved sufferer follows in turn. Donne's God allows, to the point of encouraging, the expostulator's search to find the reasons for both God's actions and his own condition.[10] This is Job's road, risking excessive complaint to '*reason with God*' ('14. Expostulation,' p. 21). Elsewhere, Donne enlists similar support from Isaiah 1:18: 'Come and *reason* with God, *argue, plead, dispute, expostulate* with *God*, come upon any conditions' (*Sermons*, VII, 88).

Characteristically, Donne tightens his rational grasp, in the uncertainties of both affliction and doctrine. Implicit faith can only loosen that grasp; thus, 'some deliberation, some consultation in our selves' as well as 'some expostulation with God himselfe,' may be excusable in us' (*Sermons*, VIII, 132). The rational processes of consideration, deliberation, and expostulation modulate naturally into one another; 'debatement' with God, however charged with affection, bent toward chiding or rebuke, or slowed by confusion, is all part of the mind's rational consideration. From the meditation to the ex-postulation, consideration turns from the 'humane condition' to conduct the debate with God, which seeks his reasons in Donne's illness.

Striking in its persistence, consideration controls the psychology of the *Devotions*. Man believes, suffers, considers; God attends, corrects, assures. Consideration is a 'minde' that vivifies the soul through 'an Actuation, an Application of the faculties of the soule to particulars' (*Sermons*, VI, 314). Unrelenting rational attention keeps the soul nervously ready for the emergent particulars of physical and spiritual existence, disregarding artificial barriers of meditation, expostulation, and prayer. The informative parallels between Protestant devotions and the *Devotions* end here. What Kaufmann calls the 'line of Hall,'[11] first reason's close order, then the stimulated affections, does not resemble closely enough how rational consideration animates the *Devotions*. Although Hall's emphasis upon reason's priority in devotional life is happily congenial to Donne's whole epistemology and psychology, the vivacity of Donne's 'consideration' suggests deeper, more traditional roots.

Here, as with other important elements in Donne's thought, his interest in Bernard of Clairvaux helps to clarify his basic assumptions. Certainly, some general similarities are suggestive enough. Donne's basic epistemological pro-gression from sense to reason to faith, at work in the *Devotions*, from sensory event to rational consideration to prayerful assurance, closely parallels Ber-nard's satisfaction of man's sense, then his reason, then his will.[12] Donne's debt to Bernard's *De Consideratione* in a 1625 sermon invites a close scrutiny of more particular similarities relating to reason's role in this epistemological framework: 'S. Bernard proposes three wayes for our apprehending Divine things: first, understanding, which relies upon reason; faith, which relies upon supreme Authority; and opinion, which relies upon probability, and verisimilitude' (*Sermons*, VI, 317).[13] Bernard's notion, that understanding, faith, and opinion are all forms of rational consideration, serves Donne in a sermon emphasizing reason's importance in perceiving and defending divine truth against false opinion. The problem for Donne, as for Bernard, is not bringing reason onto alien ground, in consideration, but simply holding it to its proper responsibility.

Consideration as the constant in opinion, faith, and understanding is important in Bernard's basic religious psychology. In *De Consideratione*, his long letter-treatise to Pope Eugenius, he defines consideration as the 'intense (intensa) exercise of thought in inquiry, or as an intense application (intentio) of the mind to the investigation of truth.'[14] As distinct from memory or will, reason's basic function is 'intention,' and 'consideration' is its basic form.[15] Donne's sense of consideration as rational attentiveness is a sympathetic parallel. An earlier sermon shows even more telling Bernardine markings: 'That which St. *Bernard* fear'd in *Eugenius*, when he came to be Pope, and so to a distraction of many worldly businesses, may much more be fear'd in a distraction of many sins, *Cave ne te trahant, quo non vis*; Take heed lest these sins carry thee farther, then thou intendest; thou intendest but Pleasure, or Profit; but the sin will carry thee farther' (*Sermons*, I, 180). In Bernard's fears, that Eugenius's rational 'intention' would be diverted, Donne clearly recognized Bernard's understanding of human psychology: 'consideration' was constant, but not its good habits.

The topical nature of Bernard's letter bears on its relationship to Donne's *Devotions*. Guided by a clear sense that life must be all of a piece, the letter gives practical, timely, tough-minded advice about the competitive demands of worldly action and spirituality. Bernard advises a 'four fold object of consideration' that dictates the formal structure of his letter; the 'objects' are respectively 'thou thyself, things beneath thee, things about thee, things above thee.'[16] Bernard's tough practicality, as ready to goad the Pope's understanding of himself, his role, and others as it is to incite him to consider God and the angels, guides attention from low to high, outer to inner, and advises a heightened awareness in all occasions. Just as consideration bears all responsibility for heightened existence in time, it is also necessary for contemplation leading to mystical refreshment. Though exiled in the world of action and necessarily engaged with material realities, consideration can through proper 'application to sensible objects'[17] also return to its natural sphere of contemplation, which Bernard treats in his fifth section. Thus, consideration guides the essential Bernardine epistemology, first the bodily senses, then gradual movement inward, through the self to mystical love and contemplation of God. But consideration can actively cross and recross those borders between sensible and spiritual, action and contemplation. Similarly, Donne's 'consideration,' placed in time, sees each event in his illness first as a material, then as a spiritual reality that engages penitential self-examination and knowledge of God, then as an occasion for prayerful communion with him.

Neither such specific influence from Bernard nor a broadly conceived role for 'consideration' in Donne need surprise us. Like Augustine, Bernard was directly influential on both sides of the theological fence, Protestant and Catholic; and we can find informative parallels to Donne's notion in Luis de Granada's widely published and influential *Of Prayer and Meditation*. Like Donne, Luis positions consideration at the heart of the devotional life. 'The verie thynge that moued me to treat of this matter was, for that I vnderstode, that one of the principall cawses of all the euilles, that be in the world, is the want of consideration.'[18] For him the devotional life, properly ordered, guarantees the constancy of consideration necessary for belief and virtue. To those who need encouragement for meditation and prayer, he recommends Bernard's 'fiue bookes of consideration' written to Pope Eugenius.[19] In *De Consideratione* he finds help in establishing his essentially Thomistic grasp of understanding as the foundation of the virtuous and affectionate life. He depicts consideration as the 'greater helper and furtherer of all other vertues,'[20] which, since they are 'affective virtues,' provoke good works. Consideration stands to affective virtues, including 'devotion,' as reason to the will. Attentively, it ponders, chews, searches, weighs, illuminates. Here, as in Donne and Bernard, we find the core of devotional consciousness, the rational attention of consideration that finds in its own constancy the means of completing the soul's responsibility.

The obvious difference in purpose between Donne's personal devotion, on one hand, and the objective formality of Bernard and Luis, on the other hand, recapitulates much said thus far. A pedagogical stance explains form in the latter two works. And, significantly, we would find the straightforward treatise an unlikely form for Donne. Instead, the *Devotions* literally enacts the role of consideration in the devotional life, while both Bernard and Luis formally and explicitly examine its relevance. The *Devotions*, however, allows no distance between the events in time and considering them. The soul's rational motions become part of the events themselves. Like Bernard, Donne assumes that consideration vivifies both action and contemplation; and for Donne it pervades the patterns of temporal life, thus stepping through any rigid boundaries between areas of existence or within devotion itself. The *Devotions* simply follows the thrust of Donne's deeply felt assumption that human existence is lived on the circumference of time's circle and, to fulfil time, to fill the circle, is to tighten the screws of the soul's attention until the erected soul finds in the temporal motions of its own immediate experience the saving patterns of Creation.

Two remaining elements in Donne's vivid temporal consciousness distinguish his notion of time in the *Devotions*. First, the demands of fulfilled time require that he recognize how his immediate bodily experience is implicated in the social Body, both the kingdom and the Church, even when he is secluded on a sick bed. Like Bernard and Luis, Donne intends his work to enter his community; more important, he sees that community actively contributing to its contents. Second, Donne's notion of time assumes that only penitential suffering, which conforms him to both God and man, sharpens the cutting edge of consideration as the means of fulfilling time. Accordingly, throughout the *Devotions* we find Donne sharply considering his bodily suffering, as well as its relationship to the community.

Donne keeps the body clearly in our mind's eye, the central datum in the material world. Thereby, both God, by giving the illness, and Donne, by interpreting its events, communicate to us. For Donne physical experience cannot be understood fully unless we understand the body's correspondences to the communal Body; thus, what happens to any member physically somehow speaks to other participating members as well. Just as a child's baptism or a member's death speaks to the experience of all members, so do the events of Donne's illness. In that specific death bell heard by Donne in the seventeenth devotion, God 'calls us all' who are 'involved in *Mankinde*'; for, 'by this consideration of anothers danger, I take mine owne into Contemplation' ('17. Meditation,' pp. 86–7). Likewise, the *Devotions* implicitly calls readers to consider their own spiritual illness and penitential suffering through involvement in Donne's. If God speaks through Donne's illness, then Donne's recreation can be fulfilled only in such effects of his illness on others. The considered moment, as the fulfilment of time, must dilate through self-awareness into the experience shared with others; Donne must recognize God's purposeful use of other members of the Body, such as the physician, in the events of the illness that catechize Donne and others through him. Donne's prolonged scrutiny here of personal events offers the vividly personal as the keenest realization of what is commonly held; and the suffering body, in the mind's eye, merging personal and communal experience, reminds us that penitential suffering considered in a participatory community of believers further describes Donne's conception of fulfilled time.

The essential link in Donne's thought between the traditional notion of the microcosm and macrocosm and his notion of epistemological progress, from the senses to reason to will, is nowhere more clearly rehearsed than in the *Devotions*. Leonard Barkan points out that the microcosm-macrocosm notion in its late maturity caused uneasiness, owing not to scepticism about its validity, but to uncertainty about man's ability to assess properly the highly articulated network of correspondences.[21] Donne holds tenaciously to this received notion, anxiously straining to assess how immediate events in either the microcosm or macrocosm should apply to the other. Further to Barkan's analysis, it needs to be noted that, for Donne, events in the body or the natural world or the social Body all occur as events in some physical medium to be perceived initially by the senses, but within the network of correspondences to be understood by reason. These correspondences between Donne's human body and the social Body, either the Church or the kingdom, point clearly to Donne's participation in the mystical Body as the individual's fulfilling reality.

This assumption emerges clearly in the correspondence between the heart in the body and the king in the kingdom. To protect the heart from the disease's venom, the physicians use cordials; and Donne observes that the heart, though most crucial to life, is more vulnerable to disease than either the liver or the brain. The heart is a strict parallel with the king, likewise the target of the 'venime & poyson of every pestilentiall disease,' of the *malignity* of ill men' ('11. Meditation,' p. 57). When considering pestilential vapours in his body, Donne darkens the lines of emphasis, for such 'pestilent, and infectious fumes' in the body are like *infectious rumors* in any *Politike body* or state. And the 'whole body' of the state suffers when these infectious vapours are aimed at *Noble parts* such as the king, its head, or the council, its brain ('12. Meditation,' pp. 63–4).

These correspondences between Donne's body and the kingdom assume his indigenous relationship to his community, introduced in an earlier comparison between kings, subjects, and God ('2. Expostulation,' p. 12) and forcefully developed when King James sends his personal physician. Like the holy French king Louis, the English Maud, and the empress Lucilla, James aids the sick Donne *as a fellow member of the body of thy Son, with them.* The comparison between James and David is similarly explicit: 'So thy servant *David* ... incorporates himselfe in his people, by calling them *his brethren, his bones, his flesh*' ('8. Expostulation,' p. 43). Donne's conception of King and Body is charged with personal history; and the correspondences between the physical and political 'hearts' are quickened by the vital memory that King James bore responsibility for Donne's taking up his Calling. Godlike, since kings are 'in' God and he 'in' them, James also becomes Christlike in sending his physician to heal Donne, an act cognate with encouraging Donne to take orders. Moreover, Donne assumes, James knows that his own participation in Christ's Body, the Church, is the signature of his own health as the kingly heart of his kingdom. Donne's belief that this king is the 'greatst upon earth' ('8. Prayer,' p. 45) straitens the fear that 'diseases' in the state may reach the kingly Heart of that political Body. Thus, Donne's fears about his own body have reminded him of a shared reality; his double consciousness of self and its shared awareness of community precludes a separation of the self from its Calling in the Body. The membership of Donne's individual body in the King's and Christ's Bodies necessarily bestows importance on the events of his illness.

Significantly, many stations of Donne's illness involve his community. The doctor arrives and is afraid; he sends for medical colleagues; the king sends his personal physician; the doctors give varied remedies; the death bells ring; the doctors warn against relapse. One movement in the *Devotions* is toward a fuller understanding of Donne's involvement. Early on, he expostulates with God for removing him from his 'calling' ('3. Expostulation,' p. 17) and laments his '*Solitude*' as illness's 'greatest misery.' This solitude blocks necessary conformity with God, angels, and men, who are all social by nature. God's 'plurality of persons' expresses a '*figure of Society*'; heaven has '*Orders of Angels*, and *Armies of Martyrs*'; and earth has '*Families, Cities, Churches, Colleges*' ('5. Meditation,' p. 25). Donne gradually dissolves the anguish of physical separation and tames his expostulation, now dangerously close to murmuring, by recognizing his continuing participation in the community. His most immediate link is his 'helper' the doctor, who fulfils the pattern of Eve's help to Adam. Then, he recognizes that God may call for man's service in unexpected ways. He asks that God '*work*' his salvation and '*declare*' it to the Militant Church ('5. Prayer,' p. 28). Donne's illness may fulfil his role in doing God's will. In the *Devotions* the record of the illness and his response will speak to the community.

The allusion to Adam and Eve is closely tied to Donne's psychology of community. Traditional paradigms for the many in the one – human marriage, the tripartite God, the social Body, the human composite of body and soul – give local forms to the mutual suffusion of individual consciousness and the strong sense of community. Fulfilled life is a movement toward conformity with God, and with other men through God, allowing a selfhood that must remind itself of essential unifying likeness. Just as God ordained a conformity between husband and wife ('20. Prayer,' p. 109), he likewise desires 'conformable affections' ('6. Prayer,' p. 34) between members of the Body; and all communal patterns are advised by conformity between Christ and his Body, and between the tripartite soul and the tripartite God. The *Devotions* manifests such designs of conformity within the psychology of membership; and the human composite remains the observable centre, the body ever in our mind's eye, explained to us by a soul brightened by consideration. The body 'dost *effigiate*' ('22. Expostulation,' p. 119) the condition of the soul, which must guide the body accordingly, in the manner of a conformable husband and wife ('20. Prayer,' p. 109). The body's resurrection shows the soul's, and that 'of both together hereafter' ('21. Expostulation,' p. 112). The composite parts are co-ordinated as one, and in this co-ordination we see the objective correlative for membership in a community.

The communion necessary for a healthy membership must be a conscious stance. It is a recognition that the self's own thoughts and its deliberative thoughts with others, respectively consideration and counsel, actively conform man to God and to other men. God himself does nothing without consultation of the whole Trinity, whether in creating man (*'let us make man'*) or preserving him ('9. Expostulation,' p. 48). Likewise, states need 'counsels' ('7. Meditation,' p. 35); and Donne's physicians consult to prescribe. Very much to the point that the *Devotions* merges the individual and communal consciousness is that consultation is a communal form of consideration. Counsel is the work of several; consideration, of one. Yet like the triune God the soul's several faculties must consult, just as the individual soul must consider. 'I was whipped by thy *rod*, before I came to *consultation*, to consider my state' ('20. Expostulation,' p. 107). Thus, by nature, the soul configures community and, by nature, must also conform to it; similarly, the healthy community in its singleness of purpose must think as one when considering its affairs. In Donne's conflation of counsel and consideration lies the double consciousness that involves the self-awareness in communal awareness.

Such a portrait of human consciousness has far-reaching thematic implications in the work. It follows that consideration, by discovering its social function as counsel, must look outward to community for fulfilment as well as within. And, in searching the moment to find the patterns that recreate the soul, consideration finds the social dimensions to fulfilling time, since the recreated self can find its own fulfilment only in the communal Body. Time can no longer exist only for the self, but as it is redefined by participation in the community. From the perspective of the shared Body, time must be seen increasingly not only as the creation of individual members, but as their mutual progress as well. Accordingly, the individual suffering body increasingly configures the participating Body, speaking clearly and directly to those who read its experience.

Here we find the final element in Donne's conception of temporal fulfilment, for corrective affliction and penitential suffering are the mode of participation. The pattern is the suffering Christ. The Body's members participate through conformity to the Head; and it is to Christ, invoked in Donne's first prayer and varyingly recalled, that the penitential form of the *Devotions* refers. Christ's suffering stamps the penitential pattern of humiliation that reforms the natural misery of the human condition; and Donne, as an assured member of Christ's Body, incarnates that imprint in which other members can participate. The penitential fulfilment of time is a participatory experience that both includes Donne's *Devotions* and is imprinted by it.

This participation guides Donne's dedicatory letter to Prince Charles, in which Donne wittily ties together essential assumptions. Donne exploits filial causality to explain the Body's temporal continuity: from the father James to son Charles, as from 'Father' Donne to his 'Sonne' the *Devotions*; and (Donne becomes more implicit when he risks Royal sensitivity) as from Donne's *Devotions* to Charles and his times. The lynch pin, that James *'vouchsafed mee his Hand'* by guiding (or forcefully nudging) Donne to take Orders, makes clear what implication politely avoids: that Donne's devotional example offered for Charles's participation continues the fruitful actions of James, invested in both Donne and Charles. Now Donne, first a 'Partaker' of James's 'time,' now of Charles's 'times,' if his work is accepted by Charles, will live 'inanimated' through Charles. That is, Donne's 'Sonne,' an 'Image *of my* Humiliation,' must be accepted by the humble. What the letter leaves implicit is made only too clear in the *Devotions* itself: 'No man is so little, in respect of the greatest man, as the greatest in respect of *God*' ('2. Expostulation,' p. 12). Yet royalty needs counsel; and Donne offers his own penitential illness as the assured believer's fulfilment through participation. Donne's work speaks to both the Body and the 'Heart' soon to inform it. For Donne, whose own gravestones will speak in his friends' voices, in the 'accents of those wordes, which their love may afford my memory' ('2. Meditation,' p. 15), individual members, spanning life and death, earth and heaven, contribute to the Body's fulfilment in time.

In the dedicatory letter a telling comparison between Donne and Hezekiah, 'who *writt the* Meditations *of his* Sicknesse,' further acknowledges the importance of the individual's repentance in communal experience. Hezekiah's prayer after his recovery was a commonplace in penitential literature.[22] In Calvin's four sermons on Hezekiah, translated into English as early as 1560, we find a detailed account of Hezekiah's meditation that shares many of Donne's emphases. In Hezekiah's illness Calvin finds God's active correction for sin emblematized by the illness. This catechistic illness points out to Hezekiah his need for humility and repentance. Yet Calvin finds the true identity of Hezekiah's song in its audience, for Hezekiah recognized in his own experience God's instruction for others as well. Significantly, even when besieged by illness, Hezekiah feared how his death would cripple his people, straitening further his own personal fear of exclusion from God's mercy. Double recognition, that his remarkable experience would recall his own sin and similarly edify his community, necessarily followed; the whole world would see his experience as 'worthy of perpetuall memory that God hath done for a man.' Calvin claims that this 'miracle' will be celebrated in the Church until the 'end of the world.'[23] Christians, 'knit together' as they are 'in one body,' would be encouraged to praise God communally.[24]

Like Donne, Hezekiah offers an exemplar of humiliation: not strength, but weakness distinguishes his value as a model. His excessive fear, complaint, and disputation repeatedly manifested his need for correction. His recovery marked his merciful pardon by a powerful and majestic God, who not only saved Hezekiah, but mercifully offered his humiliation to instruct latter days. In Hezekiah's eventual humility, obedience, and patience in bearing correction, affliction, and chastisement, Calvin finds the proper human acknowledgment of responsibility. In Calvin's discussion we find much ground common to the *Devotions*: disease as sin, correction, humility, dispute unto murmuring, God's chastisement through the individual, patience, shared repentance as time's fulfilment. Like Calvin's Hezekiah, Donne acknowledges his capacity to sin; but, also like him, he sees God's hand in his recovery. The same God who 'enlargedst *Ezechias* lease for *fifteene yeeres*' has also enlarged his. Yet, just as all men die eventually, Donne will continue to sin. A 'true *repentance* ... buried' in Christ's wounds, hence pardoned, cannot prevent all subsequent sin ('22. Prayer,' p. 120). It is as a sinful exemplar of humiliation and repentance that Donne presents his experience, Hezekiah-like, to the 'times' of Charles and to Donne's community. Like Calvin Donne finds a Providential motive in that literary gesture.

Much recent commentary on the *Devotions* examines the relationship between Donne and his audience, although the nature of that relationship needs to be examined more explicitly. Few readers can accept older assertions of Donne's singularity, of a singleminded concentration on the motions of his own psychology. The 'universal' resonates too loudly in Donne's speaking voice to maintain that position. Joan Webber excites our sensitivity to Donne's shifting and reshifting 'I' and 'we,' a symbolic self including all men.[25] Unfortunately, she then backs away to suggest that the audience really exists for Donne, not vice versa, that publication concludes the literary act, to complete the self: 'the devotions are personal; it is himself that he exposes to view.' Immediate needs of the self tend to filter out the desire 'simply to testify to God's goodness, or to provide inspiration to others.'[26] Yet his dedicatory letter to Charles, the strangeness of his convalescence spent writing and rewriting about his illness,[27] his Calling conceived as a Pauline fulfilment of Christ's sufferings in his own flesh for the Body's sake – these facts would encourage a somewhat different emphasis in answering the question of audience. His dramatization of shared experience,[28] his 'ritualization of personal misery,'[29] the symbolic self, and his Pauline Calling are all conflated in Donne's guiding belief that Christ's Body is fulfilled in time through the conformity of Members to Christ and each other. Penitential suffering is the crucial force. His vivid illness, paradoxically sin's punishment and encouragement to 'resurrection,' contains the moving centre of his belief. He offers his experience sacramentally to vivify time, not escape it, filling his work with the immediacy of recent experience. He himself fulfils time by inspiring his readers to participate in his sense of immediacy. His penitential experience repeats the conformity to Christ that integrates all members. Donne's illness and the *Devotions* are involved in this community conformed to Christ. That conformity describes fulfilled time which is, by definition, both communal and penitential.

In the immediacy of his own conformity Donne reaffirms his bond of participation with other members of the Body, and offers his experience in the *Devotions*. Donne's own nature stamps the temporal vividness that distinguishes the work. Clearly, his nature finds a congenial expression in received forms, following traditional lines of Anglican repentance,[30] a traditional theology of disease[31] and divine affliction, and conformity. Yet this nature must actualize experience in the moment. The heart longs to be battered personally, to have its rusts burned off, visibly, calculably. Specific afflictions in which God communes directly with the whole man, to the soul through the body, must preside over repentance. And the essential relationship with the Body must be experienced with the same immediacy. The necessary corrective affliction that conforms the soul to God through repentance is a traditional article of Donne's faith; it expresses the needs of his soul. Like Adam's other heirs, Donne began in '*sicknesse, punishment* for *sin*' ('23. Expostulation,' p. 125), but traditionally, this paradoxical affliction is Christ's cure. Conformity with the Physician turns the death of disease into the health of spiritual resurrection through mortifying sin. Christ's way guides both affliction and repentance. In corrective affliction, the '*brambles,* & *thornes* of a sharpe sicknesse*'* ('2. Prayer,' p. 14), Donne applies Christ's suffering, in humility, obedience, and patience. And when his illness 'brought mee to *thee* in *repentance*' ('23. Expostulation,' p. 125), Donne conformed that repentance to the Cross; in contrition and confession, he buried his sins in Christ's wounds ('22. Prayer,' p. 120) to find satisfaction in his own resurrection from disease, like Hezekiah with a new 'lease.' The received principles are there, but we find them in our vivid sense that *this* illness configures all mortal life and that time itself must conform to Christ's suffering, in which all members participate.

In Donne's seventeeth prayer, upon the ringing bells, we come close to the essential Donne. Having heard God's *'instructions*, in *another mans* to consider *mine owne condition*,' he prays that the Spirit help the dying man, that he confess, 'wrap himselfe up in the *merits*' of Christ, and receive evidence of God's forgiveness. The experience of one member of Christ's Body, having given into Donne's experience, could thus, in turn, receive back through Donne's supporting prayer. Donne further asks that the dying man then give 'outward *testimonies*' to assure those about him that the soul goes to heaven. Donne prays on the man's behalf as one of those afflicted members of the Body for whom the crucified Christ cried out on the Cross: 'This *patient*, O most blessed *God*, is one of *them*; In his behalfe, and in his name, heare thy *Sonne* crying to thee, *My God, My God, Why hast thou forsaken me*? and forsake him not' ('17. Prayer,' pp. 89–90). The suffering, now dying man so conformed to Christ the Head would participate in Christ's resurrection, to join those members of the Body in heaven. Donne's prayer applies his own conformity, incited by correction and repentance, now charitably, Christlike, facing outward to one poised between the halves of 'thy *Kingdome*.' The pattern he applies is Christ's. But also he is a *'patient*,' a diseased sufferer,[32] one who needs Christ's cure, even when embodying that cure at the point of death. Patience rephrases Donne's concept of fulfilled time; for patience is conformity with Christ: humility, obedience, penitential suffering and death to sin, concern for community, waiting for the God-given moment. 'But, *O Lord*, I am not *wearie* of thy *pace*, nor *wearie* of mine owne *patience*' ('19. Prayer,' p. 103). By 'patiently' considering each immediate moment, through conformity to Christ's pattern, Donne finds the recreation of time and must continue to find it every moment until death. The dying Donne, vividly manifested in the pulpit for *Deaths Duell*, follows accordingly.

CONCLUSION

9

Conformity as Conclusion:
Deaths Duell

The event of *Deaths Duell* was remarkable even by the standards of Donne's day. He had been appointed to preach on 'his old constant day, the first *Friday* in *Lent*,' at Whitehall before the king. Though wasted by illness, Donne 'passionately denied' the requests of concerned friends that he not preach. His text was Psalm 68:20: '*And unto God the Lord belong the issues of death*. i.e. *from death*' (*Sermons*, X, 230). Isaak Walton captures a very special drama: 'Many that then saw his tears, and heard his faint and hollow voice, professing they thought the Text prophetically chosen, and that Dr. Donne *had preach't his own funeral Sermon*.'[1] But it is not just the drama of a wasted, dying man who embodies his own words about death that is remarkable. Even more so is that the event of Donne's delivery and the sermon itself, taken together, represent a coherent and fulfilling conclusion to his life and thought.

The vivid sight of the dying man could have made the sermon itself anticlimactic if not for its own powerful effects. A forceful statement of omnipresent mortality and vivid images of putrefaction and vermiculation relentlessly aggravate fear of death. Donne's dying body becomes only the most immediate example of the principle of mortality and of the inevitability of material decay and putrefaction:

Our very *birth* and entrance into life is *exitus à morte*, an *issue from death*, for in our mothers *wombe* wee are *dead* so, as that wee doe *not know* wee *live*, not so much as wee doe in our *sleepe*, neither is there any *grave* so close, or so *putrid* a *prison*, as the *wombe* would be unto us, if we stayed in it *beyond* our time, or dyed there *before* our time. In the *grave* the *wormes* doe not kill us, wee *breed* and *feed*, and then *kill* those wormes which wee our selves produc'd. In the wombe the dead *child* kills the *Mother* that conceived it, and is a murtherer, nay a *parricide*, even after it is dead. And if wee bee not dead so in the *wombe*, so as that being dead, wee kill her that gave us our first life, our life of *vegetation*, yet wee are dead so, as *Davids Idols* are dead. (*Sermons*, x, 231–2)

And the portrayal of the crucified Christ that concludes the sermon remains amongst the most powerful statements in Donne's religious prose.

To say that the sermon itself was not anticlimactic is not to say that it can have the same power for us as for the actual audience. Both the dying man and the artifact would have been important. Even for a spellbinder like Donne, his presence in the pulpit then would have been a rare moment; and in his very self-conscious staging of it can be found much of the intended effect on his audience. Walton's account of Donne's final days – his return from Essex to deliver the sermon, the delivery itself before the king and the Whitehall audience, his order that a life-size burial effigy be drawn prematurely, his contemplation of that drawing as his 'hourly object'[2] – reveals parts of a whole. There is a consciousness of the interrelationships between his own person, the artifacts embodying or expressing it, and the communal Body including both person and artifacts. Familiar assumptions here reach back to Donne's beginnings. His abiding sense of the body as a legitimate medium of truth and of the human need to read its experience were revealed in the conception of the body as a 'book' as early as the love poetry in 'To his Mistris Going to Bed' and 'The Extasie' and later in the verse letter 'To Sir Edward Herbert, at Julyers.' The body's experience must be understood and known by an attentive reason. Likewise, we find the assumption that artifacts are surrogate bodies necessary for expressing truth. Such diverse works as 'The Canonization,' 'The Relique,' *The Anniversaries*, the verse letters, and the *Devotions* reveal this assumption.

Walton's nervous estimate of Donne's order for the burial effigy as showing 'a desire of glory or commendation ... rooted in the very nature of man'[3] is not the only interpretation that can be given of Donne's motives. In the *Devotions* Donne assumes that his own diseased body has significance for other members of the participating Body. This significance is embodied in the literary artifact, which must be considered rationally by members of Donne's audience just as Donne must consider the events of his immediate experience. In *Deaths Duell* Donne's own person is not explicitly expressed in the artifact, but it would have been tangibly present. As members of the same Body as Donne, his auditors could have participated, in a very immediate way, in the significance of his dying body. The burial effigy, also an artifact, embodies the image of Donne, shrouded and prepared spiritually to meet Christ. Thus, the body, diseased but alive in the *Devotions*, then wasted and dying in *Deaths Duell*, then configured in its death image in the effigy, 'be-

longs' to members of the participating Body, who must consider its significance. The fact that Donne spent his final days contemplating the charcoal
drawing reveals, in a most dramatic and characteristically extreme way, his
sense that his own body and its artificial images have continuing value for
the communal Body, no less for Donne himself than for other members.

At bottom is operating the elemental bodily consciousness that we have
seen to be one key factor in Donne's epistemology and psychology and which,
in *Deaths Duell*, provokes the fear of physical death and dissolution of bodily
identity. The imminence of Donne's own death would exacerbate that fear
in members of his audience. The fearful appeal to this bodily consciousness
is answered by the climactic image of the crucified Christ, with its assurance
that through identification with death itself, in the pattern of Christ's suffering
death, fear can be transformed into hope. Only through conformity to Christ
that bends man's will to God's through penitentially crucifying sin, in humility, obedience, and patience, can one escape the fear of death. Donne's
assurance of his own resurrection from sin through conformity to Christ in
the *Devotions* and Walton's account of his joyful assurance of salvation during
the days before his death[4] suggest that Donne would have viewed his own
wasted body as an example of penitential conformity to Christ's suffering
death. Thus, the vivid image of the dying man is fulfilled in the vivid depiction
of the suffering God as its pattern. The audience is invited, implicitly, to
participate in Donne as one exemplary member of the Body and, explicitly,
to conform to the suffering and death of Christ the Head. In accordance
with his Lenten purposes, '*Crucifying* of that *sinne* that governes thee' to
achieve conformity (*Sermons*, X, 247), Donne pulls tight the strings of bodily
consciousness with his image of the suffering, incarnate Word: 'There wee
leave you in that *blessed dependancy*, to *hang* upon *him* that *hangs* upon the
Crosse, there *bath* in his *teares*, there *suck* at his *woundes*, and *lye downe in peace*
in his *grave*, till hee vouchsafe you a *resurrection*, and an *ascension* into that
Kingdome, which hee hath *purchas'd for you*, with the *inestimable price* of his
incorruptible blood. Amen' (*Sermons*, X, 248). Only this palpable image of Christ
can change bodily fears into hope through acceptance of the body's own
necessary death and resurrection.

Donne keeps our attention on Christ's bodily suffering as, increasingly,
the sermon, like the development of Donne's own thought, converges on
the Cross. Divine love inspires Christ's freely given love:

Many waters quench not love, Christ tryed many; He was *Baptized* out of his *love*, and
his love determined not there; He wept over *Jerusalem* out of his *love*, and his love
determined not there; He *mingled blood* with *water* in his *agony* and that determined

not his love; hee *wept pure blood*, all his blood at all his eyes, at all his pores, in his *flagellation* and *thornes (to the Lord our God belong'd the issues of blood)* and these *expressed*, but these did *not quench his love.*' (*Sermons*, X, 243)

Love of Christ, in return, inspires penitential conformity in body and tripartite soul, thereby converting the forces of annihilation and recreating man the damaged goal of Creation. In the suffering of the Cross that pays sin's debt, God shows to man the pattern in body and soul that mortifies sin. Donne's emphasis upon the humanity of the Word, his very palpable physical and psychological suffering, brings the specifically human together with the larger metaphysical power of the Word. In the explicit conformity built on love, humility, obedience, patience, and acceptance of suffering and death, being is recreated. And Donne, in offering his own accomplished suffering to the audience, exemplifies this recreation for others, thereby, like Paul, fulfilling the suffering of Christ in his own flesh for the Body's sake.

Consistent with his earlier works, Donne stresses that this meeting of the personal and metaphysical occurs in time. Donne ends *Deaths Duell* at the end of his own circle with yet another meditation on time that places importance on the given moment. In the sermon the movement from fear to conformity with Christ, from death of the body to the resurrection of hope, recreates time. The sermon's initial weight on the omnipresence of death points to the negativity of fallen time: 'We celebrate our owne funeralls with cryes, even at our own birth, as though our *threescore and ten years life* were spent in our mothers labour, and our circle made up in the first point thereof' (*Sermons*, X, 233). Similarly, the progression of fallen time is crippled and reversed: 'That which we call life, is but *Hebdomada mortium, a week of deaths*, seaven dayes, seaven periods of our life spent in dying, *a dying seaven times over*; and there is an end. *Our birth dyes* in *infancy*, and our *infancy* dyes in *youth*, and *youth*, and the rest dye in *age*, and *age* also dyes, and *determines all*' (*Sermons*, X, 234).

Against the degeneration of time through death, Donne, fittingly himself a dying man nearing his own last day, offers the model of Christ's last day. Gradually, the sermon conforms time itself to Christ, thereby re-informing time according to the Incarnate Word:

Take in the *whole day* from the *houre* that *Christ received* the *passeover* upon *Thursday*, *unto* the *houre* in which hee *dyed* the *next day*. Make *this* present *day* that *day* in thy *devotion*, and consider what *hee did*, and remember what *you have done*. Before hee *instituted* and *celebrated* the *Sacrament*, (which was *after* the *eating of the passeover*) hee proceeded to that *act* of *humility*, to *wash his disciples feete*, even *Peters, who* for a while *resisted* him; In thy *preparation* to the holy and blessed *Sacrament*, hast thou with a sincere *humility* sought a *reconciliation* with all the *world*, even with those that have been *averse* from it, and *refused* that *reconciliation* from thee? If so (and not else) thou hast spent that *first part* of this his *last day* in a *conformity* with him. (*Sermons*, X, 245–6)

The day of Donne's sermon and the day before Christ's death are both special days. For Donne, it is his last sermon before an expected and welcome death,[5] a point close to the Omega of his circle of time. For Christ, it is the period of a single day immediately before his Crucifixion, likewise a point close to the Omega of his exemplary circle. The auditors, like Donne and Christ, must face the continuing possibility that each day may end their circles. Each day is a '*criticall* day' (*Sermons*, X, 241)[6] that must be regarded as potentially man's last, to be brought into conformity with Christ's last day. Donne's visible conformity to Christ's pattern will dilate this particular moment in the respective lives of his listeners. Thus, *Deaths Duell* speaks to the immediate moment, to both individuals and to the communal Body, applying these special days of Donne and Christ. As in the *Devotions* Donne is speaking to members of the Body, the Church, invoking the image of Christ the Head; and he is speaking to members of the Body, the kingdom, here in the presence of its regal Heart. All members hear the same pattern for fulfilling time.

As elsewhere in Donne's works, time is fulfilled within the human soul. The reference points are psychological and epistemological; and the guiding conformity to Christ, which is so crucial in Donne's theology of participation, works within a larger conformity of the tripartite human soul to the tripartite God. In the *divisio* in preparation for 'these three considerations' of the three meanings of '*exitus mortis*' that make up the sermon, Donne establishes parallels to the three Persons of the Trinity:

In all these three lines then, we shall looke upon these words; *First*, as the *God of power*, the *Almighty Father* rescues his servants from the jawes of death: *And then*, as the *God of mercy*, the glorious *Sonne* rescued us, by taking upon himselfe this *issue of death: And then* betweene these two, as the *God of comfort*, the *Holy Ghost* rescues us from all discomfort by his blessed impressions before hand, that what manner of death soever be ordeined for us, yet this *exitus mortis* shall be *introitus in vitam* our *issue in death*, shall be an *entrance into everlasting life*. (*Sermons*, X, 231)

Similarly, the sermon works on all members of the tripartite Image in the human soul: on the reason in the frequent request that the auditors consider the matter of the sermon, especially the experience of Christ; on the will in the stimulation of love for Christ's loving sacrifice; and on the memory in the request that believers remember their own sinful actions in comparison with Christ's example. The recreation of time requires attentive efforts by the entire soul.

In the *Devotions* reason considers each moment in time according to the principles informing it. The same assumption in *Deaths Duell* makes conformity to Christ dependent on the soul's keen rational awareness. The audience is asked to consider the significance of moments in Christ's 'day' ending with his death. 'Make *this* present *day* that *day* in thy *devotion*, consider what *hee did*, and remember what *you have done*' (*Sermons*, x, 245). Donne repeatedly points to the importance of considering the matter of the sermon, 'to consider with mee how to *this God the Lord belong'd the issues of death*' (*Sermons*, x, 243), explicitly sharpening the audience's rational attention. Implicitly, the audience is also being asked to consider the dying preacher standing before them, just as they are asked to consider his diseased body in the *Devotions*. The dramatic force of the given moment in Donne's works develops in these later works into a full-blown sense of temporal events as a form of communication from God to man, to be understood and known. When Donne speaks of God as Logos, who necessarily proceeds logically (*Sermons*, v, 103), for whom a minute in time is a 'syllogisme' (*Sermons*, x, 111), he is emphasizing the rational dimension in that communication. The audience in *Deaths Duell* must consider not only Donne's spoken words, but also his presence in the pulpit as a form of temporal communication from God. This is necessarily the domain of reason's same bright attention emphasized throughout Donne's works as the condition for fulfilling temporal life. Reason must also attentively arbitrate the will's experience in love and examine anew what memory comprehends.

That Donne would expect the members of his audience to consider not only his words but also himself as part of the same event returns us to a matter with which we began in Chapter One, namely, Donne's own person as a factor in his works. The complexities of Donne's nature have set off varied and, at times, conflicting responses. Clearly, Donne was unsettled as a young man; it is nonetheless possible to determine those elements which dominate his essential nature even at that time. Merritt Hughes's clear warning against 'kidnapping' Donne in our own modern preconceptions[7] still exhorts us to see Donne as he wished to be seen. Behind the restlessness and the chafing in Donne there was a yearning for constancy. The preceding chapters have assumed that this yearning must be understood in terms of the basic impulses in Donne's nature and thought that continue to manifest themselves in his works. Donne's nature, at times so obtrusive, is most assessable in what he continues to say. As we have seen, his need for constancy required that man's full nature, composite material body and rational soul, establish a working relationship to a communal Body that accepts suffering as the necessary condition of fulfilment. In Donne's restatement of Paul's joyous fulfilment of Christ's suffering in his own flesh for the Body's sake, Donne expressed a Calling that, in the received forms of his Faith, fulfilled his yearning for constancy.

Walton's chronicle of Donne's final days, an account which his modern counterpart R.C. Bald regards as unexceptionable,[8] suggests that Donne's faith was fulfilled in his death. But death does not compromise his abiding sense that the Body of Christ, the physical and spiritual community that contributes to the constancy of Donne's mature being, would continue to span heaven and earth after his death. Though Donne himself was spiralling closer to his circular God, whose mercy ever moved perpendicularly above the believer (*Sermons*, VI, 175),[9] he recognized even in his last acts the responsibility to other participating members. Donne's relationship to the community was not always so resolved, and his life on the circumference of his temporal circle was not always so fulfilled. In the third satire there is the incompleted search for a 'true religion' (43), the injunction to 'doubt wisely' (77)[10] in a progress spiralling upward ('about must goe') to Truth on a 'huge hill' (79–81).[11] In 'A Valediction: forbidding Mourning,' its calmness a marked contrast to other love poems of Donne, is expressed the conviction that mutual love bonded by spiritual union can make an individual, private circle just.[12] And in 'Goodfriday, 1613. Riding Westward' he affirms the need for affliction to turn his sinful soul in its circular, westward movement back to its eastern origin, in conformity with the suffering Christ. However, in Donne's maturity, in his priestly Calling, he did achieve a personal assurance and constancy that fulfilled life along the circumference of his circle. In his assurance of his conformity with Christ, he offered his bodily presence to fulfil Christ's suffering for the sake of the communal Body. And in his literary works he embodied his sense of the epistemological and psychological immediacies that make up that conformity.

To conclude, it is the two major artifacts in his last remains, the sermon *Deaths Duell* and the death effigy in St Paul's, that we can find the final measure of the Calling that fulfilled his life. The sermon, although it now lacks the startling ambience centred in the dying man, still leaves its deep imprint on readers in the way it emboldens the problems of mortality and time. The death effigy likewise leaves its imprint, with its composed face accepting the inevitability of death. Donne would have appreciated time's witty justification of his personal value for the Body; the marble effigy remains, but the original building was destroyed by fire. Many modern readers would say that both the sermon and the effigy, like his other literary works, have outlasted the system of belief that inspired Donne. Yet it is not too fanciful to suggest – and we can perhaps appreciate this irony better than Donne – that his artifacts still inform a kind of Body in so far as they unite us in asking that we know and feel the large forces that shape us. That Donne's own works accomplish this successfully, often in the most immediate ways, make them a coherent and understandable achievement that can be said to help fulfil life on the circumference of time's circle.

NOTES

INDEX

Editions Used

The editions of Donne's works listed on this page have been used throughout this study. The necessary volume, page, or line numbers are given parenthetically within my text.

LOVE POETRY

The Elegies and The Songs and Sonnets, ed. Helen Gardner. Oxford: Clarendon Press, 1965

DIVINE POETRY

John Donne: The Divine Poems, ed. Helen Gardner. Oxford: Clarendon Press, 1978. (For the *Holy Sonnets* I have used Grierson's consecutive numbering given parenthetically by Gardner.)

OTHER POETRY

John Donne: The Epithalamions, Anniversaries and Epicedes, ed. W. Milgate. Oxford: Clarendon Press, 1978
John Donne: The Satires, Epigrams and Verse Letters, ed. W. Milgate. Oxford: Clarendon Press, 1967

PROSE

Devotions upon Emergent Occasions, ed. Anthony Raspa. Montreal and London: McGill-Queen's University Press, 1975
Essays in Divinity, ed. Evelyn M. Simpson. Oxford: Clarendon Press, 1967
The Sermons of John Donne, eds. George R. Potter and Evelyn M. Simpson. 10 vols. Berkeley and Los Angeles: University of California Press, 1953–61

Any departures from these editions are indicated in the notes. All references to Grierson are to *The Poems of John Donne*, ed. H.J.C. Grierson. 2 vols. Oxford: Clarendon Press, 1912

Notes

CHAPTER ONE

1 The terms 'epistemology' and 'psychology' are not used here in their strictest senses. 'Epistemology' refers more broadly to Donne's repeated examination of kinds of knowing and knowledge. He ranges widely from the shared knowledge of mutual love in 'The Exstasie' to the experiential knowledge of 'Christ crucified' in the sermons. The roots of his 'psychology' are Augustinian faculty psychology, which necessarily leads reason, memory, and will into spiritual and theological domains. The rational soul's dependence upon the body implicates the body as well.

2 For one refutation of claims that there is intellectual relativism in Donne's poetry, see Helen Gardner, 'Introduction' in *John Donne: A Collection of Critical Essays* (Englewood Cliffs, N.J.: Prentice-Hall, 1962), 12. Also, see Barbara Kiefer

Lewalski, *Donne's 'Anniversaries' and the Poetry of Praise: The Creation of a Symbolic Mode* (Princeton: Princeton University Press, 1973), 7–8. For the most recent statement of the contrary view, see John Carey, *John Donne: Life, Mind and Art* (London and Boston: Faber and Faber, 1981), 13–14, 219, 250.

3 For a useful discussion of the dating problem, see Richard E. Hughes, *The Progress of the Soul: The Interior Career of John Donne* (New York: William Morrow and Co., 1969), 130–2.

4 For the Spirit's 'overshadowing' see '14. Prayer,' in *Devotions*, p. 76; for the notion of conception, see *Sermons*, VII, 70, 133, 155.

5 The hexameral metahistory follows a Trinitarian scheme, two thousand years each of Nature, Law, and Grace. See *Sermons*, VI, 331.

6 For general Renaissance background and also more explicit, but related, Puritan applications, see Geoffrey F.

Nuttall, *The Holy Spirit in Puritan Faith and Experience* (Oxford: Blackwell, 1946).

7 See J.B. Endres, 'Appropriation,' in *New Catholic Encyclopedia* (New York: McGraw Hill Book Company, 1967), I, 708–9.

8 Cf. *Sermons*, VI, 129.

9 Not only the Greek but the Latin contributions to this tradition are discussed in A.H. Armstrong and R.A. Markus, *Christian Faith and Greek Philosophy* (London: Darton, Longman, and Todd, 1964), 16–29. Also, see Harry A. Wolfson, 'Extradeical and Intradeical Interpretations of Platonic Ideas,' *JHI*, 22 (1961), 3–32.

10 For Donne's distinction between the essential and the uttered Word at Creation, see *Sermons*, VI, 216.

11 See *Sermons*, IV, 98–9; *Essays in Divinity*, 29.

12 For examples of (1) the roles of both the Spirit and the Word and (2) Donne's use of the Scriptural support, see *Sermons*, IV, 102; IX, 98. Mrs Simpson notes (*Sermons*, X, 325) that Donne uses several Biblical versions freely. Whenever possible, I have simply quoted Donne's local renditions, unless noting otherwise.

13 For the Platonist background, see Roy W. Battenhouse, 'The Grounds of Religious Toleration in the Thought of John Donne,' *Church History*, 2 (1942), 246–7.

14 Cf. Augustine, *De Civitate Dei*, XI, 28; Bonaventure, *De reductione artium ad theologiam*, 12; Thomas

Aquinas, *Summa Theologica*, I, q. 45, a. 7.

15 '2. Annunciation,' lines 7–8 in *La Corona*.

16 For a discussion of Donne's Covenant thought, see E. Randolph Daniel, 'Reconciliation, Covenant and Election: A Study in the Theology of John Donne,' *Anglican Theological Review*, 48 (1966), 14–30. More general discussions of this widely shared, but varied, notion include: Herschel Baker, *The Wars of Truth* (Cambridge, Mass.: Harvard University Press, 1952), 203–14, 291–302; John S. Coolidge, *The Pauline Renaissance in England: Puritanism and the Bible* (Oxford: Clarendon Press, 1970), 77–140; Everett H. Emerson, 'Calvin and Covenant Theology,' *Church History*, 25 (1956), 136–44; Perry Miller, 'The Marrow of Puritan Divinity' in *Errand into the Wilderness* (Cambridge, Mass.: Harvard University Press, 1956), 48–98; *The New England Mind: The Seventeenth Century* (Cambridge, Mass.: Harvard University Press, 1954), 365–97; John von Rohr, 'Covenant and Assurance in Early English Puritanism,' *Church History*, 34 (1965), 195–203; Leonard J. Trinterud, 'The Origins of Puritanism,' *Church History*, 20 (1951), 35–57; A. Yonick, 'Covenant (In the Bible)' in *New Catholic Encyclopedia*, IV, 401–6.

17 Donne sidesteps the controversy 'whether Gods Decree of Reprobation and Salvation, were before his Decree of Creation.' Such mysteries

are beyond human comprehension (*Sermons*, IV, 305). Nonetheless, his assertion that God's intention to create Donne preceded his intention to elect him may indicate where Donne's real sympathies lay (*Sermons*, VIII, 282). In any event Donne's emphasis upon God as the Creator is consistent with the importance which Creation plays in his whole metaphysic.

18 Donne's Scriptural basis for the notion of the Spirit's seal includes Ephesians 1:13; 2 Corinthians 1:22; Romans 8:16 (*Sermons*, X, 62–3); Revelation 7:2–3 (*Sermons*, X, 41).

19 Lewalski, *Donne's 'Anniversaries' and the Poetry of Praise*, 161.

20 See *Sermons*, VI, 328.

21 These teachings flow out of the 'fulnesse' of the Incarnate Christ, in whom *'it pleased the Father, that in him should all fulnesse dwell'* (Colossians 1:19). Donne explicates this Pauline conception of fullness, first, as all the attributes and qualities of the Godhead; second, Christ's fulfilment of righteousness through perfected suffering that satisfied God's judgment; third, the fullness of the Church, his Body, through the merits and mercies of its Head (*Sermons*, IV, 288). The language of 'filling' and 'fullness,' interchangeably applied to both Persons, pronounces their closeness of function (e.g., *Sermons*, IX, 240).

22 See n. 21 above.

23 The spiral that constitutes human and temporal circles translates the perfect, unending circularity of God into motions appropriate to creation. The spiral pulls the natural rectilinear movement of matter toward the centre, which is God. The spiralling circles become increasingly fulfilled the closer they transcribe the circular fullness of God and Eternity. The history of circular motion receives admirably concise treatment in John Freccero, 'Donne's "Valediction: Forbidding Mourning," ' *ELH*, 30 (1963), 335–76. Especially see p. 340.

24 John Dryden, *A Discourse Concerning the Origin and Progress of Satire*, 1693, in *The Poems of John Dryden*, ed. James Kinsley (Oxford: Clarendon Press, 1958), II, 604.

25 'Elegie on Prince Henry,' lines 65–6. See p. 207, n. 18 regarding these lines.

26 See Donald M. Friedman, 'Memory and the Art of Salvation in Donne's Good Friday Poem,' *ELR*, 3, (1973), 418–42; Robert L. Hickey, 'Donne's Art of Memory,' *TSL*, 3, (1958), 29–38; Janel M. Mueller, 'Introduction,' in *Donne's Prebend Sermons* (Cambridge, Mass.: Harvard University Press, 1971), 33–5; Dennis Quinn, 'Donne's Christian Eloquence,' *ELH*, 27, (1960), 289–91; Joan Webber, *Contrary Music: The Prose Style of John Donne* (Madison: University of Wisconsin Press, 1963), 22, 31; John S. Chamberlin, *Increase and Multiply: Arts-of-Discourse Procedure in the Preaching of Donne* (Chapel Hill: University of North

Carolina Press, 1976), 16–18, 26–8, 115–18.

27 See William Empson, ' "A Valedic-tion: of Weeping" ' in *John Donne: A Collection of Critical Essays*, ed. Helen Gardner (Englewood Cliffs, N.J.: Prentice-Hall, 1962), 52; Judah Stampfer, *John Donne and the Meta-physical Gesture* (New York: Funk and Wagnalls, 1970), 163–70.

CHAPTER TWO

1 Irving Lowe, 'John Donne: the Middle Way. The Reason-Faith Equation in Donne's Sermons,' *JHI*, 22 (1961), 396.
2 Thomas Wilson, *The Rule of Reason: Conteinyng the Arte of Logique*, ed. Richard S. Sprague (Northridge, California: San Fernando State College, 1972), 8.
3 For a useful résumé see Earl Miner, 'Wit: Definition and Dialectic,' in *The Metaphysical Mode from Donne to Cowley* (Princeton: Princeton University Press, 1969), 118–58.
4 See the following: Rosemond Tuve, *Elizabethan and Metaphysical Im-agery: Renaissance Poetic and Twen-tieth Century Critics* (Chicago: University of Chicago Press, 1947); A.J. Smith, *Donne: The Songs and Sonets* (London: Edward Arnold, 1964), 63–9; Murray Roston, *The Soul of Wit: A Study of John Donne* (Oxford: Clarendon Press, 1974), 71–107; Una Nelly, *The Poet Donne: His Dialectic Method* (Dublin: Cork University Press, 1969), 59–109;

J.B. Leishman, *The Monarch of Wit: An Analytical and Comparative Study of the Poetry of John Donne* (New York: Harper and Row, 1965), 41–51, 145–241; Dwight Cathcart, *Doubting Conscience: Donne and the Poetry of Moral Argument* (Ann Arbor: University of Michigan Press, 1975), 1–12.
5 Leishman says that Donne liked what children call 'dressing up' (*The Monarch of Wit*, 147). Cf. Louis Martz, *The Wit of Love* (Notre Dame and London: Notre Dame University Press, 1969), 19–26. For Martz, Donne's penchant to pose for numerous portraits suggests a manifold personal reality.
6 Robert Ellrodt, *L'Inspiration Person-elle et l'Esprit du Temps chez Les Poètes Métaphysiques Anglais* (Paris: Librarie José Corti, 1960), I, 82–94. Ellrodt's denial that Donne's poetry embraces temporal progress cannot accommodate progression in the argument itself.
7 Anne Ferry, *All in War with Time: Love Poetry of Shakespeare, Donne, Jonson, Marvell* (Cambridge, Massa-chusetts and London, England: Harvard University Press, 1975), 65–126.
8 Cf. Miner, *The Metaphysical Mode*, 48–93.
9 The timelessness of perpetuity need not exclude change. For Donne, it was imprinted with his strong sense of sequential movement learned in time.
10 See A.E. Malloch, 'The Techniques

and Function of the Renaissance
Paradox,' *SP*, 53 (1956), 191–203. He
has described the instigative intention of Donne's formal paradoxes,
noting that 'their being remains
unfulfilled until they become part of
a dialectic action. They do not become themselves until they are over-
thrown' (195).

11 Gardner, *The Elegies and The Songs
and Sonnets*, 208.

12 See Leonard Barkan, *Nature's Work
of Art: The Human Body as Image
of the World* (New Haven and London: Yale University Press, 1975),
46–51; Joseph Antony Mazzeo,
'Metaphysical Poetry and the Poetic
of Correspondence' in *Renaissance
and Seventeeth-Century Studies* (New
York: Columbia University Press,
1964), 44–59.

13 Gardner, *The Elegies and The Songs
and Sonnets*, 207, lines 25–8.

14 See Louis I. Bredvold, 'The Religious Thought of Donne in Relation
to Medieval and Later Traditions,'
197 in *Studies in Shakespeare, Milton
and Donne* by members of the English Department of the University
of Michigan (New York: Haskell
House, 1964), 224; Herschel Baker,
The Image of Man (New York: Harper and Brothers, 1961), 217, n. 50;
Hiram Haydn, *The Counter-Renaissance* (New York: Charles Scribner's
Sons, 1950), 111f. The Baker and
Haydn discussions are two examples
of Bredvold's continuing influence
on discussion of Donne and reason.

15 'Reason, Faith, and Just Augustinian

Lamentation in Donne's Elegy on
Prince Henry,' *SEL*, 13 (1973), 53–60.

16 Donne's central dramatic movement
is an elegiac pattern of shock, disruption of value, and consolation all
worked out within an epistemological *schema*. An extended delineation
of reason and faith (3–16) and their
relationship to the prince (17–24)
is followed by an anatomy of those
powers, first faith (25–44), then
reason (63–76). There is an intervening suicidal aside (45–62). The consolation (77–98) reinstates the
threatened powers through a tribute
to the prince's lady built on sceptical
reasoning and evaluation of grief.

17 Ruth Wallerstein, *Studies in Seventeenth Century Poetic* (Madison: University of Wisconsin Press, 1950), 70.

18 The 'connexion / Of causes' of
Sylvester's edition and not the 'connexion / With causes' adapted by
Milgate is true to the poem's Augustinian foundation discussed in this
chapter. See Milgate's discussion
of the special manuscript problems
in assessing Donne's intentions (*The
Epithalamions, Anniversaries and Epicedes*, 191).

19 Augustine, *The City of God*, tr. Dods,
Wilson, Smith (New York: The
Modern Library, 1950), v, 8; bracketed Latin citations are from *Patrologiae Cursus Completus, Series Latina*,
ed. J.P. Migne, 221 vols. (Paris,
1844–64); hereafter cited as *City* and,
with appropriate book and section,
given parenthetically within the text.

20 Cf. *Sermons*, VIII, 225.

21 The rational basis of Augustinian thought is ignored in Donne scholarship about Augustine's influence. First, in *Against the Academicians*, then later (e.g., *City*, XI, 26), Augustine refuted rational scepticism. Etienne Gilson's summary of Augustine's reason-faith formula is instructive: 'In its final form the Augustinian doctrine concerning the relationships between reason and faith comprises three steps: preparation for faith by reason, act of faith, understanding of the content of faith' (*The Christian Philosophy of Saint Augustine*, tr. L.E.M. Lynch [London: Victor Gollancz, 1961], 29).

22 Much distortion of Donne's attitude to reason stems from Louis I. Bredvold's still influential assertions that Donne's Thomistic confidence in reason waned as his Augustinism grew. Bredvold readily admits that Donne's rational impulse walks beside his spiritual impulse, but he sees Donne's reasonings as the residual compulsion from an outgrown intellectualism, not as the essential sinew in a reasoned belief ('The Religious Thought of Donne'). Bredvold's disciples have been even less willing to acknowledge an elemental reasoning impulse in Donne's religion. See: Haydn, *The Counter-Renaissance*, II; 129, n. 149; Charles M. Coffin, *John Donne and the New Philosophy* (New York: Humanities Press, 1958), 264; George Williamson, 'The Libertine Donne,' in *Seven-teenth Century Contexts* (London: Faber and Faber, 1960), 42–62. Also in Bredvold's lengthened shadow is the recent discussion by John Carey, *John Donne: Life, Mind and Art* (London and Boston: Faber and Faber, 1981), 231–60.

Other commentary agrees that reason does not set the essential direction of Donne's thought. See: Joan Webber, *Contrary Music: The Prose Style of John Donne* (Madison: University of Wisconsin Press, 1963), 4–12, 22; Richard E. Hughes, *The Progress of the Soul* (New York: William Morrow and Co., 1969), 141–57, 185–7.

23 Thomas Aquinas, *Summa Theologica*, tr. Dominican Fathers (London: Black Friars, in conjunction with Eyre and Spottiswoode, 1968), I, xii, 12.

24 Thomas Aquinas, *Summa Contra Gentiles*, tr. A.C. Pegis (Garden City, N.Y.: Doubleday, 1955), I, 7.

25 Bredvold, 'The Religious Thought of Donne,' 228.

26 Frank Manley, 'Introduction' in *John Donne: The Anniversaries* (Baltimore: Johns Hopkins Press, 1963), 46.

27 See Gilson, *The Christian Philosophy of Saint Augustine*, 269–70, n. 1; 303–4, n. 19. Also, see Augustine, *On the Trinity*, tr. A.W. Haddan and W.G.T. Shedd (Grand Rapids, Michigan: Wm. B. Eerdmans Publishing Company, 1956), XII, ii, 2; XII, xiv, 22–3; XII, xv, 25; XIII, i, 1–4; XIII, xix, 24; XIV, i, 1–3.

28 Augustine, 'Letter 147,' ch. 7, in

Letters 131–53, tr. W. Parsons, vol. 20 in *The Fathers of the Church* (Washington, D.C.: Catholic University of America Press, 1965); here Augustine asserts that acts of belief depend upon trustworthy evidence, which demands the use of reason.

29 Gilson, *The Christian Philosophy of Saint Augustine*, 29; also, see Augustine, *On the Predestination of the Saints*, I, v, tr. R.E. Wallis, in *Basic Writings of Saint Augustine*, I, ed. Whitney J. Oates (New York: Random House, 1948): 'For however suddenly, however rapidly, some thoughts fly before the will to believe, and this presently follows in such wise as to attend them, as it were, in closest conjunction, it is yet necessary that everything which is believed should be believed after thought has preceded; although even belief itself is nothing else than to think with assent.'

30 Augustine, *On the Trinity*, XII, xiv, 23.

31 Ibid., XIV, i, 3.

32 Webber, *Contrary Music*, 12–13.

33 Ibid., 4–12.

34 Ibid., 22, 31.

35 For a more detailed analysis of this syllogistic substratum see my 'Reason in Donne's Sermons,' *ELH*, 39 (1972), 361–2.

36 In regard to the merging of meditation and sermon, see Barbara Kiefer Lewalski, *Donne's 'Anniversaries' and the Poetry of Praise* (Princeton: Princeton University Press, 1973), 73–107; Terence C. Cave, *Devotional Poetry in France c. 1570–1613* (Cambridge: Cambridge University Press, 1969), 20, 36–48.

37 Webber, *Contrary Music*, 22, 140–2. Cf. Dennis Quinn, 'Donne's Christian Eloquence,' *ELH*, 27 (1960), 283.

38 Quinn, 'Donne's Christian Eloquence,' 284.

39 Augustine, *On the Trinity*, XIII, xix, 24.

40 Augustine, *On Christian Doctrine*, tr. D.W. Robertson, Jr (Indianapolis: Bobbs-Merrill, 1958), II, xvi, 23–4.

41 Augustine's most significant treatment of memory occurs in Book X of the *Confessions*. Not just a storehouse or an agent of active recall, the Augustinian memory has the capaciousness and diversity that distinguishes consciousness itself, including some elements of the unconscious, even the imagination. The influence of the *Confessions* on Donne is indisputable, but Donne's works simply do not show that he granted such epistemological and psychological range to memory. The choice is not a bald memory vs. reason; rather it lies in finding the proper emphasis that accommodates not only memory's importance to Donne and his difference from many contemporaries in this regard, but also the role of rational 'consideration.' Donne draws a line between remembering and considering: 'First *remember*; which word is often used in the Scripture for considering

and taking care ... But here we take not remembring so largly, but restrain it to the exercise of that one faculty, the memory' (*Sermons*, II, 236). This distinction agrees with his continuing emphasis on consideration as a function of reason. Yet the interaction between these two faculties can blur the boundary between their repsective domains. On one hand, memory functions like the conclusion of a syllogism (*Sermons*, VIII, 262); on the other hand, he says the Spirit 'hath taught you all things, that is, awakened your memories, to the consideration of all that is necessary to your present establishment' (*Sermons*, VIII, 255). In deliberately overlapping his categories, Donne assumes the close coordination between the two faculties. However, strictly speaking, Donne's reason considers, understands, knows; memory stores what reason knows, growing in comprehension. What memory 'knows' is first known by reason and, once recalled, is considered again. The 'nearest way to lay hold upon God, is the consideration of that which he had done already' (*Sermons*, VII, 63). And such 'consideration' is reason's job.

42 John Calvin, *Institutes of the Christian Religion*, tr. F.L. Battles (Philadelphia: Westminster Press, 1973), I, xv, 7; Latin citations are taken from *Joannis Calvini Opera*, II, in *Corpus Reformatorum*, XXX, ed. G. Baum, E. Cunitz, and E. Reuss

(Brunswick: 1864). Hereafter cited as *Institutes*.

43 *Institutes*, I, xv, 8.
44 *Institutes*, II, ii, 18.
45 *Institutes*, II, ii, 13ff.
46 *Institutes*, III, ii, 7.
47 *Institutes*, III, ii, 14.
48 *Institutes*, II, ii, 20.
49 *Institutes*, II, iii, 10.
50 *Institutes*, III, ii, 33.
51 *Institutes*, III, ii, 36.
52 *Institutes*, III, ii, 34.
53 Barbara Lewalski, *Protestant Poetics and the Seventeenth-Century Religious Lyric* (Princeton: Princeton University Press, 1979), 13–27.
54 *Sermons*, VII, 235.
55 Donne's deep uneasiness about 'implicit' faith is a corollary of congenital ratiocination. 'Explicit' belief demands rational expression of faith's contents. Cf. *Sermons*, VIII, 166; X, 71.
56 The soul's essential form, its tripartite faculties, is ineradicable, even in Hell. Cf. *Sermons*, IX, 81.

CHAPTER THREE

1 See Leonard Barkan, *Nature's Work of Art: The Human Body as Image of the World* (New Haven and London: Yale University Press, 1975), 46–60. He discusses Donne's expression of the traditional notion that studying cosmology was a form of self-knowledge.
2 Cf. '18. Prayer, in *Devotions*, 96.
3 Augustine, *Confessions*, XIII,

xxxii–xxxiii, 47–8.

4 John Calvin, *Institutes of the Christian Religion*, I, V, 1–2.

5 See Barkan, *Nature's Work of Art*, 61–115.

6 'To Sir H. Goodere' in John Donne, *Letters to Severall Persons of Honour*, ed. C.E. Merrill, Jr (New York: Sturgis and Walton Company, 1910), 44.

7 See John S. Coolidge, *The Pauline Renaissance in England: Puritanism and the Bible* (Oxford: Clarendon Press, 1970), 35–9, 48, 50, 61–2, 67–8, 79, 145.

8 Barkan, *Nature's Work of Art*, 44, 51, 55.

9 Both the dedicatory letter to Prince Charles and the eighth devotion refer to James's role in Donne's taking orders. When James sends his own physician, Donne finds more evidence thereby that this Christian David actively incorporates himself in his people.

10 See '5. Meditation,' *Devotions*, p. 25; *Sermons*, III, 246. In regard to marriage as the basis of the family, the family of community, see *Sermons*, II, 336.

11 Donne's most dramatic adaptation of the marriage between Christ and the Church is the best known, in his 'Holy Sonnet, XVIII.'

12 Cf. John Carey, *John Donne: Life, Mind and Art* (London and Boston: Faber and Faber, 1981), 131–66. Unfortunately, Carey's perceptive discussion does not connect the body to the community.

13 Helen Gardner, 'General Introduction' in *The Elegies and The Songs and Sonnets of John Donne*, xxix.

14 See John Donne, *The Satires, Epigrams and Verse Letters*, ed. W. Milgate, 117.

15 Louis I. Bredvold, 'The Naturalism of Donne in Relation to Some Renaissance Traditions,' *JEGP*, 22 (1923), 480: 'he refers constantly to nature ... as the justification of individual desires, as the denial of all universal moral law.'

16 See Gardner, *The Elegies and The Songs and Sonnets*, 133, line 46.

17 See Barbara Lewalski, *Donne's 'Anniversaries' and the Poetry of Praise: The Creation of a Symbolic Mode* (Princeton: Princeton University Press, 1973), 128.

18 The two observers stationed by Donne respectively before and after the lovers' ecstasy justify the lovers as examples. The first, already spiritually refined, could demonstrate by further spiritual gain these pure lovers' effects on others. The presence of the second ('such as wee,' 73) partially democratizes pure love, denying the lovers' uniqueness, hence humanizing their claims.

19 See *Sermons*, X, 112. The background for understanding the correspondences between language, body, and other material objects as the incarnation of truth is Creation: 'God spoke so, in his language of *Workes*, as that all men may understand them' (p. 110).

20 Cf. Grierson's remarks: 'Donne as

usual is pedantically accurate in the details of his metaphor. The canonized lovers are invoked as saints, i.e., *their prayers are requested*. They are asked to beg from above a pattern of their love for those below' (*Poems*, II, 16).

21 A particularly good example of this longing can be found in 'To all my friends: Sir H. Goodere' in *Letters*, 37–8.

22 See Milgate, 'General Introduction' in *The Satires, Epigrams and Verse Letters*, xxxiii–xl; Lewalski, *Donne's 'Anniversaries' and the Poetry of Praise*, 42–70.

23 See n. 6 above.

24 Milgate, *The Satires, Epigrams and Verse Letters*, xxxvi.

25 Ibid., 266.

26 Grierson, *Poems*, I, 288–90.

27 'To the Countesse of Bedford' ('Honour is so sublime perfection'), 33.

28 Lewalski, *Donne's 'Anniversaries' and the Poetry of Praise*, 248.

29 For Lewalski 'the two poems emphasize, respectively ... the miseries of this world and the joys and benefits accruing to us by death' (ibid., 303). The poet is a 'spokesman for a community' and his meditation on these joys and benefits is a 'model and stimulus' for his readers (276). She does not emphasize the paradoxical implications that fullness for both the glorified soul like Elizabeth Drury and the regenerate soul like the poet is increased through continuing influence on the living.

30 In *Sermons*, V, 358–9 the assimilation of man's 'bones' to Christ's renders this conformity forcefully.

31 Bernard, *Sermones in Cantica Canticorum*, XXXVI, 4.

32 Bernard, *Sermones de diversis*, CVIII.

33 Bernard, *Sermones de diversis*, CXVI, as quoted in translation in Bernard, *The Steps of Humility*, tr. G. Burch (Cambridge, Mass.: Harvard University Press, 1940), 8.

34 Bernard, *Sermones de diversis*, CXVI.

35 Cf. Bernard, *Sermones in Cantica Canticorum*, L, 6; LXXXV, 8.

36 Ibid., XXXIII, 2–3.

37 For the theology of the Word manifest in history, see Ronald S. Wallace, *Calvin's Doctrine of the Word and Sacrament* (Edinburgh and London: Oliver and Boyd, 1953), 27–32, 40–60.

38 Cf. '21. Meditation' in *Devotions*, 110–11.

CHAPTER FOUR

1 See Charles M. Coffin, *John Donne and the New Philosophy* (New York: Humanities Press, 1958), 104f; Edmund Gosse, *The Life and Letters of John Donne*, (Gloucester, Mass.: Peter Smith, 1959), II, 6–7; John Donne, *Poems*, ed. H.J.C. Grierson (London: Oxford University Press, 1963), II, 205; R.C. Bald, *John Donne: A Life* (Oxford: Clarendon Press, 1970), 269.

2 Cf. Donne's verse letter, 'To Sir Henry Wotton' ('Sir, more then

Kisses'), 7–10.

3 B.F. Nellist, 'Donne's "Storm" and "Calm" and the Descriptive Tradition,' *MLR*, 59 (1964), 511–15.

4 See W. Milgate, 'General Introduction' in *The Satires, Epigrams and Verse Letters*, xxii.

5 N.J.C. Andreasen, *John Donne: Conservative Revolutionary* (Princeton: Princeton University Press, 1967).

6 Cf. *Sermons*, VI, 232.

7 Donne viewed the martyr's self-display as a perverted awareness of audience and a pleasure in suffering. In *Pseudo-Martyr* (London: 1610), his attack upon Romanists who would not take the Oath of Allegiance to James is more than political in its rejection of this mentality. For example, see II, i–ii, pp. 9–11.

8 In regard to the Prince Henry elegy, see: Ruth Wallerstein, *Studies in Seventeenth Century Poetic* (Madison: University of Wisconsin Press, 1950), 70–1; for a broader discussion of this merger of private and public, see Barbara Kiefer Lewalski, *Donne's 'Anniversaries' and the Poetry of Praise: The Creation of a Symbolic Mode* (Princeton: Princeton University Press, 1973), 42–107; also, for a related discussion of Donne's merger of the devotional and the homiletic, see Janel M. Mueller, 'The Exegesis of Experience: Dean Donne's *Devotions upon Emergent Occasions*,' *JEGP*, 67 (1968), 1–19.

9 See above, Chapter Three, p. 100, for a discussion of 'place' as a notion

of being that includes space and motion. Here, the notion of 'triumph' (178), which is movement in space, is a figure for the fulfilment of time in 'place.'

10 See Milgate, 'General Introduction,' in *The Satires, Epigrams and Verse Letters*. For the 'integrity' of virtue, see p. xxxvi; for the relationship of faith to good works and discretion, see p. xxxvii.

11 '17. Prayer,' p. 90; '19. Prayer,' p. 103.

12 See F.M. Catherinet, 'Conformité à la volonté de Dieu,' in *Dictionnaire de Spiritualité: Ascétique et Mystique Doctrine et Histoire*, II, 1441–69. Essentially, conformity is voluntary obedience to God's will, both in actions and through the full powers of the soul. Augustinian psychology, in emphasizing sin as a condition of the will, finds the basis of conformity in the turning of the will to God.

13 Douglas L. Peterson, 'John Donne's *Holy Sonnets* and the Anglican Doctrine of Contrition,' *SP*, 56 (1959), 504–18.

14 Patrick Grant, *The Transformation of Sin: Studies in Donne, Herbert, Vaughan and Traherne* (Montreal and London: McGill-Queen's University Press; Amherst: University of Massachusetts Press, 1974), 40–65.

15 Gerard H. Cox III, 'Donne's *Devotions*: A Meditative Sequence on Repentance,' *Harvard Theological Review*, 66 (1973), 331–51.

16 For one explication of the knowledge of Christ crucified, see *Sermons*, V, 276.

17 E.g., George Herbert's 'Affliction (v),' 13–24.

18 E.g., *Sermons*, VI, 60, 237–8.

19 For one compelling example see *Sermons*, II, 300.

20 See Evelyn M. Simpson, 'Introduction' in *Sermons*, III, 34, n. 63.

21 Donne's conviction of the importance of the individual identity is tenacious: '*Ego*, I, I the same body, and the same soul, shall be recompact again, and be identically, numerically, individually the same man. The same integrity of body, and soul, and the same integrity in the Organs of my body, and in the faculties of my soul too; I shall be all there, my body, and my soul, and all my body, and all my soul' (*Sermons*, III, 109–10). Suffering for the Body according to Paul's model in Colossians 1:24 maintains this personal identity: 'Since I am bound to take up my crosse, there must be a crosse that is mine to take up' (*Sermons*, II, 301).

CHAPTER FIVE

1 See Edgar Hill Duncan, 'Donne's Alchemical Figures,' *ELH*, 9 (1942), 280–4; Joseph Mazzeo, 'Notes on John Donne's Alchemical Imagery,' in *Renaissance and Seventeenth-Century Studies* (New York: Columbia University Press, 1964), 79–80;

W.A. Murray, 'Donne and Paracelsus: An Essay in Interpretation,' *RES*, 25 (1949), 115–23; Charles Nicholl, *The Chemical Theater* (London: Routledge and Kegan Paul, 1980), 122–35.

2 Murray, 'Donne and Paracelsus,' 122.

3 J.B. Leishman, *The Monarch of Wit* (New York: Harper and Row Publishers, 1966), 175; Judah Stampfer, *John Donne and the Metaphysical Gesture* (New York: Funk and Wagnalls, 1970), 194.

4 John Donne, *Biathanatos* (London: Printed for Humphrey Moseley, 1648), 216–17.

5 Allen Debus, *The English Paracelsians* (London: Oldbourne, 1965), 24–6.

6 *The Hermetic and Alchemical Writings of ... Paracelsus the Great*, tr. Arthur Waite (New Hyde Park, New York: University Books, 1967), I, 72; hereafter cited as *Paracelsus*.

7 *Paracelsus*, I, 231–2; Cf. Murray, 'Donne and Paracelsus,' 122.

8 Cf. *Essays in Divinity*, 19.

9 *Paracelsus*, I, 58.

10 For examples see *Paracelsus*, I, 231; II, 87.

11 *Othello*, III, iv. 36, 39.

12 Jay Arnold Levine, ' "The Dissolution": Donne's Twofold Elegy,' *ELH*, 28 (1961), 309. Levine cites George Ripley's 'The Mistery of Alchymists' in *Theatrum Chemicum Brittannicum*, ed. Elias Ashmole (London, 1652), 385.
For whereas a Woman is in presence,

There is much moysture and
accidence,
Wetnes and humours in her be
The which would drown'd our
Quality;
Perceive well ... by *Noahs* flood,
To much moysture was never good.

13 Levine, ' "The Dissolution": Donne's
Twofold Elegy,' 309.

14 Ibid., 306; Levine cites *Paracelsus*, I,
86 as an example of widespread
use of this term.

15 Paracelsus argues that the unborn
foetus is 'fruit' shaped by the
'impression' of the mother's imagination (*Paracelsus*, I, 122). Similarly,
the heavenly stars can 'imprint' the
foetus. However, abortive 'impressions' from either the mother or the
stars can create 'hermaphrodites,
androgyni' (I, 173). In 'Weeping' the
speaker's 'Pregnant' tears 'beare' the
'stampe' of the lady's image and
are androgynous 'Fruits' of suffering.
Her 'impression' (16) informs the
globular tears that miscarry through
flooding.

16 *Paracelsus*, I, 193.

17 William Empson, ' "A Valediction:
of Weeping" ' in *John Donne: A
Collection of Critical Essays*, ed.
Helen Gardner (Englewood Cliffs:
Prentice-Hall, 1962), 54.

CHAPTER SIX

1 For different elements in that Au-
gustinian legacy revealed in the *Holy
Sonnets*, see the following: Patrick
Grant, *The Transformation of Sin:
Studies in Donne, Herbert, Vaughan
and Traherne* (Amherst: University
of Massachusetts Press; Montreal
and London: McGill-Queen's Uni-
versity Press, 1974), 40–72; William
H. Halewood, *The Poetry of Grace:
Reformation Themes and Structures in
English Seventeenth-Century Poetry*
(New Haven and London: Yale
University Press, 1970), 33–70, 80–5;
Richard E. Hughes, *The Progress
of the Soul: The Interior Career of John
Donne* (New York: William Morrow
and Co., 1969), 177ff.

2 Augustine, *Confessions*, tr. E.B.
Pusey (London and New York:
Everyman's Library, 1970), X, xxx, 41.

3 E.g., the Whore of Babylon, who
lives by fornication (Rev. 17), assumes Babylon the idolatrous city
(e.g., Jer. 50:2, 38).

4 *An Homilie Against perill of Idolatrie,
and superfluous decking of Churches*
in *Certaine Sermons or Homilies Appointed to be Read in Churches In
the Time of Queen Elizabeth I* (1547–
1571). London, 1623. *A Facsimile
Reproduction of the Edition of 1623*,
intro. by M.E. Rickey and T.B.
Stroup (Gainesville, Florida: Scholars Facsimiles and Reprints, 1968),
63.

5 *Confessions*, II, ii, 2.

6 See R.C. Bald, *John Donne: A Life*
(Oxford: Clarendon Press, 1970),
122–3.

7 See Halewood, *The Poetry of Grace*,
41, 66; Charles Trinkaus, *In Our
Image and Likeness: Humanity and
Divinity in Italian Humanist Thought*

(Chicago: University of Chicago Press, 1970), I, 3–50.

8 Petrarch, *Sonnets and Songs*, tr. Anna Marie Armi (New York: Universal Library, 1968). All quotations are from this edition, with poem numbers given parenthetically within the text.

9 See Terence C. Cave, *Devotional Poetry in France c. 1570–1613* (Cambridge: Cambridge University Press, 1969), 138.

10 Ibid., 81.

11 Antoine Favre, *Centurie premiere de sonets spirituels de l'amour divin et de la pénitence* (Chambéry, 1595); all quotations are from this edition, with sonnet numbers given parenthetically within the text.

12 See Petrarch, *Sonnets and Songs*, CCCLX.

13 Quoted in Louis L. Martz, *The Poetry of Meditation: A Study in English Religious Literature* (New Haven and London: Yale University Press, 1965), 185.

14 Ibid., 179–93.

15 Gardner, *The Divine Poems*, xlix–l.

16 Douglas L. Peterson, 'John Donne's *Holy Sonnets* and the Anglican Doctrine of Contrition,' *SP*, 56 (1959), 508.

17 Peterson's representation of Catholic teaching is slightly off target here (p. 506). Although sorrow because of fear is sufficient for absolution in the Sacrament of Penance, it is regarded as imperfect contrition. For a discussion of this distinction see P. De Letter, 'Contrition,' *New Catholic Encyclopedia* (New York: McGraw-Hill Book Co., 1967), IV, 280–1.

18 J.B. Leishman, review of Helen Gardner, *The Divine Poems* in *RES.*, n.s. 5 (1954), 74–83; A.J. Smith in his edition, *John Donne: The Complete English Poems* (Harmondsworth, Middlesex: Penguin education, 1973), 625.

19 Richard Hooker, *Of the Laws of Ecclesiastical Polity*, VI, iii, 5.

20 Grant, *The Transformation of Sin*, 52–3.

21 See David L. Jeffrey, *The Early English Lyric and Franciscan Spirituality* (Lincoln: University of Nebraska Press, 1975), 43–72.

22 Cf. Petrarch, *Sonnets and Songs*, II.

23 William Kerrigan, 'The Fearful Accommodations of John Donne,' *ELR*, 4 (1974), 354.

24 The pun on *make* can work several ways: begetting, fashioning, repentance, siege, conversion; *make*, the old synonym for *mate*. See *OED*. Also, cf. 'First travaile we to seeke and then make love?' ('Holy Sonnet, XVIII').

25 Cf. Lorenzo Scupoli, *The Spiritual Combat and a Treatise on Peace of the Soul*, rev. tr. W. Lester and R. Mohan (Westminster, Maryland: Newman Bookshop, 1945), ch. 14. This widely popular work establishes a useful context for assessing Donne's use of the *topos*.

26 See William R. Mueller, 'Donne's Adulterous Female Town,' *MLN*, 76 (1961), 312–14.

27 John Calvin, *Commentaries on Jeremiah*, tr. John Owen (Edinburgh, 1851), Lecture IX (Jeremiah 2:33), 140.

28 Bernard, *The Steps of Humility*, tr. G.B. Burch (Cambridge, Mass.: Harvard University Press, 1940), I, 2.

29 *The Steps of Humility*, VII, 21; bracketed Latin citations are from *Patrologiae Cursus Completus, Series Latina*, ed. J.P. Migne, 221 vols. (Paris, 1844–64), CLXXXVII, 953–4.

30 *The Steps of Humility*, VII–VIII, 21–2; *PL*, CLXXXVII, 953–4.

31 Martz, *The Poetry of Meditation*, 52.

32 For an assessment of Petrarch's sinful will, but lucid reason, see Kenelm Foster, 'Beatrice or Medusa: the Penitential Element in Petrarch's *Canzoniere*' in *Italian Studies Presented to E.R. Vincent*, ed. C.P. Brand, K. Foster, U. Limentani (Cambridge: W. Heffer and Sons, 1962), 41–56.

33 Sir Philip Sidney, *Poems*, ed. W.A. Ringler, Jr (Oxford: Clarendon Press, 1962); sonnet numbers are given parenthetically within the text. See Ringler's comments on the conventional Reason vs. Love debate, p. 464.

34 Martz, *The Poetry of Meditation*, 43.

35 Ibid., 45–6.

36 For the contrary view see Richard E. Hughes, *The Progress of the Soul*, 185–6. Terence Cave, *French Devotional Poetry*, 48, notes that 'analysis,' the exercise of reason, included

'question, argument, paradox, antithesis.'

37 Martz, *The Poetry of Meditation*, 76–7.

38 Peterson, 'John Donne's *Holy Sonnets* and the Anglican Doctrine of Contrition,' 512.

39 Barbara Kiefer Lewalski, *Protestant Poetics and the Seventeenth-Century Religious Lyric* (Princeton: Princeton University Press, 1979), 265. Her approach to the sonnets suffers from a major shortcoming of her Calvinistic view of Donne. Conformity between God and man in love is at the heart of Donne's theology, but not Calvin's.

CHAPTER SEVEN

1 Regarding this paradox see A.B. Chambers, ' "Goodfriday, 1613. Riding Westward": The Poem and the Tradition,' *ELH*, 28 (1961), 50ff.

2 See William H. Halewood, *The Poetry of Grace* (New Haven and London: Yale University Press, 1970), 67: 'conversion is the device in Reformation theology for ending the rebellion of the self and bringing man into harmonious relation with God.'

3 The profound influence of both Paul and Augustine on Donne necessarily inspires consideration why that 'Goodfriday' does not speak to such a conversion experience. Donne's sermons leave little opportunity to doubt his interest in sud-

den conversion, particularly Paul's, to demonstrate God's power and the human need for Grace. See *Sermons*, I, 255; VI, 265. However, it is not the experiential element in the sudden conversion that engages Donne's attention, but its manifestation of divine power.

4 'Conversion Psychology in John Donne's Good Friday Poem,' *Harvard Theological Review*, 72 (1979), 101–22.

5 See John Calvin, 'To the Reader' in *Commentaries on the Psalms of David and Others*, tr. Arthur Golding (London, 1571).

6 François Wendel, *Calvin: The Origins and Development of His Religious Thought*, tr. P. Mairet (London, 1963), 191.

7 John Calvin, *Institutes of the Christian Religion*, tr. F.L. Battles (Philadelphia: Westminster Press, 1973), II, iii, 8.

8 Calvin, *Institutes*, III, iii, 5. Latin citation is taken from *Johannis Calvini Opera*, II, in *Corpus Reformatorum*, XXX, ed. G. Baum, E. Cunitz, and E. Reuss (Brunswick: 1864).

9 Calvin, *Institutes*, II, iii, 6.

10 Augustine, *Confessions*, tr. E.B. Pusey (London: J.M. Dent and Sons, 1970), II, i; Latin citations are from *Patrologiae Cursus Completus, Series Latina*, ed. J.P. Migne, 221 vols. (Paris, 1844–64), XXXII, 675. This work is hereafter cited as *PL*.

11 Augustine, *Confessions*, VIII, v, 10; *PL*, XXXII, 753.

12 Augustine, *Confessions*, VIII, xii, 30; *PL*, XXXII, 762.

13 Augustine, *On Free Will*, tr. J.H.S. Burleigh, in *Augustine: Earlier Writings* (London: SCM Press, 1953), III, i, 2; *PL*, XXXII, 1272.

14 Donald M. Friedman, 'Memory and the Art of Salvation in Donne's Good Friday Poem,' *ELR*, 3 (1973), 418–42.

15 Augustine, *Enarratio in Psalmum*, XCIII, 18 in *PL*, XXXVII, 1206.

16 Augustine, *Enarratio in Psalmum*, XLIV, 17 in *PL*, XXXVI, 503–4.

17 Bernard, *Eighty-six Sermons on the Song of Solomon*, in *Life and Works*, IV, tr. S.J. Eales (London, 1896), XXXVI, 5, p. 237; *PL*, CLXXXIII, 970. This work is hereafter cited as *Song of Solomon*.

18 Bernard, *Song of Solomon*, LXXXIII, 2–3, p. 508; *PL*, CLXXXIII, 1182.

19 One of Calvin's variations on the theme of bending in conversion depicts God's role: 'God begins his good work in us, therefore, by arousing love and desire and zeal for righteousness in our hearts; or, to speak more correctly, by bending, forming, and directing, our hearts to righteousness' (*Institutes*, II, iii, 6).

20 'That I may rise, and stand, o'erthrow mee,'and bend / Your force, to breake, blowe, burn and make me new' (3–4). The position of 'bend' enables it to act on both 'mee' in line 3 and 'Your force' in line 4, with the meaning shifting in line 4 accordingly.

21 Cf. *Sermons*, II, 87.

22 Bernard, *Song of Solomon*, XLII, 4, p. 261; *PL*, CLXXXIII, 989.

23 Bernard, *Song of Solomon*, LXIX, 2,

p. 422.

24 Augustine, *Expositions on the Book of Psalms*, IV, tr. C.E. Pritchard and H.M. Wilkins (Oxford, 1850), XCIV, 18, p. 367.

25 Bernard, *Song of Solomon*, XXI, 10–11, p. 122.

26 John Downame, *The Christian Warfare*, (London, 1613), Pt. III, Lib. 2, Ch. xxiii, Sect. 2.

27 Downame, *The Christian Warfare*, Pt. III, Lib. 2, Ch. xxiii, Sect. 6; also, cf. the following: 'For as afflictions doe notably helpe forward our effectual callings and first conversion unto God, so do they much further our repentance, and provoke us continually to renew the act thereof after our many relapses and daily slips into sin' (Pt. III, Lib. 2, Ch. xxiii, Sect. 1).

28 Richard Sibbes, *The Christian Work*, in *Works*, V, ed. Alexander Grosart (Edinburgh, 1863), 26.

29 Sibbes, *The Saints Refreshing*, in *Works*, VI (1863), 84.

30 Friedman, 'Memory and the Art of Salvation in Donne's Good Friday Poem,' 439.

31 Cf. Augustine, *Confessions*, VIII, v, 10; *PL*, XXXII, 753: 'my own iron will' (ferrea voluntate).

32 This often used image goes at least as far back as *De virginitate* by Gregory of Nyssa, written before he became a bishop in 371 (Augustine's first work is thought to have been written in 386). See Gerhard B. Ladner, *The Idea of Reform: Its Impact on Christian Thought and Action in the Age of the Fathers* (New York,

Evanston, and London: Harper and Row, 1967), 92. Cf. Bernard, *Song of Solomon*, LVII, 8; Downame, *The Christian Warfare*, Pt. III, Lib. 2, Ch. vi, Sect. 3.

33 Friedman, 'Memory and the Art of Salvation in Donne's Good Friday Poem,' 420–37.

34 Winfried Schleiner, *The Imagery of John Donne's Sermons* (Providence, R.I.: Brown University Press, 1970), 137.

35 See Patrick Grant, *The Transformation of Sin* (Montreal and London: McGill-Queen's University Press; Amherst: University of Massachusetts Press, 1974), 40–65.

36 F.J.E. Raby, *A History of Christian-Latin Poetry from the Beginnings to the Close of the Middle Ages* (Oxford: Clarendon Press, 1953), 440–1.

37 Quoted in David L. Jeffrey, *The Early English Lyric and Franciscan Spirituality* (Lincoln: University of Nebraska Press, 1975), 31.

38 See Raby, *A History of Christian-Latin Poetry*, 419, n. 2; Jeffrey, *The Early English Lyric and Franciscan Spirituality*, 31–2, 50, 57, 88.

39 As background for these lines, Jeffrey (ibid., 31–2) draws attention to Bernard's commentary on John 10:27–8 ('My sheep hear my voice and I the Lord acknowledge them, and they follow me; and I give to them eternal life').

40 Unlike Donne, Bernard distinguishes between 'Image' and 'Likeness' in the Biblical affirmation that man was made 'to his Image and likeness' (Gen. 1:26). The Image

refers to the essential powers of the soul; the Likeness, to the accidental ability to use these powers without impediment. (See Gilson, *The Mystical Theology of Saint Bernard*, 46–53). Donne views the terms to be 'illustration of one another ... to be all one' (*Sermons*, IX, 73).

41 Bernard, *Song of Solomon*, LXXXIII, I, p. 506; *PL*, CLXXXIII, 1181.

42 Etienne Gilson, *The Mystical Theology of Saint Bernard*, tr. A.H.C. Downes (London, 1955), 99.

43 Bernard, *Song of Solomon*, LXXXII, 8, p. 507.

44 Bernard, *The Steps of Humility*, tr. G.B. Burch (Cambridge, Mass.: Harvard University Press, 1940), III, 6.

45 Bernard, *The Steps of Humility*, III, 7.

46 Grierson and Smith adopt 'turne'; Gardner, 'tune.' Despite this minor textual skirmish regarding those Donne manuscripts which read 'tune' versus those which read 'turne,' there is little doubt that, in either case, Donne intends to depict Christ as the hand that creates and maintains the universe, the Logos, the instrument of Creation, and principle of order. Given the other 'turns' in 'Goodfriday' and given the Augustinian influence (see nn. 49 and 50 below) strengthening the poem, 'turne' is more consistent. We can at least assume, as did Grierson when put to defend 'turne,' that it would be implicit in 'tune' anyway (see Gardner, *The Divine Poems*,

p. 99, line 22, for the details of the disagreement). Since, as Gardner herself notes, 'authority is evenly divided on the matter,' and since 'turne' is more broadly consistent with the poem, Grierson was probably right to begin with.

47 John Donne, *The Complete English Poems*, ed. A.J. Smith (Harmondsworth, Middlesex: Penguin Books, 1973), 654, n. 22.

48 For examples see Hosea 14:2, 4 and Zechariah 1:3 in the Geneva Bible.

49 Augustine, *De Genesi ad litteram*, I, iii, 7, in *PL*, XXXIV, 248–9.

50 Augustine, *De Genesi ad litteram*, I, iv, 9, in *PL*, XXXIV, 249.

CHAPTER EIGHT

1 Aristotle, *Physics*, IV, II, 219b; Augustine, *Confessions*, XI, xxiv, 31; Thomas Aquinas, II *Sent.* d.1, q.1, a.5, arg. 7.

2 Augustine, *Confessions*, X, xv–xxviii, 18–38.

3 Cf. *Deaths Duell*, *Sermons*, X, 241.

4 Gerard H. Cox III, 'Donne's *Devotions*: A Meditative Sequence on Repentance,' *Harvard Theological Review*, 66 (1973), 345–7.

5 Barbara Kiefer Lewalski, *Donne's 'Anniversaries' and the Poetry of Praise: The Creation of a Symbolic Mode* (Princeton: Princeton University Press, 1973), 142–73.

6 See Chapter Two, p. 41.

7 Lewalski, *Donne's 'Anniversaries' and the Poetry of Praise*, 83.

8 U. Milo Kaufmann, *The Pilgrim's*

Progress and Traditions in Puritan Meditation (New Haven and London: Yale University Press, 1966), 122–4.

9 Joseph Hall, *The Art of Divine Meditation* in *The Works*, VI (New York: AMS Press, 1969; reprint from 1863 Oxford edition), 65.

10 Cf. *Sermons*, II, 154–5.

11 Kaufmann, *The Pilgrim's Progress and Traditions in Puritan Meditation*, 130–3.

12 Cf. Etienne Gilson, *The Mystical Theology of Saint Bernard*, tr. A.H.C. Downes (London and New York: Sheed and Ward, 1955), 109.

13 Cf. Bernard, *Treatise on Consideration*, tr. A Priest of Mount Melleray (Dublin: Browne and Nolan, 1921), V, iii, pp. 153–4.

14 Ibid., II, ii, p. 39; Latin citations are from *Patrologiae Cursus Completus, Series Latina*, ed. J.P. Migne, 221 vols. (Paris, 1844–64), CLXXXII, 745.

15 See George B. Burch, 'Introduction: An Analysis of Bernard's Epistemology,' in Bernard, *The Steps of Humility* (Cambridge, Massachusetts: Harvard University Press, 1940), 26–35.

16 Bernard, *Treatise on Consideration*, II, iii, p. 40.

17 Ibid., v, i, p. 146.

18 Luis de Granada, *Of Prayer, and Meditation*, tr. Richard Hopkins (Paris, 1582), 3; facsimile edition (Menston, Yorkshire: Scolar Press, 1971).

19 Ibid., 5.

20 Ibid., 8.

21 Leonard Barkan, *Nature's Work of Art: The Human Body as the Image of the World* (New Haven and London: Yale University Press, 1975), 46–60; for the contrary view see Joan Webber, *Contrary Music: The Prose Style of John Donne* (Madison: University of Wisconsin Press, 1963), 188.

22 See Terence C. Cave, *Devotional Poetry in France c. 1570–1613* (Cambridge: Cambridge University Press, 1969), 96–8.

23 'The thyrde sermon' in *Sermons of John Calvin, upon the songe that Ezechias made after he had bene sicke, and afflicted by the hand of God, conteyned in the 38. Chapter of Esay* (London, 1560), 59.

24 Ibid., 'The fourth sermon,' 74.

25 Joan Webber, *The Eloquent 'I': Style and Self in Seventeenth-Century Prose* (Madison, Milwaukee, London: University of Wisconsin Press, 1968), 34ff.

26 Ibid., 21.

27 For the details see R.C. Bald, *John Donne: A Life* (Oxford: Clarendon Press, 1970), 450–5.

28 N.J.C. Andreasen, 'Donne's *Devotions* and the Psychology of Assent,' *MP*, 62 (1965), 209.

29 Richard E. Hughes, *The Progress of the Soul: The Interior Career of John Donne* (New York: William Morrow and Co., 1969), 264.

30 See Cox, 'Donne's *Devotions*: A Meditative Sequence on Repentance,' 331–51.

31 See Jonathan Goldberg, 'The Understanding of Sickness in Donne's *Devotions*,' *RQ*, 24 (1971), 507–17.

32 Donne keeps us aware of the close

relationship between suffering and patience, between *suffero* and *patior*. Cf. '11. Meditation,' pp. 57–8; *Sermons*, II, 299; *Sermons*, VIII, 185.

CHAPTER NINE

1 Izaak Walton, *The Life of Dr. John Donne* in *Lives* (London, 1670), 70–1; facsimile edition (Menston, Yorkshire: Scolar Press, 1969).
2 Ibid., 75.
3 Ibid., 74.
4 Ibid., 73.
5 Ibid., 72.
6 Cf. Donne's variations on the notion of critical days in '14. Devotion' in *Devotions upon Emergent Occasions*.
7 Merritt Y. Hughes, 'Kidnapping Donne' in *Essays in Criticism*, second series, by members of the Department of English, University of California (Freeport, New York: Books for Libraries Press, 1969; first published 1934), 61–89. Hughes is taking aim particularly at modern readers who mistakenly find in Donne a mirror for their own scepticism.
8 R.C. Bald, *John Donne: A Life* (Oxford: Clarendon Press, 1970), 528.
9 'This then is the course of Gods mercy, He proceeds as he begun, which was the first branch of this second part; It is always in motion, and always moving towards *All*, alwaies perpendicular, right over every one of us, and always circular, always communicable to all' (*Sermons*, VI, 175).

10 In the following passage from a 1627 Christmas sermon, Donne categorizes doubt with deliberation and consideration, which are activities of reason: 'But then, for extraordinary things, things that have not their evidence in the word of *God* formerly revealed unto us, whether we consider matters of Doctrine, and new opinions, or matter of Practise, and new commands, from what depth of learning soever that new opinion seeme to us to rise, or from heighth of Power soever that new Command seeme to fall, it is still *in genere deliberativo*, still we are allowed, nay still wee are commanded to deliberate, to doubt, to consider, before we execute' (*Sermons*, VIII, 135).
11 See Louis L. Martz, *The Wit of Love* (Notre Dame and London: University of Notre Dame Press, 1969), 32–3. Martz finds an analogue for the spiralling ascent upon Truth's hill in a fifteenth-century Florentine painting, which 'represents perfectly the agonized effort of Donne's mind to rise above the world of flux represented, from beginning to end, in his poetry – that world of change, corruption, decay, self-seeking, betrayal, disease, and death, which forms the somber ground from which his questing mind seeks to arise.'
12 See n. 23, p. 205 for a discussion of spiralling circles in Donne's 'A Valediction: forbidding Mourning.'

Index

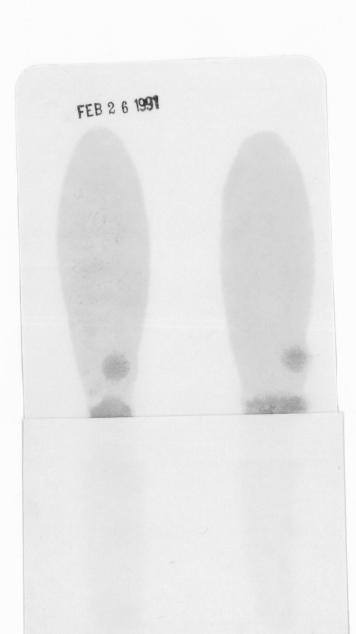

FEB 2 6 1991